The Politics of European Competition Regulation

The Politics of European Competition Regulation provides an original and theoretically informed account of the political power struggles that have shaped the evolution of European competition regulation over the past six decades.

Applying a critical political economy perspective, this book analyses the establishment and development of competition regulation at European Community and national level since the 1950s. It puts forth the central argument that competition regulation came to reflect the broader shift towards a neoliberal order since the 1980s. Buch-Hansen and Wigger argue that this shift, which took place against the background of the gradual transnationalisation of capitalist production and the economic crisis of the late 1970s, was driven by the European Commission in alliance with the emerging transnational capitalist class.

The authors examine the political responses to the current global economic crisis in the fields of state aid, cartel prosecution and merger control and conclude that an alternative type of competition regulation, which forms part of a much broader transformation of the current socioeconomic order, is needed. This book will be of interest to students and scholars of global political economy, European integration and competition law.

Hubert Buch-Hansen is Assistant Professor of International Political Economy at Copenhagen Business School Denmark.

Angela Wigger is Assistant Professor of Global Political Economy at the Institute of Management Research at the Radboud University, The Netherlands.

RIPE SERIES IN GLOBAL POLITICAL ECONOMY

This series, published in association with the *Review of International Political Economy,* provides a forum for current and interdisciplinary debates in international political economy. The series aims to advance understanding of the key issues in the global political economy, and to present innovative analyses of emerging topics. The titles in the series focus on three broad themes:

- the structures, processes and actors of contemporary global transformations
- the changing forms taken by governance, at scales from the local and everyday to the global and systemic
- the inseparability of economic from political, social and cultural questions, including resistance, dissent and social movements.

The series comprises two strands:

The *RIPE Series in Global Political Economy* aims to address the needs of students and teachers, and the titles will be published in hardback and paperback. Titles include:

Transnational Classes and International Relations
Kees van der Pijl

Gender and Global Restructuring:
Sightings, sites and resistances
Edited by Marianne H Marchand and Anne Sisson Runyan

Global Political Economy
Contemporary theories
Edited by Ronen Palan

Ideologies of Globalization
Contending visions of a new world order
Mark Rupert

The Clash within Civilisations
Coming to terms with cultural conflicts
Dieter Senghaas

Global Unions?
Theory and strategies of organized labour in the global political economy
Edited by Jeffrey Harrod and Robert O'Brien

Political Economy of a Plural World
Critical reflections on power, morals and civilizations
Robert Cox with Michael Schechter

A Critical Rewriting of Global Political Economy
Integrating reproductive, productive and virtual economies
V. Spike Peterson

Contesting Globalization
Space and place in the world economy
André C. Drainville

Global Institutions and Development
Framing the world?
Edited by Morten Bøås and Desmond McNeill

Global Institutions, Marginalization, and Development
Craig N. Murphy

Critical Theories, International Relations and 'the Anti-Globalisation Movement'
The politics of global resistance
Edited by Catherine Eschle and Bice Maiguashca

Globalization, Governmentality, and Global Politics
Regulation for the rest of us?
Ronnie D. Lipschutz, with James K. Rowe

Critical Perspectives on Global Governance
Rights and regulation in governing regimes
Jean Grugel and Nicola Piper

Beyond States and Markets
The challenges of social reproduction
Edited by Isabella Bakker and Rachel Silvey

The Industrial Vagina
The political economy of the global sex trade
Sheila Jeffreys

Capital as Power
A study of order and creorder
Jonathan Nitzan and Shimshon Bichler

The Global Political Economy of Intellectual Property Rights, Second Edition
The new enclosures
Christopher May

Corporate Power and Ownership in Contemporary Capitalism
The politics of resistance and domination
Susanne Soederberg

Savage Economics
Wealth, poverty and the temporal walls of capitalism
David L. Blaney and Naeem Inayatullah

Cultural Political Economy
Edited by Jacqueline Best and Matthew Paterson

Gender and Global Restructuring Second Edition
Sightings, sites and resistances
Edited by Marianne H. Marchand and Anne Sisson Runyan

Routledge/RIPE Studies in Global Political Economy is a forum for innovative new research intended for a high-level specialist readership, and the titles will be available in hardback only. Titles include:

1. **Globalization and Governance ***
   Edited by Aseem Prakash and Jeffrey A. Hart
2. **Nation-States and Money**
   The past, present and future of national currencies
   Edited by Emily Gilbert and Eric Helleiner
3. **The Global Political Economy of Intellectual Property Rights**
   The new enclosures?
   Christopher May
4. **Integrating Central Europe**
   EU expansion and Poland, Hungary and the Czech Republic
   Otto Holman
5. **Capitalist Restructuring, Globalisation and the Third Way**
   Lessons from the Swedish model
   J. Magnus Ryner
6. **Transnational Capitalism and the Struggle over European Integration**
   Bastiaan van Apeldoorn
7. **World Financial Orders**
   An historical international political economy
   Paul Langley
8. **The Changing Politics of Finance in Korea and Thailand**
   From deregulation to debacle
   Xiaoke Zhang
9. **Anti-Immigrantism in Western Democracies**
   Statecraft, desire and the politics of exclusion
   Roxanne Lynn Doty
10. **The Political Economy of European Employment**
    European integration and the transnationalization of the (un)employment question
    Edited by Henk Overbeek

11. **Rethinking Global Political Economy**
Emerging issues, unfolding odysseys
Edited by Mary Ann Tétreault, Robert A. Denemark, Kenneth P. Thomas and Kurt Burch

12. **Rediscovering International Relations Theory**
Matthew Davies and Michael Niemann

13. **International Trade and Developing Countries***
Bargaining coalitions in the GATT & WTO
Amrita Narlikar

14. **The Southern Cone Model**
The political economy of regional capitalist development in Latin America
Nicola Phillips

15. **The Idea of Global Civil Society**
Politics and ethics of a globalizing era
Edited by Randall D. Germain and Michael Kenny

16. **Governing Financial Globalization**
International political economy and multi-level governance
Edited by Andrew Baker, David Hudson and Richard Woodward

17. **Resisting Intellectual Property**
Debora J. Halbert

18. **Neoliberal Hegemony**
A global critique
Edited by Dieter Plehwe, Bernhard Walpen and Gisela Neunhöffer

19. **Global Standards of Market Civilization**
Edited by Brett Bowden and Leonard Seabrooke

20. **Beyond Globalization**
Capitalism, territoriality and the international relations of modernity
Hannes Lacher

21. **Images of Gramsci**
Connections and contentions in political theory and international relations
Edited by Andreas Bieler and Adam David Morton

22. **Global Public Policy**
Business and the countervailing powers of civil society
Edited by Karsten Ronit

23. **The Transnational Politics of Corporate Governance Regulation**
Edited by Henk Overbeek, Bastiaan van Apeldoorn and Andreas Nölke

24. **National Currencies and Globalization**
Endangered specie?
Paul Bowles

25. **Conflicts in Environmental Regulation and the Internationalization of the State**
Contested terrains
Ulrich Brand, Christoph Görg, Joachim Hirsch and Markus Wissen

26. **Governing International Labour Migration**
Current issues, challenges and dilemmas
Edited by Christina Gabriel and Hélène Pellerin

27. **The Child in International Political Economy**
    A place at the table
    Alison M. S. Watson

28. **Global Citizenship and the Legacy of Empire**
    Marketing development
    April Biccum

29. **Development, Sexual Rights and Global Governance ***
    Resisting global power
    Amy Lind

30. **Cosmopolitanism and Global Financial Reform**
    A pragmatic approach to the Tobin tax
    James Brassett

31. **Variegated Neoliberalism**
    EU varieties of capitalism and international political economy
    Huw Macartney

32. **The Politics of European Competition Regulation**
    A critical political economy perspective
    Hubert Buch-Hansen and Angela Wigger

33. **The European Union, Civil Society and Conflict**
    Edited by Nathalie Tocci

**Also available in paperback*

The Politics of European Competition Regulation

A critical political economy perspective

Hubert Buch-Hansen and Angela Wigger

Routledge
Taylor & Francis Group
LONDON AND NEW YORK

First published 2011
by Routledge,
2 Park Square, Milton Park, Abingdon, Oxon, OX14 4RN

Simultaneously published in the USA and Canada
by Routledge
711 Third Avenue, New York, NY 10017

Routledge is an imprint of the Taylor & Francis Group, an informa business

British Library Cataloguing in Publication Data
A catalogue record for this book is available from the British Library

Library of Congress Cataloging-in-Publication Data
Buch-Hansen, Hubert.
The politics of European competition regulation : a critical political economy perspective / Hubert Buch-Hansen and Angela Wigger.
p. cm.—(RIPE series in global political economy)
Includes bibliographical references and index.
1. Trade regulation—Europe. 2. Competition—Europe.
3. Industrial policy—Europe. 4. Europe—Commercial policy.
I. Wigger, Angela. II. Title.
HD3616.E853B83 2011
382'.3094—dc22

2010039440

ISBN: 978–0–415–60579–3 (hbk)
ISBN: 978–0–203–82852–6 (ebk)

Typeset in Times New Roman
by RefineCatch Limited, Bungay, Suffolk

Contents

Preface and acknowledgments

This book is not solely about competition and competition regulation. Instead, it retells the history of more than 60 years of capitalist development in Europe. It does so by locating the evolution of the content, form and scope of European competition regulation in the context of shifting social power balances within the broader political economy. Its aim is to stimulate critical and heterodox thinking about the central and often unchallenged position of competition and its regulation in the broader regulatory ensembles of advanced capitalist economies.

The book builds on several years of research that we conducted as part of our PhD studies at Copenhagen Business School and the Vrije Universiteit Amsterdam. But it also moves well beyond that. It is the outcome of an intellectual journey that has proceeded through dialogues with different bodies of literature. Of these dialogues, three particularly deserve mentioning here: first, our work greatly benefited from an interchange with critical realist philosophy of science. The theoretical perspective advanced in this book is underpinned by the social ontology of critical realism, according to which history and social phenomena are the open-ended and contingent outcomes of dynamic interplays between material structures, discourses and agents. We are very much indebted to the works of scholars such as Margaret Archer, Roy Bhaskar, Andew Sayer and Colin Wight. Second, this book draws on a dialogue with historical materialist perspectives on capitalism, its inherent contradictions and transformation, classes and class fractions, regulation and the state. Contemporary scholars whose theoretical works have inspired us include Bob Jessop, Bastiaan van Apeldoorn, Henk Overbeek, William I. Robinson, Alain Lipietz, David Harvey, Robert Cox, Magnus Ryner, Alan Cafruny and Kees van der Pijl. Third, at a lower level of abstraction, this book entered a dialogue with various empirical sources and studies on competition regulation. We have learned a lot from personal conversations with, and the work of, political scientists such as Michelle Cini, Lee McGowan, Stephen Wilks, Marie-Laure Djelic, Umut Aydin, Brigitte Leucht, Hussein Kassim, and Chad Damro. Likewise, engaging with the works of historians and legal scholars such as Laurant Warlouzet, Volker Berghahn, Tony Allan Freyer, Daniel Goyder, David J. Gerber and Giorgio Monti has enriched our understanding of competition regulation in important ways. Our gratitude moreover goes to all the people from the European

Commission, organised labour and business groups, as well as competition law experts who generously agreed to be interviewed by us.

On a more personal level, we would like to thank our friends and families for all their love and support and our esteemed colleagues for their constructive critique and advice on ongoing work. Special thanks go to the members of the Amsterdam Research Centre for International Political Economy: Henk Overbeek, Bastiaan van Apeldoorn, Andreas Nölke, Laura Horn, James Perry, Nana de Graaff, and Arjan Vliegenthart, as well as to Morten Ougaard, Peter Nielsen, Susana Borrás, Robbert Maseland, Jan Orbie, Otto Holman and Duncan Wigan. We have also benefited from many conversations with our colleagues from the Politics Department at the Radboud University in Nijmegen and the Department of Intercultural Communication and Management at Copenhagen Business School. We are also grateful to the audiences at several conferences and workshops for their valuable inputs and to Richard Harvey for checking our use of the English language. Finally, we would also like to thank the editors and the anonymous reviewers for their valuable suggestions and thoughtful comments, as well as Hannah Shakespeare, Harriet Frammingham and the rest of the Routledge team for their enthusiasm and professionalism.

The central argument of this book has also been published as an article titled 'Revisiting 50 years of market-making: The neoliberal transformation of European competition policy' in the *Review of International Political Economy.* For the record, we would like to emphasise that we have contributed equally to this work and that our names appear in the alphabetical order of our surnames.

Hubert Buch-Hansen and Angela Wigger
June 2010
Amsterdam and Copenhagen

Foreword

As the authors argue in this insightful and timely book, competition has become the unifying principle of the European integration process. The neoliberal myth that competition alone produces efficiency and economic growth, and that bringing ever more areas of social life under the discipline of market competition will enhance welfare for all, has cast a spell on the integration process since the 1980s. Indeed in the original, but in the end rejected (in France and the Netherlands), European constitution 'free and undistorted competition' had been listed as one of the Union's fundamental objectives. However, the policy aimed at promoting free market competition – as part of a broader *marketisation* project – had already become part of the EU's *de facto* 'constitution' as a result of a process that forms the central and compelling story of this book, that is, the neoliberal transformation of the European competition regime.

This first book-length analysis of European competition regulation from a critical political economy perspective, is a very welcome contribution to the understanding of not only this key policy area but also of the European project as a whole. Welcome because it presents an empirically solid, theoretically consistent, tightly argued explanation of the transformation of European competition regulation, one that throws a truly novel light on these regulatory developments and thus takes us beyond the more conventional (institutionalist) approaches. It does so by adopting a perspective that puts the regulation of competition, as its central research problem, squarely in the context of capitalism and its constituent social relations. It thus recognises that competition and competition policy cannot be abstracted from the capitalist economic system, and its contradictory dynamic of capital accumulation, of which it is part, nor from what the authors call the *ensemble of regulation* that is critical to the reproduction of that system. It is this then that allows the authors to reveal the broader social purpose served by competition regulation, showing how its content reflects underlying unequal social power relations.

Taking the dialectical interplay of structure and agency over time as an important point of departure, the authors show how the struggle over the transformation of EU competition regulation has been shaped by four contending regulatory discourses in turn shaped by rival social forces, in particular those organically linked to prevailing (transnational) fractions of the capitalist class.

This sophisticated analysis – taking agency as well as the mediating power of ideas seriously without lapsing into voluntarism or idealism, and taking (economic) structures seriously without succumbing to an unwarranted determinism or economism – thus produces an historically and empirically rich narrative that reveals how competition regulation in the EU has been undergoing a neoliberal transformation that has clearly served the interests of transnational capital more than that of other social groups. From this critical perspective, then, the social costs of competition that remain hidden in the orthodox neoclassical account come sharply into focus.

This study is all the more welcome because of its timeliness. It comes at a moment in which the whole European project, of which competition regulation has been and still is such an important part, has arguably entered its most serious crisis yet. This crisis, and the new constraints it imposes as well as the new opportunities it offers, makes it all the more important to understand how we got here, as well as, on that basis, to gain insight into both the potential for, as well as limits to, the transformation of the current socio-economic order.

Arguably, the neoliberal model of European governance is now near collapsing under the weight of its own contradictions, or at least has been entering into a multi-level legitimacy crisis. The unravelling of neoliberal hegemony started with the aforementioned popular rejections of the Constitution in 2005 in the context of a heightening Euro-scepticism. Since then, the neoliberal policy orthodoxy, including the quasi-religious dogma of competition, has naturally come under heavy fire in the wake of the near total collapse of the global economy that for more than two decades had been premised on the precepts of neoliberal governance and neoclassical economics. The current crisis presents real dilemmas for Europe's ruling elite. From the perspective of Europe's capitalist class the whole *raison d'être* of the European integration process is that it promotes marketisation and commodification through applying the principle of competition above everything else. Yet it is precisely this which also is most damaging to the legitimacy of the whole project. This then hints at some of the deepening social contradictions of the prevailing paradigm of competition regulation and of the neoliberal project more widely. This comes on top of a contradiction that is in fact inherent in all types of capitalist competition regulation and of which the authors display an astute awareness, which is that although competition is the lifeblood of capitalism as well as an opportunity to individual firms seeking to enter new markets, those same firms will always strive for monopoly. As is evidenced by the analysis of this book, calls for increased (free) competition are thus often accompanied by calls for policies that facilitate greater concentration and protection against outsiders (maybe increasingly from East Asia as the current economic power balance is shifting away from the West?).

Reading this book will contribute greatly to understanding these contradictions and resultant regulatory dilemmas. As regards the neoliberal project, the EU appears to be at a crossroads. Although the legitimacy of neoliberal governance has been seriously weakened by the crisis, and although its underlying growth model has turned out to be a (near fatal) failure, there are also signs that neoliberalism within the EU is Phoenix-like arising from the ashes. Thus for instance, Europe's successor strategy to the Lisbon agenda called 'Europe 2020' entails much of the same old neoliberal content. In the case of competition regulation this book shows how, thus far, the neoliberal discourse, despite waning societal legitimacy, continues to inform the policies of the authorities in Brussels. However, taking a somewhat longer-term view, the contradictions of the neoliberal finance-led growth model that now have become manifest appear to run so deep as to present insurmountable limits – that is, this model has proven to be unsustainable. Yet, as the authors correctly point out, to move beyond protracted crisis management and restore growth on a different basis, an alternative model first has to be presented as well as supported by a new configuration of social forces. This is not yet in the offing: instead of a counter-project to neoliberalism that departs from a critique of the social destruction wrought by 'undistorted competition', much of the current social discontent seems to finds its expression above all in the rise of (radical) right-wing populist forces. But inasmuch as politics is also a battle of ideas, one pre-condition is that indeed ideas that contain genuine alternatives to neoliberalism are available for social forces to draw upon. The authors must be commended for ending their book with such a set of ideas, presenting an outline in which they make a forceful case for a new competition regulation that would form part of a more ecologically balanced, more democratic and more just social order.

Let me thus conclude by congratulating the authors with this important book that, representing critical scholarship in the field of European political economy at its best, deserves to be widely read. I have no doubt that its readers will be enriched by the novel insights this book offers into what is, and is likely to remain, one of the crucial areas of European supranational socio-economic regulation at a moment in which the European project is at such a critical juncture, economically, socially and politically.

Bastiaan van Apeldoorn
September 2010
Vrije Universiteit Amsterdam

Introduction

The assumption that competition is good and more competition is even better has reached the status of a mantra among policy-makers, businesspeople and academics alike. Never before in the history of mankind has faith in competition enjoyed such an exalted, almost religious, standing and never before have more dimensions of social reality been immersed with its logic. With the ascendancy of neoliberal doctrines in the 1980s, previously shielded public utility sectors, such as energy, water, transportation, postal services and telecommunications were privatised and exposed to the necessity to compete. The imperative of competitiveness is not only limited to the domain of private companies competing for profits and markets however. A sweeping marketisation has embraced ever more public service sectors, ranging from social welfare, health care, housing and increasingly also education. Universities compete for students and funding for research projects, hospitals compete for patients and local townships, cities, regions and even entire countries compete for mobile taxpayers, tourists and corporate investments. At the same time, the unemployed compete for jobs, whilst the employed vie to keep their jobs and further their career opportunities. The vast prominence of disciplinary policy tools, such as performance indexes, scoreboards and benchmarking 'best practices' are a tangible manifestation of competition as a totalising and all-pervasive logic. Exposed to continuous comparative evaluation, contemporary capitalist societies have transformed into true competition societies.

The European Union (EU) is at the forefront of promoting competition as inherently positive. Competition is featured as a panacea for almost everything: it is believed to boost economic competitiveness, enhance social welfare, produce sustainable economic growth and currently even to cure the global economic crisis. The idea that more competition automatically leads to more competitiveness was first endorsed in the European Commission's *White Paper on Competitiveness, Growth and Employment* in 1993. In the Lisbon Agenda of 2000, the goal to outcompete the rest of the world by becoming the world's most competitive and knowledge-based economy in 2010 was declared official EU policy (European Council 2000). In the same vein, the recently published follow up, the *Europe 2020 Strategy*, also centre-staged the 'competition for competitiveness' spirit in its headline targets. Somewhat paradoxically, the new strategy seeks to reconcile the rigours of capitalist competition with 'high employment', 'social and territorial cohesion', as well as a 'greener' and 'more resource efficient' economy (European Commission 2010a: 3). Competition, it seems, has evolved into the central unifying principle for the European integration project, bearing solutions to the global economic crisis, the environmental crisis and the EU's enduring legitimacy crisis. Romano Prodi, former President of the European Commission, even went as far as giving equal weighting to competition with democracy and human rights when stating that the EU's ultimate goal was to guarantee European citizens 'prosperity and peaceful co-existence on the basis of democracy, competition, solidarity and unconditional respect for human rights' (Prodi 2001).

The belief that competition is sacred and that its effects are merely positive finds its ideological and social scientific precept in (neo)classical economics. Ever since Adam Smith, mainstream economic theories have assigned a metaphysical status to capitalist competition as the most efficient organising mechanism of markets. Acquired profits are considered well deserved and the resulting social order of inequality 'just'. In the words of two neoclassical economists, 'competition benefits almost everyone' and is 'the permanent driving force behind individuals as it rewards successful activities and penalises laziness and failure' (Eekhoff and Moch 2004: 1). According to the prevailing gospel, consumers are the main beneficiaries of capitalist competition. Next to forcing companies to innovate and improve the quality of the products and services, competition is believed to exert a downward pressure on prices. Prices are expected to move towards a point at which profits are eliminated and at which revenues mainly cover the production costs. In line with the alleged equilibrium dynamics of supply and demand, according to neoclassical economics we are all reaping the benefits of competition when we go out and shop, make a phone call or travel somewhere.

This rather one-dimensional view might be intuitively appealing and politically motivating, but it ignores the failures of competition of which we seldom hear. What is often forgotten is that people need to have a job first before they become consumers. Consumers are (in most cases) also employees who usually pay the price of competition in the form of lower wages, longer working days, pressure to increase productivity and poorer working conditions. In the face of competitive pressures, employers may choose to adopt labour saving technologies or relocate the production to cheap labour areas, which inevitably leads to redundancies, leaving many people left in dire straits about their future careers and living standards. Furthermore, the centrifugal forces of capitalist competition cause companies to coalesce and fuse into ever larger units. Economic concentration often goes together with radical corporate 'restructurings' in the form of large-scale job losses, especially if companies from the same industry are involved. Rationalisation and the elimination of duplicate job functions frequently constitute the downside of the much-praised synergy effects. This is even more pertinent considering that the number of mergers and acquisitions has grown exponentially over the past decades, while overall levels of Green-field investments and the concomitant production of jobs have decelerated.

Competition may be the driving force of the corporate profit-seeking venture that keeps capitalism alive; yet it is also the source of many of its problems. The competitive race for economic survival and the continued accumulation of capital is never a smooth process, but proceeds in an uncoordinated and unbalanced fashion. Through competition the social contradictions that are inherent to the capitalist system are exacerbated. Recurrent economic crises, social disruptions, the exhaustion of nature's resources and environmental degradation, as well as obscene poverty are its ineluctable toll. Competition in other words, affects the material conditions of everyone – not just the companies that are directly subjected to it. Arguably, also neoclassical economists acknowledge that competition is tenuous and often resisted. However, they often remain oblivious to the wider consequences of competition for society at large. In neoclassical economics, competition-distorting behaviour, such as cartels and other forms of restrictive corporate practices, including the corporate tendency to monopolise markets, is believed to interfere merely with the self-regulating mechanics of the equilibrium tendency. Most neoclassical economists thus agree that competition cannot be taken for granted, but effectively needs to be enforced upon the market and its agents by regulation.

In the European context, regulation that exposes companies to the disciplinary forces of competition was introduced in the aftermath of the Second World War at both national and supranational level. It evolved into one of the most prominent features of economic governance in Europe. Competition regulation formed a core area in the European Coal and Steel Community (ECSC), which was established in 1951 and the subsequent European Economic Community (henceforth the EC) of 1957. The European Commission, in practice its Directorate General (DG) for Competition, was made responsible for enforcing the EC competition rules and gradually came to enjoy extensive powers in the prosecution of cartels, the abuse dominant positions, state aid and later also the control of mergers. To date, there is no comparable regulatory field in which the Commission enjoys similar wide-ranging competences and in which the Council of the European Union and the European Parliament have so little to say.

The question of how competition in Europe should be regulated has raised fierce political controversies throughout the entire post-war era. Also today, the status of competition as capitalism's juggernaut stays contested. As French President Nicolas Sarkozy remarked in 2007: 'Competition as an ideology, as a dogma, what has it done for Europe? Fewer and fewer people who vote in European elections and fewer and fewer people who believe in Europe' (in Financial Times 2007a). Particularly in the wake of the current global financial and economic crisis, pressures have increased to relax competition rules. So far the prevailing status of competition as a central foundation of European integration project has nevertheless remained largely unaffected by criticism.

This book inverts the orthodoxy promoted by the conventional creed that competition is solely a good thing. It exposes the political power struggles among agents who have contested and shaped the evolution of European competition regulation over the past six decades. Applying a critical political economy perspective, the book takes the broader context of capitalist development in Europe as a point of departure. The central argument put forth is that the content, form and scope of European competition regulation underwent a neoliberal transformation since the 1980s, and that this transformation was driven by the European Commission in alliance with the emerging transnational capitalist class. The book explains the establishment of competition regulation at EC and national level in the 1950s, and locates its evolution in the 1960s and 1970s in the social order of 'embedded liberalism' that was underpinned by Fordist production methods and a broader Keynesian-inspired, macroeconomic welfare vision. It argues that as part of the gradual transnationalisation of capitalist production and the enduring economic crisis of the late 1970s, the content, form and scope of competition regulation came to reflect the broader shift towards a neoliberal order. It shows furthermore that the neoliberal tenets, which consolidated through a series of reforms throughout the 1990s and early 21st century, continue to prevail also in the current global economic crisis. Despite the growing contestation of the suggested post-Lisbon growth model as outlined in the *Europe 2020 Strategy*, up to now, the EU crisis management in the field of competition regulation does not pose a serious challenge to the hegemony of neoliberalism.

How this book differs ...

There is certainly no shortage of books on European competition regulation. The contributions by economists and legal scholars, in particular, are copious, dealing with a myriad of different technical and judicial aspects of competition and its regulation. Although this literature surely has its merits, most of it adopts a strictly mono-disciplinary approach. It provides a somewhat narrow and self-contained perspective on competition regulation, which is generally conceptualised as if it was untainted by politics and social power relations. Economists and legal scholars do not enjoy an undisputed monopoly in the academic literature on competition regulation however. Since the mid-1990s, a number of political science studies on EC competition regulation have surfaced (cf. Bulmer 1994; McGowan 2005; Wilks 2007; Damro 2006a; Büthe 2007; Wigger and Nölke 2007; Cini and McGowan 2008; Baskoy 2008). Yet compared to other market regulatory domains of European governance, competition regulation still suffers from a chronic lack of attention from political scientists. Although many of these studies provide astute and detailed insights into the institutional and regulatory dimensions, they also tend to analyse competition regulation as an atomistic policy field that is cut off from broader societal developments.

This book goes beyond generic discussions of competition regulation. What sets this book apart is, first, that it approaches European competition regulation from a critical political economy perspective. This perspective seeks to overcome the shortcomings that can be identified in other theoretically informed political science studies of competition regulation in the EU. As hinted above, a characteristic feature of these theories is that developments in competition regulation are not located in the context of the dynamic nature of capitalism and the way capitalism is regulated at different historical junctures. This is the case for accounts building on intergovernmentalism (Schwartz 1993), neofunctionalism (Büthe 2007; McGowan 2007a), principal-agent theories (Schmidt 1998; Wilks and Bartle 2002; Damro 2006a), as well as sociological institutionalism (Bulmer 1994). The sociological institutionalist perspective for example, links major changes in competition regulation to the way 'EC institutions have mediated various pressures at critical stages in the integration process' (Bulmer 1994: 426), but consigns the 'various pressures' to a status of exogenous variables that are not further theorised. In contrast, the critical political economy perspective developed here theorises competition and considers competition regulation a contingent feature in the broader regulatory architecture that is designed to stabilise the continued accumulation of capital.

A common feature of the aforementioned theories is that they neglect the importance of social foundations of political power. Sociological institutionalism and principal-agent theories tend to be preoccupied with institutions and institutional agents rather than the political influence of fractions of capital and labour and the underlying relations of power. Intergovernmentalism, as a state-centric theory, acknowledges the importance of domestic producers, but fails to account for the emergence and growing influence of transnational corporations. Neofunctionalism in turn, highlights subnational actors, including organised business interests, but due to the absence of a theory of capitalism, it ignores the transformation of such interests over time. Another problematic aspect common to these theories is that they do not fully, if at all, consider the importance of ideas and discourses in relation to competition regulation. This mainly applies to the theories infused with rational choice logics, namely neofunctionalism, intergovernmentalism and principal-agent theories. In contrast, the critical political economy perspective advanced here, highlights the importance of competing ideas about (competition) regulation and stresses how such ideas relate to the general discourses and power balances between social forces that prevail at a given juncture.

Second, this book fundamentally reconsiders the history of European competition regulation. With the notable exception of Freyer (2006), Gerber (1998), and Harding and Joshua (2003), few scholars have analysed the broader historical developments in this field. The overwhelming majority of scholars have focused instead on historically more delimited but nonetheless crucial developments, such as the adoption of new treaties, key regulations or court rulings. Such studies commonly tell the story of how European competition regulation, despite occasional setbacks, turned into an increasingly efficient and sophisticated regulatory tool that was vital for the successful management of the European integration project. Thereby they faithfully echo the speeches and reports issued by those in charge of competition regulation. Undoubtedly, competition regulation in Europe has become more sophisticated in recent decades. As this book demonstrates though, a much more important and profound transformation of the content, form and scope of European competition regulation has taken place, which has important repercussions on the organisation of capitalism in Europe (see also Buch-Hansen and Wigger 2010). This transformation, which is largely ignored in the existing literature or not explored in sufficient depth, is not a story of evolutionary progress, but rather the result of a major shift in underlying social power relations that paired with the transnationalisation of production.

Third, this book breaks with the tendency in the existing literature to obscure, or downplay, the profoundly political nature of competition regulation through seemingly apolitical and static conceptualisations. These are entrenched with the belief that competition, as the Holy Grail of capitalism, benefits everyone in society. Exemplary of this tendency are Motta (2004: 30), who defines competition policy as 'a set of policies and laws ensuring that competition in the marketplace is not restricted in such a way as to reduce economic welfare', or Neumann (2001: 5) who, by referring to Adam Smith, opines that '[t]o provide scope for the invisible hand to accomplish its task, competition policy must aim at securing undistorted competition'. This book challenges such deficient understandings of competition regulation. Different agents have different interests and any given type of competition regulation benefits some groups and segments in society more than others. This renders competition regulation inherently political from the outset. Behind seemingly detailed judicial and technocratic issues of competition rules and their enforcement lurk important political questions regarding the distribution and concentration of economic power and wealth, not only in domestic markets but also in an ever more globalised world. Although the political dimension receives mentioning in passing and is not entirely dismissed in the existing literature (see e.g. Monti 2007: 4–6; Motta 2004: 27), its broader implications generally remain at the margins of most scientific analyses. This is the case not only with legal and economic scholars, but also with political scientists, mirroring a broader tendency within contemporary political science to reduce politics to mere policy-making. That is, a tendency to remain at the descriptive surface of political processes, while failing to ask the essential question of *cui bono*: who benefits and who loses?

Fourth, as already indicated above, this book analyses competition regulation from a critical vantage point, whereas the bulk of the literature adopts what Cox (1996) called a problem-solving perspective. The latter 'takes the world as it finds it, with the prevailing social and power relationships and the institutions into which they are organised, as the given framework for action' (ibid.: 88). Scholars who take for granted that the current type of competition regulation is desirable without further questioning whether competition is indeed a blessing, also tend to be preoccupied with finding solutions to problems that emerge from the everyday enforcement practices. Cases in point are the contributions by legal scholars, who publish foremost in the specialised journal article sector. Voluminous commentaries address questions of interpretation of existing competition regulation and case law, legal consistency and procedural equity, as well as predictability and transparency – concerns generally also shared by the wider business community that is subject to competition regulation (Dörn and Wilks 1996: 3). Similarly, economists tend to be preoccupied with sophisticated econometric tools for analysing market shares, market efficiencies, consumer welfare and developing models for detecting competition-distorting conduct. The branch of both legal scholars and economists often drive the academic debate by inaugurating new legal questions, or responding to judicial problems encountered in changing market situations. They often aspire to prescribe more efficient regulatory practices, which feeds back into the actual regulatory developments of the field.

The critical perspective adopted here is not inherently more 'normative' than a problem-solving perspective. Any problem-solving perspective 'is value-bound by virtue of the fact that it implicitly accepts the prevailing order as its own framework' (Cox 1996: 89–90). In contrast, a critical perspective 'does not take institutions and social power relations for granted but calls them into question by concerning itself with their origin and how and whether they might be in the process of changing' (ibid.: 89). The ambition of this book is to provide a valid and comprehensive *explanation* of the evolution of European competition regulation by focusing on the nexus of social power relations and prevailing discourses at different historical junctures. To this end, the analysis is based on a wide range of reliable empirical sources. The book is however also explicitly normative as it serves a critical emancipatory purpose. Social science should go beyond explanation and function as one of the motors of human emancipation by questioning the mechanisms that produce and reproduce material inequality. In this spirit, the book complements explanation with critique after having exposed the social purpose and the resulting societal consequences of the current type of European competition regulation.

Given the broad focus on social struggles between agents adhering to different ideas and discourses in the context of the dynamics of capitalist development, a meticulous analysis of the different technical debates that have shaped regulatory developments of European competition regulation is beyond the scope of this book. The empirical analysis rather moves back and forth between the concrete and the general, making it necessary to sometimes paint with a broad brush. For more detailed discussions of specific judicial technicalities and regulatory developments, we refer to the existing textbook literature.

The structure of the book

The book consists of eight chapters. Chapter 1 outlines the critical political economy perspective that informs the empirical analyses in the subsequent chapters. By drawing on historical materialist accounts in the field of Global Political Economy (cf. Van Apeldoorn 2002; Overbeek 1990) and Bob Jessop's version of regulation theory to explain broader material socioeconomic and ideational changes (cf. Jessop 2002a; Jessop and Sum 2006), this perspective theorises the particular dynamics that follow from the competitive processes, and explains why the content, form and scope of competition regulation reflects, albeit imperfectly, the underlying power balances in society. Chapter 2 traces and explains the emergence of competition regulation systems in Europe, thereby focusing specifically on developments taking place in Germany, France and the UK, paying special attention to the pivotal role of the political pressures exerted by US authorities at that time. In addition to a brief account of the macroeconomic background and the nature of the US antitrust system, it assesses the importance of cartels and monopolies in Europe's industrial organisation in early twentieth century, as well as their role in the rise of the German Nazi regime. Chapter 3 unravels the particular socioeconomic power configuration that brought competition regulation into the realm of the Coal and Steel Community and the subsequent European Economic Community. It challenges the widespread view that the competition provisions of the European integration project were merely a reflection of ordoliberal thinking and instead demonstrates that the content, form and scope of the European competition regime were shaped by both a 'national mercantilist' and a 'neoliberal' discourse of regulation.

Chapter 4 analyses the development and enforcement of competition regulation in Europe in the 1960s and 1970s, the heyday of the post-war social order of 'embedded liberalism' and the so-called 'American challenge'. It shows that in this era and most notably in the wake of the economic crisis, social forces advocating positions informed by 'centre-left' and 'Euro-mercantilist' discourses challenged neoliberal and national mercantilist ideas. Competition regulation was politically legitimised with references to social inclusion, full employment goals and inter-class solidarity, thereby reflecting the wider class compromise between organised labour and industrial capital fractions of the mixed economies in Europe. Chapter 5 highlights the growing influence of the emerging transnational capitalist class that shaped the transformation of the content, form and scope of European competition regulation in the context of the enduring economic crisis of the 1970s, and the subsequent neoliberal market-oriented regulatory restructuring in the 1980s. It argues that in the presence of political counterforces, the neoliberal turn in EC competition regulation did not take place over night. Rather, it went through a transitional phase in which elements of the neoliberal discourse were gradually incorporated in the enforcement of competition rules. Overall, the neoliberal turn led to a more stringent prosecution of cartels, the prohibition of state aid schemes, the adoption of privatisation directives that aimed at liberalising state-owned key utility and infrastructure sectors, and the adoption of the EC merger control regulation in 1989.

Chapter 6 explains the consolidation of the neoliberal discourse of regulation throughout the 1990s on the basis of its dialectical relation with the manifestation of transnational accumulation structures and enhanced processes of financialisation. It locates the neoliberal content, form and scope of the regulatory practices in the various fields of competition regulation, such as cartels, state aids, dominant positions, privatisation and mergers and acquisitions in the fundamentally changed context of the transnational restructuring of capitalist production and the related socioeconomic power relations. Furthermore, the chapter demonstrates that EC level neoliberal practices had important repercussions on domestic competition regulation, which underwent a process of Europeanisation in this period. Chapter 7 explores the nature and main causes of the 2004 modernisation of EC competition regulation. It argues that even though the content, form and scope of EC competition regulation were transformed in important respects, the reform process merely underscored the further consolidation of the neoliberal discourse of regulation by institutionally anchoring a more marked-based, free competition orientated system. The chapter reveals that neoliberal forms of regulation increasingly came under political pressure, in particular since the global economic crisis in 2007.

Chapter 8 explains why EC level competition regulation increasingly acquired an external dimension in the course of the 1990s through the conclusion of various bilateral and multilateral competition agreements. Particular attention is paid to how the transatlantic interagency cooperation in competition matters facilitated commercial cross-border transactions in the transatlantic marketplace, and why the Commission evolved as a vanguard in attempting to orchestrate a multilateral agreement on global competition rules. The chapter displays the contestation to the establishment of multilateral competition rules and with it, the contestation to give free market access to new product, labour, public procurement and investment markets on a worldwide scale. It explains why alternative routes were chosen, corresponding with the interests of the transnational capitalist class.

The concluding remarks recapitulate the main findings of the analysis and assess the EU level political responses to the global economic crisis while speculating on whether the crisis management marks the beginning of a new transformation of competition regulation. A few critical reflections upon the nature of competition and neoliberal competition regulation provide a point of departure for the outline of an alternative vision of competition and it regulation.

1 Theorising competition regulation

A critical political economy perspective

This chapter outlines the theoretical perspective underpinning the analysis of the politics of six decades of competition regulation in Europe. It begins by spelling out the ontological assumptions of this perspective and explicating the ensuing theoretical implications. Section two conceptualises competition as a central feature of capitalism and as a phenomenon with both positive and negative societal consequences. Section three presents a novel perspective on competition regulation, which links the regulation of competition to capitalist market regulation more generally. It highlights that the content, form and scope of competition regulation is never given beforehand, but always discursively shaped, reflecting, albeit imperfectly, social power relations. Section four addresses the importance and nature of classes and class fractions, whilst section five links the preferences of such fractions to different discourses of competition regulation. The final section conceptualises states and supranational institutions, highlighting the degree of operational autonomy they enjoy.

1.1 Ontological reflections

All social scientific theories and, for that matter, all explanations of phenomena in the social world, entail a particular social ontology – understood as an abstract articulation of social being (Patomäki 2002: 77). The theoretical perspective outlined here embodies insights from a social ontology associated with critical realism (see Bhaskar 1979). At the heart of this ontology is an account of the agency-structure relationship, with agency denoting the capacity of agents to act, and structure referring to the relational context within which agents operate (Hay 2002: 94). Structures are always the outcome of human activities undertaken in the past. This means that, at any given point in time, agents are confronted with pre-existing structures that either facilitate or constrain their social activities. Bhaskar (1979: 51) introduces the notion of the *position-practice system* to highlight that agents occupy structural positions associated with particular resources, constraints, predicaments and powers, which motivate their 'occupiers' to engage in specific social practices. Importantly, this does not imply a deterministic understanding of structure and agency. Agents reproduce or transform social structures through their practices (Archer 1995; Bhaskar 1979). As social reality is populated by real human beings who have different characteristics and inclinations, events and phenomena are never predetermined before they happen, meaning that 'the future remains pregnant with a surplus of opportunities' (Jessop 2005: 53).

Agents and structures do not stand in a one-to-one relationship with each other. Rather 'society must be regarded as an ensemble of structures, practices and conventions' (Bhaskar 1979: 45). Agents are thus faced with a complex web of interrelated (political, economic, social, communicative) structures of which they only have partial knowledge. This means that unacknowledged structural consequences can follow from intentional activities, and that agents rely on particular (fallible) interpretations of social reality when formulating their preferences and strategies (Hay 2002: 209–10). In the political economy sphere, such interpretations are informed by discourses, defined as structured sets of ideas that 'provide a cognitive filter, frame or conceptual lens or paradigm through which social, political and economic developments might be ordered and rendered intelligible' (Hay and Rosamond 2002: 151). In other words, such ideas or discourses exist independently of agents, but can be internalised and deployed in rhetoric (ibid.: 150–2). Importantly, agents always interpret the world from the structural positions they occupy and this impacts on their ideational inclinations. As a consequence, 'it is very likely to make a difference for your ideological predisposition or world view whether you are the Chief Executive Officer (CEO) of Shell or one of that company's low-skilled employees' (Van Apeldoorn 2002: 19).

The theoretical implications of this social ontology are manifold. First, theoretical reductionism is ruled out from the outset. Only a theoretical perspective that ascribes genuine importance to agents, material structures and ideas or discourses can be considered acceptable. Second, if society comprises an ensemble of interrelated structures, the particular subject of investigation needs to be studied as a component of the greater whole of which it forms part. Rather than conceptualising the social world 'as an assemblage of clearly bounded objective entities which exist independently of each other' (Dean *et al.* 2006: 24), a theory has to support dialectical research, namely research that places the particular part that we are studying in the context of the broader whole in order to arrive at an improved understanding of both (see also Ollman 2003: 14).

Finally, the social ontology also has implications for the form the theoretical perspective takes. Taking agency seriously, and accepting the related assertion about the complex and open-ended nature of social reality, involves rejecting theories that purport to explain social phenomena by means of generally valid laws about social regularities and a small number of 'independent variables'. Such theories constitute a straitjacket that distorts the dynamic nature of social reality by pretending that the world is essentially static (Buch-Hansen 2008: 46).[1] In addition to this, they 'are apt to provide scientific legitimacy for particular forms of political practice' (Wight 2006: 8), often in favour of maintaining the status quo, and ruling out the emancipatory role of social science as a practice with the potential to change the world (Cox 1996: 89). A theoretical perspective rather has to 'point us towards the most important factors which conjointly shape that "complex synthesis of multiple determinations"' we are studying (Jessop

1990: 249). At the same time, it has to provide room for a significant degree of flexibility. The critical political economy perspective of this book has been specifically designed 'to allow for' genuine changes in the nature of competition and competition regulation at different junctures and for different types of agents to play decisive roles.

1.2 Capitalism and competition

> Free competition brings out the inherent laws of capitalist production, in the shape of external coercive laws having power over every individual capitalist.
>
> Karl Marx (1965 [1887]: 270)

Contemporary Western societies are capitalist societies. This does not mean that all phenomena in such societies can be reduced to manifestations of capitalism and the imperatives of its functioning. However, in social spaces where the economic sphere is capitalist, this sphere is dominant over other spheres, and thus able to impose its primary logic on institutions in other spheres more than such other spheres are able to impose their primary logics on the economic sphere (see also Jessop 2000; Lipietz 1983: 19). The overshadowing logic in capitalist economies is that of capital accumulation, with 'capital' denoting accumulated wealth that can be used to accumulate more wealth. Indeed, '[c]apitalism as a historical system is defined by the fact that it makes structurally central and primary the endless accumulation of capital' (Wallerstein 2000: 147; see also Jessop 1990: 152 on the notion of capital).

Any attempt to provide a general description of capitalism runs into the problem that the particular forms of capitalism have varied from location to location and also over time. In fact, 'capitalist relations are themselves subject to profound historical alteration and to major variations between one socio-economic formation and another, depending on the history of struggle and social movements' (Lipietz 1983: 19; see also Robinson 2004: 4–5).[2] Capitalism thus has no 'final telos': it is historically contingent and 'its future remains open in the face of structural changes and social struggles' (Jessop 1997: 561). Nonetheless, at a very general level, capitalism can be defined as an economic system in which a large number of companies, using privately owned capital, goods and wage-labour, produce and sell goods and services with the intention of making profit (Jessop 2002a: 12). The main source of real added value is the labour power consumed in the production process. It ultimately makes possible a process where capital expands through the successful reinvestment of past profits.[3] The commodification of labour is a distinguishing feature of capitalism: workers exchange their capacity to work for a wage and accept the right of their employer (the capitalist) to reap the profits (or absorb losses) that result from the sale of the produced goods and services.

The process of capital accumulation generally takes place in the context of competition. Competition is a crucial aspect of capitalist systems, and it is thus not surprising that it constitutes a key concept in most economic theories. (Neo-)classical theories depart from David Ricardo's and/or Adam Smith's positive sum idea, which associates competition with a number of desirable effects such as economic progress and innovation, the creation of wealth and the reduction of poverty.[4] Competition is seen as a driving force of capitalism that, as spelled out in Smith's *The Wealth of Nations* (2003[1776]: 623) 'is advantageous to the great body of the people'. It drives 'every man to endeavour to execute his work with a certain degree of exactness' (ibid.: 963). Consequently, '[i]n general, if any branch of trade, or any division of labour, be advantageous to the public, the freer and more general the competition, it will always be the more so' (ibid.: 420). Competition in other words, is assumed to result in the maximisation of social wealth and welfare. Neoclassical theories share this view and base their understanding on the notion of 'perfect competition', an imaginary state of affairs, in which a large number of small companies are unable to influence the market conditions to their own benefit. This presumes a harmonious equilibrium situation in which no further welfare increases are possible, neither for buyers or sellers, nor for the final consumers (cf. Eekhoff and Moch 2004; Neumann 2001).

The critical political economy perspective outlined here insists on taking a more critical and balanced view on the effects of capitalist competition, understood as the process of rivalry between particular companies in their struggle for profits. Certainly, intercompany competition can trigger a dynamic interplay with positive effects, such as giving companies a strong incentive to invest in R&D, improve the quality of the products and services whilst keeping prices down, hereby benefitting consumers. Yet at the same time, competition has a range of significant negative consequences that are far from trivial. It exerts direct pressures 'to the sphere of production, and particularly labour to deliver higher profitability, be it by higher productivity, longer working days or lower wages' (Bryan and Rafferty 2006: 162; see also Marx 1965[1887]: Chapter 20). Companies thus tend to impose the costs on labour when responding to competitive pressures. This means that not everybody can profit equally from competition. The critical question is *for whom* wealth is increased.

There is no such thing as a politically innocent capitalist market (Sklar 1988: 88). The extension and intensity of competition lays at the very foundation of conflict of capitalist relations. It generates incompatible interests with regard to the surplus created in the process of production. Moreover, it also prompts companies to act in ways that have profoundly negative societal consequences. As Stanford (2008: 135–8) notes, '[s]ome of the downsides are exactly opposite to the upsides, indicating the complex and often contradictory character of real-world competition'. Among other things, companies may seek to improve their competitive position by 'externalising' their costs, for instance by polluting or selling unsafe products, thereby shedding their liabilities outside the market place. Likewise, they may seek to differentiate their products 'in ways that are wasteful, useless, or even destructive: massive (and often misleading) advertising, excess packaging (to make products look "bigger"), and artificial obsolescence (where products are artificially designed to wear out or become useless prematurely)' (ibid.: 137). Moreover, there are no guarantees that competition results in innovation. To the contrary, competition can get so intense that companies are not making sufficient profit for new investments in R&D, and opt for a wasteful duplication of their competitors' products instead.

In marked contrast, the neoclassical perspective elevates competition to a force that leads to 'a high degree of wealth in society' (Eekhoff and Moch 2004: 4). This very biased and one-sided view ignores that there are no guarantees that competition in today's globalised capitalist economy has positive effects at societal level. It also ignores that competition does not only take place in markets, but also for markets. Competition prompts a process of commodification, namely the subjugation of ever-more facets of human existence and interaction to the logics of the market and thus, the price mechanism (Overbeek 2004: 4). As far as labour is concerned, the extended logic of competition reveals itself in the individualisation of the wage relationship, individual performance evaluations with the prospect of salary increases, bonuses and individual career advances (Bourdieu 1998). Furthermore, entire territories (states, regions, or cities) compete with each other, striving to create a business-friendly regulatory climate that attracts and secures capital. Winners and losers are not distributed evenly. As a result 'some companies, sectors, regions and even entire countries grow and prosper while others decline' (Stanford 2008: 136). Endorsing a macro-view lays bare that competition is not only an essential driving force of capitalism, but also results in a number of absurdities. It erects a hierarchy of socioeconomic relations marked by inequalities in wealth and power, which extend from the individual to groups or classes and to geographical regions in the world. The social costs of competition are significant and thus should not be ignored.

Another defining feature of the process of competition is that it is highly fragile. A major contradiction in the process of capital accumulation arises because '[c]apitalism is driven by competition, yet capital must always seek to thwart competition' (Wood 2003: 22). In its strongest form competition confronts companies as an objective threat, 'which strikes not at the margins of the profits and the outputs of the existing firms but at their foundations and their very lives' (Schumpeter 1947: 84). In the long run, only the most powerful survive, while weaker companies are either absorbed by other companies or simply perish. To put it metaphorically, competition forces market players to swim or to sink, and competition takes place only between the swimmers. It is not a game in which everyone who plays can win (see Arnold in Kolasky 2002a). In the vicious struggle to secure profits and economic survival, many capitalists are thus inclined to avoid or reduce the 'feverish agitation' of price and product rivalry (see Marx 2006[1891]: 44). Companies can evade the vicissitudes of the competitive process by engaging in cartels and other forms of collusive arrangements, or by seeking to receive various types of state aid. Another option is to secure a competitive market position by means of economic concentration through mergers and acquisitions or to out-compete competitors by temporarily reducing the price of produced goods or services.

Competition and the attempt to monopolise the market are irreversibly coupled. Mergers and the conclusion of collusive agreements are both responses to, and elements of, the concentration of capital. Fierce competition intensifies the trend towards economic power concentration: the more economic power concentrates, the more onerous it is for smaller competitors to keep up, and the more the option of a merger is a viable solution for corporate survival. This can trigger a self-perpetuating mechanism in which jumping on the merger bandwagon becomes a necessity for companies in dire straits. At the same time, shockwaves created by enhanced concentrations may eventually result in the oligopolisation or monopolisation of market power – at the expense of competition and market diversity. As Marx (1965[1887]: 626) observed, 'competition rages in direct proportion to the number, and in inverse proportion to the magnitudes, of the antagonistic capitals. It always ends in the ruin of many small capitalists, whose capitals partly pass into the hands of their conquerors, partly vanish'. Economic concentration in the form of monopolies or oligopolies, with no or only few competitors left, concomitantly reveals the inherent contradictions of the capitalist system.[5] Wanniski (1992: 18) captured this contradiction well by noting that 'Marx was extremely close to the truth' when he discovered that '[c]apitalism could not succeed because capitalists would sow the seeds of their own destruction. That is, if capitalism requires relentless competition, yet capitalists are doing everything they can to destroy competition, we have a system that is inherently unsustainable'. This and other contradictions, explain why capitalism's expanded reproduction cannot be secured by markets and market actors alone, but depends on various forms of regulation (cf. Polanyi 1992[1944]).

1.3 Theorising competition regulation

Markets are not natural facts that represent some sort of God-given order that existed prior to and despite of various extra-economic interferences. On the contrary, markets are social constructs that only exist because of the existence of extra-economic spheres such as education, nature, security, the family and the interventions by legal-regulatory and political institutions (see also Van Apeldoorn and Horn 2007: 211–15). The reproduction of capitalism thus 'depends on its achieving an inherently unstable balance among market-oriented economic supports whose efficacy depends on their location beyond market mechanisms' (Jessop 2002a: 19). This 'balance' is by definition unstable because of the contradictions that lie at the heart of capitalism and its dynamic nature. Over time, the continued accumulation of capital depends on gradual transformations, and possibly the replacement of the various 'supports'.

In what follows, the concept of regulation refers to different types of interventions in (parts of) the economic sphere by political and legal-regulatory institutions.[6] The totality of regulatory practices in a given social space, such as a country or a region, and the institutions performing those regulatory tasks are referred to as the *ensemble of regulation*, while the part of this social space that is subject to regulation is denoted as the *field of regulation* (see Figure 1). Alongside other extra-economic factors, ensembles of regulation can contribute

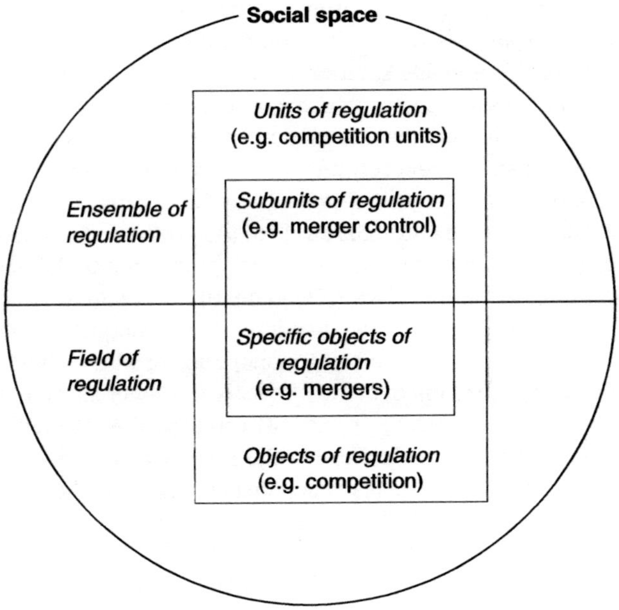

Figure 1 Conceptualising regulation.

to stabilise and sustain particular *growth models*, namely sets of economic logics, techniques and practices associated with a relatively stable period of economic growth. A given ensemble of regulation is made up of multiple *units of regulation*, each defined in relation to some *object of regulation* forming part of the wider field (such as competition, trade, environment or monetary issues).[7] Moreover, a particular unit of regulation consists of various *subunits of regulation* that relate to a number of more *specific objects of regulation.* For instance, competition regulation may involve the regulation of 'objects', such as mergers, cartels and state aid. Conceptualised in these terms, the European Commission's Competition DG and its regulatory practices (which are obviously based on various rules) constitute a unit of regulation, made up of various subunits. Importantly, these and other (sub)units are not isolated entities, but often connected to other (sub)units of regulation in a given social space, as well to (sub)units of other social spaces. It is therefore necessary to analyse them in the context of both the transformation of capitalism and the way in which capitalism is regulated.

Competition units of regulation do not emerge as an automatic or functionalist response to the needs of the economic system. That is, capitalism cannot 'speak for itself' and articulate its preferences for or against particular interventions in the economic sphere. Only agents can have opinions about how to regulate capitalism and subsequently act on them. Such opinions are informed by discourses that exist independently of the individual agent and that may or may not become institutionalised. Competition regulation, like all regulation, is based on particular discourses, and the latter are, in turn, related to broader regulatory discourses that prevail at a given juncture. It is therefore insufficient to look at regulation only in terms of ensembles, units and subunits. Rather, different levels of ideas of regulation need to be taken into account. On the basis of their relative level of concreteness, two levels of 'ideas of regulation' can be distinguished, namely general discourses and unit-specific discourses.

General discourses of regulation entail more encompassing perspectives or structured sets of ideas, on how the economy in a given social space ought to be regulated. They relate to the overall nature of the ensemble of regulation and prescribe particular 'models' of capitalism. For example, neoliberalism is a general discourse that *inter alia* prescribes a market-oriented type of regulation, resonating well with the Anglo-Saxon model of capitalism, whereas mercantilism ascribes an important role to states in protecting and promoting domestic industries through active industrial policies, reverberating with the model of state-capitalism (cf. Coates 2000; Van Apeldoorn 2002: 72–8). *Unit-specific discourses of regulation* emerge from general discourses, and translate them into perspectives on how to deal with the various objects making up the field of regulation.[8] In the competition area, such discourses entail perspectives on the purposes of competition units and the specific objects they ought to target (content), how competition rules ought to be enforced (form), and what jurisdiction competition units ought to cover (scope).

Regarding *content*, a given competition unit can have various objects of regulation, such as cartels, market dominance, mergers or state aid and in regulating these objects, serve different social purposes that benefit certain societal groups more than others. It can strive to make entire economies more competitive, or focus on competition between single companies. It can problematise and constrain economic power (concentration), or enable private market power to emerge. It can enhance or restrict competition among market players, be more or less market-interventionist, more or less business-friendly or more or less free-market orientated. Regarding *form*, competition rules can be enforced by politically independent competition authorities, involve political decision-makers or be left to private market actors litigating before the courts, generally referred to as private enforcement. The question of *scope* concerns the demarcation of the jurisdictional reach of the competition unit in question: it can be national, regional, or global. When looking at concrete ensembles of regulation, or (sub) units of regulation in a given social space, it can be possible to identify traits of different discourses. Consequently, such ensembles or (sub)units can contain a number of 'irrelevant, residual, marginal, secondary, and even potentially contradictory elements' (Jessop 2002b: 106).

It follows that definitions of 'competition regulation' with a claim to capture its universal essence are futile. Rather, competition regulation is a label that can be attached to regulation serving various social purposes and involving different ideas. This is not to say that its nature is completely ambiguous, and that it is impossible to distinguish competition regulation from other forms of regulation.

Generally, its declared purpose is to preserve or bring about competition in a market place. How and to what extent this is accomplished and whether competition units of regulation also incorporate features that remedy some of the negative effects of competition cannot be answered in a general way however. The critical political economy perspective outlined here advocates for this reason a flexible and open-ended conceptualisation of competition regulation, which takes its multidimensional, dynamic and political nature into account.

The ascendancy of a discourse of regulation proceeds through moments of deconstruction, construction and consolidation (Overbeek 2000: 248–9). In a *deconstructive moment*, articulators of a new discourse challenge prevalent ideas, and promote new ones that threaten to undermine the ideational position of an existing discourse. Once a vast majority of the parties involved subscribe to these ideas, a *constructive moment* follows in which the discourse gets implemented in social practices, policy solutions and structural adjustments. Such a transition never entails a total rupture of previous structures at once, but is shaped by 'the paradoxical simultaneity of continuity/discontinuity in the flow of historical time' (Jessop and Sum 2006: 324). In a situation of relative continuity, regulatory changes are in line with the structural coherence of a given period. Once new regulatory ideas are incorporated (to pacify oppositional forces), this coherence is disrupted. A phase of transition begins in which relative continuity alternates with relative discontinuity. Such transitions are 'moments of disjunction and relative openness' in which different social forces search for new patterns of structural coherence in an experimental manner (ibid.: 326). Once contradictions exacerbate, a phase of restructuring begins, leading eventually to a *moment of consolidation*, which is marked again by relative continuity: the discourse becomes hegemonic and deeply engrained in institutions and regulatory ensembles.

1.4 Classes and class fractions

Competition units of regulation are based on particular ideas on how to organise a market place. These ideas are related, albeit imperfectly, to the general discourses that prevail at a given juncture, which in turn, are related to the underlying balance of power between various social forces. The notions of class and capital fractions are essential in this regard. Even though capitalism is premised on the exploitation of one class by another, this does not imply that politics in contemporary late-modern societies can meaningfully be reduced to a struggle between capital and labour. Already Marx noted that the stratification of classes does not appear in its pure form 'as the lines of demarcation are obliterated by 'middle and intermediate strata' (Marx 1966[1894]: 885). Moreover, not all social struggles are necessarily connected to class, let alone to class awareness. Yet such social struggles, even though not consciously directed at class interests, may nonetheless have 'conjuncturally determined' class relevance (Jessop 2002a: 32), particularly once they impact on dominant class interests. Importantly, the polar opposites of the fundamental classes (capital and labour) do not constitute unified wholes, but are internally fractionalised in various ways. As spelled out by political economy scholars associated with the 'Amsterdam Perspective', the defining feature of a class fraction is that its members perform similar economic functions in the process of capital accumulation and concomitantly, tend to have specific ideological inclinations related to these functions (Van der Pijl 1989: 11; see also Overbeek 2004).

The different outlook and preference of capital fractions can result in class struggles between these capital fractions.[9] As noted by Overbeek (1990: 25), '[c]onflicts between fractions of capital tend to transcend the competition between individual capitalists, because these conflicts do not take place within the existing framework of the economic, political and ideological conditions for capital accumulation but are concerned with changing these conditions'. The fractionalisation of capital can take place along different axes and thus give rise to different conflicts, such as between industrial versus money capital (Overbeek 1990: 25–7; Overbeek and Van der Pijl 1993: 3–5), between monopoly and non-monopoly capital (e.g. Poulantzas 1975: 144–5), and between nationally versus transnationally oriented capital (Overbeek and Van der Pijl 1993: 5–7; Robinson 2004: 49–53).

Furthermore, it is important to distinguish between the structural aspect of classes/class fractions and the process of class formation, 'that is, the moment when class becomes the basis for collective action; a movement from class structure to class agency' (Van Apeldoorn 2002: 21). At first, a class is defined with reference to the position of its members in the economic structure: 'A person's class is established by his objective place in the network of ownership relations [...]. His consciousness, culture, and politics do not enter the definition of his class position' (Cohen 1978: 73). This is the objective, or structural dimension of class. Classes however, only become driving forces of history when a circle of their 'members' unite – that is, when a group of agents occupying similar class positions, constituting what Marx called a 'class-in-itself', develop a common class consciousness, articulate common preferences and work for their realisation, thereby becoming a 'class-for-itself'.

Economic concentration across national borders, be it in the form of mergers and acquisitions, or commercial intercompany agreements, constitute one of the most important mechanisms through which the material basis for the formation of class agency at the transnational level comes into being (Robinson 2004: 57–62). Transnational class fractions in the structural sense emerge and consolidate when companies with a previously national orientation engage in cross-border economic transactions and thereby transnationalise. As structure is prior to agency, the transnationalisation of capital can result in the emergence of transnational class agency. In other words, classes are not static and the significance of particular fractions changes in a dialectical interplay with the transformation of capitalism.

The class fraction approach is indispensable when trying to understand fundamental changes in the broader capitalist development, such as overall changes in ensembles of regulation. When studying more narrow phenomena such as the establishment and transformation of European competition units of regulation, it is also limited however. Functional distinctions and conflicting preferences between different capital fractions, each defending a distinct position in a political battle, do not necessarily surface in clear-cut ways. Some social groups may cut across the axes that define class fractions and represent both national and transnational capital interests. It is not a foregone conclusion that national business federations necessarily defend the interests of nationally oriented capital. Also the distinction between productive and money capital can be blurred. This has consequences for the way the concepts are used in the chapters that follow. To complement the concepts of 'the capitalist class' and 'capital fractions' and related notions such as 'industrial' or 'financial capitalists', the concept of 'organised capital' will be applied to denote business associations and similar organisations/groups that are not clearly associated with specific fractions.

1.5 Social forces and discourses of competition regulation

When seeking to explain the transformation of European competition regulation over time, the critical political economy perspective outlined in this book ascribes particular importance to the members of the prevailing fraction(s) of the capitalist class. Next to enjoying a 'privileged position' in capitalist societies (Lindblom 1977), the owners and managers of companies are affected by market regulation more directly than others.[10] Hence, they have a genuine interest in influencing competition rules and their enforcement. At the same time, they have an ambiguous and almost paradoxical relationship with competition regulation. In principle, every law or regulatory rule can constrain economic freedom, as efforts to comply always cause transaction costs. Yet, competition regulation goes further than this as it can both enable and constrain private market power. It can function as a constructive force for some and impose constraints on the economic freedom of others. This is why the capitalist class is not a unified group, but is more likely to be divided over the desirability of a particular type of competition regulation. The particular preferences of capital fractions are generally contingent upon a range of different aspects, including the degree of market openness and the broader macroeconomic market structure, the integration of companies and/or business sectors in the world economy and their trade orientation.

Members of different fractions can be expected to formulate their position with respect to the desired content, form and scope of competition regulation on the basis of different unit-specific discourses. In order to understand the overall evolution of competition units of regulation over time, it is therefore vital to look at the relative power balance between fractions of capital at different junctures. Such power balances are not stable, but shaped by the prevailing form of capital accumulation, which impacts on the relative ability of capital fractions to influence what type of (competition) regulation they are subjected to.

In the chapters that follow, four unit-specific discourses are identified, namely a neoliberal, a national mercantilist, a Euro-mercantilist and a centre-left discourse.[11] It is argued that the nature of competition units of regulation at different junctures reflects, albeit imperfectly, the relative power balances of the configurations of agents formulating their positions on the basis of these discourses. Certainly, these configurations did not only include the owners, managers and representatives of various forms of capital, but also political decision-makers at ministerial and parliamentarian level, trade unions and institutional actors, such as various diplomats and bureaucrats. Moreover, economic or legal experts from the academia or from the professional services branch have been involved in the processes leading up to important developments in the history of European competition regulation. The remainder of this section explicates the nature of the four unit-specific discourses, and links them to the preferences of different social forces, notably fractions of capital and labour, thereby moving from the theoretical to the empirical domain. This is crucial to keep in mind because the number and nature of significant discourses cannot be determined exclusively at the level of theory.

The **neoliberal discourse** is based on the assumption that competition is inherently desirable, because it is believed to produce efficiency gains in the allocation of resources and in the production process and ultimately to increase the welfare of consumers. This is also the assumption underlying (neo)classical economics, which is regularly called in to scientifically legitimise the type of competition regulation prescribed by this discourse. Neoliberalism however, is also a '*rascal concept* – promiscuously pervasive, yet inconsistently defined, empirically imprecise and frequently contested' (Brenner *et al.* 2010a). In the context of competition regulation, different neoliberal schools of thought co-exist, such as German ordoliberalism, the Austrian and the Chicago school, each with their own theoretical core concepts, principles and values (cf. Budzinski 2009; Giocoli 2009). Notwithstanding these differences, a basic core of the neoliberal unit-specific discourse can be identified, prescribing a distinctive content, form and scope of competition regulation.

As regards *content*, primacy is given to 'pure' and objective competition criteria, rather than broader societal considerations, such as industrial and social policy goals. Such criteria serve the purpose of removing all sorts of private and public obstacles that are considered a hinder to free market access and the efficient allocation of resources. The use of price theories and price modelling generally serves as a central reference point for determining anticompetitive conduct. This implies that cartels and various forms of state aid are considered intolerable, particularly as such practices foreclose market access for competitors and distort the free pricing mechanism. The stance towards economic concentration however, is more ambiguous, especially as it can be the natural result of the continuous competitive dynamics. On the one hand, economic concentration can create the necessary economies of scale and scope, leading to enhanced efficiency gains, which in turn can be passed on to consumers in the form of lower prices and higher quality products. On the other hand, it reduces the number of competitors and thus also competition. Thus, as competition is celebrated as a highest good, this creates a fundamental tension. Some versions of neoliberalism, such as German ordoliberalism, therefore argue against the concentration of economic power (Gerber 1998: 240–1; see also Chapter 2).

Most proponents of the neoliberal discourse however, favour merger subunits that allow for significant degrees of concentration.

As regards *form*, the neoliberal discourse advocates that politically independent institutions, rather than political decision-makers, enforce competition regulation. This viewpoint is closely related to the notion that competition needs to be regulated on the basis of pure competition criteria in order to prevent policy-makers from obstructing unpopular decisions on social or industrial policy grounds. Overall, this discourse proposes to restrict public market intervention to a minimum, which means that, insofar as economic concentration is furthered, mergers and acquisitions ought to be merely passively facilitated rather than actively encouraged. Finally, as regards *scope*, the neoliberal discourse can serve as the basis for competition regulation both at national and supranational level. Yet, in order to establish uniformity in the enforcement of competition regulation and to avoid the transaction costs for companies that result from a multijurisdictional overlap, the neoliberal discourse generally favours to move regulatory competences from the national to the supranational or global level.

Those who are interested in the right to compete freely and undisturbed by state interferences and privately erected market barriers, tend to formulate their position on the basis of the neoliberal discourse. Export oriented companies seek open markets abroad and will consequently tend to favour neoliberal type competition units of regulation, even if they may still prefer domestic barriers for foreign competitors as a way to secure their competitive strength. In fact, the more companies are engaged in transnational transactions, the more their owners and managers favour competition regulation that protects the right to compete freely. In the contemporary era of economic globalisation, transnational corporations have the strongest interest in neoliberal competition regulation, preferably in the form of supranationally or globally centralised, or then nationally harmonised competition units of regulation. Reversely, those vulnerable to the exposure of fierce outside competition, such as declining industries, import-competing and/or small and medium-sized enterprises, tend to seek protection from the anarchy of free-market play by the visible hand of the state (see also Van Apeldoorn 2002: 27–9). Rather than free competition and open borders, the owners and managers of such companies tend to favour competition regulation based on a national or a Euro-mercantilist discourse. Although these discourses are based on the assumption that a certain degree of competition is desirable, they do not promote the preservation of competition at all costs.

According to the **national mercantilist discourse,** the top priority is to secure the competitiveness of key domestic companies or industrial sectors vis-á-vis foreign competitors. To this end, it prescribes interventionist industrial policies that foster national champions – that is, domestic flagship companies that are able to compete in global markets. This has strong implications for the nature of competition regulation. As regards *content*, competition regulation tends to be subsumed under national industrial policy strategies, which prioritise the global competitiveness of key national companies and industrial sectors above a high degree of competition in domestic markets. From this vantage point, competition units of regulation consequently ought to adopt a discriminatory enforcement strategy, which is to the benefit of domestic corporations and which does not interfere with state aid, tax reductions, guaranteed procurement and other supporting policies. Economic concentration is considered necessary and thus, needs to be actively encouraged by public market intervention. It follows that merger control subunits are considered redundant or then, ought to be designed in a way that ensures that mergers and acquisitions for the most part are not obstructed. Likewise, in order to reduce domestic corporate rivalry, cartels and other restrictive business practices ought to be tolerated in some cases. As regards *form*, the national mercantilist discourse reserves an important role for political decision-makers in the regulatory processes, particularly as political discretion allows for the necessary flexibility to streamline the regulation of competition with industrial policy strategies. Finally, competition regulation has to be national in *scope,* as European or global level regulation might contradict or undermine domestic industrial policies.

Competition regulation informed by the **Euro-mercantilist discourse** shares similarities with the national mercantilist discourse, most notably in terms of *content*. The main difference concerns the question of *scope*: primacy is given to EC level industrial policies that foster 'European champions' – that is, globally competitive companies based in the EC/EU. Accordingly, all subunits making up the EC competition unit of regulation have to be compatible with the realisation of EC industrial policy. As regards *form*, far-reaching discretionary powers in the regulation of competition have to be entrusted upon officials of EC institutions, particularly in the Commission. Generally, this discourse is likely to be articulated by the owners and managers of companies with a national or European market orientation.

Similarly to the two mercantilist discourses, the **centre-left discourse** is based on the assumption that the beneficial effects of competition are limited and that it should therefore not be preserved at all costs. A point of concern is the potentially negative consequences for labour. As this suggests the main advocates of this discourse are likely to be unions and centre-left parties. In terms of *content*, it is held that social policy aspects, such as employment effects and labour rights ought to be taken into account in the regulation of competition. In terms of *form*, labour representatives and political decision-makers, rather than independent authorities with no or little democratic accountability, have to ensure that the viewpoints of labour are accommodated. Unlike the other discourses, the centre-left discourse does not prescribe a particular *scope* of competition regulation. Table 1 summarises the content, form and scope prescribed by the four discourses.

1.6 Conceptualising the state and supranational institutions

When dealing with the phenomenon of European competition regulation, the role played by the European Union (EU) and its member states cannot be

Table 1 Discourses of competition regulation

	Neoliberal discourse	*National mercantilist discourse*	*Euro-mercantilist discourse*	*Centre-left discourse*
Content	Competition-only focus, entailing a consumer welfare and efficiency rhetoric	National industrial policy focus, aiming at fostering national champions	EC industrial policy focus, aiming at fostering European champions	Social policy focus, entailing a full employment and labour rights rhetoric
Form	Regulation by politically independent institutions	Involvement of national political decision-makers in regulatory processes	Far-reaching discretionary powers given to EC institutions/ officials	Involvement of labour and democratically accountable decision-makers
Scope	Both national and EC, yet preferably EC and beyond	National	EC	No clear preference

ignored. Much has been written about their nature and functions. For example, the EU has been conceptualised as a regime (Hoffmann 1982), a federation (Burgess 2000), a political system (Hix 1999), as well as a new form of political domination (Schmitter 1991). Likewise, the state has been theorised and conceptualised in a variety of different ways (for an overview see Hay *et al.* 2006). As the tasks performed by the capitalist states are manifold (see Hudson 2005: 98; Jessop 2002a: 45), state institutions relate in numerous ways to a particular field of regulation. This can vary greatly from institution to institution, from one social space to another and from epoch to epoch (Hay 1996: 5; see also Flinders 2006). Capturing the essence of the state and the EU in a single theoretical mechanism is therefore impossible. Instead, it is necessary to distinguish between various 'moments of stateness' (Hay 1996: 9), or, 'aspects of statehood' (Ougaard 2004: 66).

In the present context, the focus is on the role of states and state-like organisations, such as the EC/EU, as providers of regulation and some degree of social cohesion, as well as their function as key locations for political contestation. Both states and state-like organisations are conceptualised here as ensembles of institutions, that form part of various (sub)units of regulations making up the wider ensemble of regulation. Institutions contain webs of related positions occupied by agents, and are characterised by their capability to communicate and act as one agent when interacting with their environment, which in part consists of other institutions. To be sure, all decisions in an institution are made by agents; yet they do so in the 'in the name' of the institution, which allows the institution to appear as one agent. In line with neo-Gramscian perspectives, states and state-like institutions are argued to be crucially influenced by underlying class compromises, and to receive a large degree of their power from social forces in civil society (Cox 1987). As outlined in a previous section, this means that the content, form and scope of units of regulation are affected by socioeconomic power balances. Notwithstanding, states or state-like organisations cannot be reduced to arenas, structures, or terrains, as some neo-Gramscian scholars have done (see Bieler and Morton 2001: 18; Van Apeldoorn 2004: 168; 2002: 46–7). Institutions and institutional ensembles also enjoy some degree of independence, or 'operational autonomy' (Jessop 2000: 330), which is a necessary precondition for them to perform their tasks. Non-state actors can provide ideational input into policy processes, but they rarely get to design the rules that regulate the objects in a particular field of regulation in their entirety. Political decision-makers and bureaucrats can behave in ways that contradict the preferences of prevailing social forces. Thus, states and state-like institutions 'act as a distorting mirror to reproduce a highly imperfect reflection of these conflicts and one that imprints its own image on their resolution' (Hall 1986: 233).

The relation between states and supranational institutions has been a central theme in literature on European integration since the 1950s, giving rise to the famous supranationalist-intergovernmentalist dichotomy (Branch and Øhrgaard 1999). Ultimately, the question about this dynamic relationship can only be answered empirically. Suffice it to say that the EU has developed into more than just an international organisation or a regime. National governments, however, remain the primary 'scale managers' that have a decisive say when determining at what level to place the regulation of particular objects (Hudson 2005: 110). The supranational institutions, in turn, are related to institutions at national, regional and international levels. Thus, institutions at various levels may share the responsibility for the management of the same unit of regulation within Europe. As such, the EC/EU can be best seen 'as one element within a more complex multiscalar and multidimensional system of governance and regulation in Europe' (Hudson 2003: 58; see also Holman 2004).

Conclusion

> [F]rom day to day there are both winners and losers. Still in the long run all can become winners unless the right to participate in market activities is curtailed. Freedom to join the competitive process must therefore be safeguarded by law.
>
> Neumann (2001: 3)

This quote, taken from a textbook on competition policy written by a prominent economist, provides a good illustration of the way competition and competition policy are perceived of in the bulk of the literature. Competition is seen as a gift to mankind, as something that will benefit everyone, if not distorted. As emphasised in this chapter, competition however also produces negative effects at societal level, benefitting some individuals and groups more than others. Moreover, it was stressed that the fragile nature of the competitive process makes competition regulation necessary; yet it can vary in its content, form and scope. This is because competition regulation is based on particular ideas, more specifically unit-specific discourses that are related to general discourses of regulation. Various agents can promote positions informed by such discourses. The theoretical perspective outlined here however ascribes particular importance to capital fractions and their power relations that change over time in dialectical interplay with the transformation of capitalism. Finally, the chapter argued that states and supranational institutions are not just passive structures, but rather ensembles of institutions, populated with real agents, and possessing a significant degree of operational autonomy from class fractions. Consequently, the precise content, form and scope of a given competition regulation is never just a pure reflection of the outcome of struggles between such fractions.

2 The origins of European competition regulation I

National level developments

This chapter traces and explains the emergence of competition units of regulation in Europe after the Second World War, focussing particularly on the political struggles at national level in West Germany (henceforth Germany), France and the United Kingdom (henceforth UK). It argues that these competition units resulted from political compromises between agents formulating their positions on the basis of the national mercantilist or the neoliberal discourse of regulation. As accounted for in the theory chapter, these discourses entail radically different views with respect to the content and form of competition regulation. This divergence was reflected in the nature of the competition units that were established in these European core countries.

The chapter demonstrates that political pressures exerted by the US authorities were pivotal in the adoption of competition rules in Europe in the 1950s, especially in Germany but also in France and the UK. Section one therefore accounts for the macroeconomic background and nature of the US competition unit of regulation. Section two addresses the importance of cartels and monopolies in Europe's industrial organisation in the early twentieth century. Section three analyses the role of cartels in the rise of the Nazi regime in Germany, whilst section four explores the influence of US authorities in the institutional rebuilding of post-war Germany. The last three sections locate the political processes that led to the competition units of regulation that were established in Germany, France and the UK in the context of emerging national models of capitalism.

2.1 The US antitrust movement and the 1890 Sherman Act

Rules on competition as a component of the wider regulatory ensemble were undoubtedly a US invention, dating back to the late nineteenth century processes of rapid industrialisation. The extension of the US railroad system facilitated transportation and trade, whilst new technologies led to increased industrial productivity and improved communication. As a result, markets rapidly expanded, leading to unprecedented economic growth. When an economic depression hit the economy in 1883 and stagnating demand resulted in overproduction, competition intensified. In response, giant trusts emerged, a sort of inter-firm network between several legally independent companies that institutionalised on a more or less permanent basis the control over operation and investment decisions, fixed prices, imposed output limitations and divided local and regional markets among themselves.[1] Such trusts wielded monopolistic control over entire industries such as steel, cattle, lead, oil, sugar, whiskey and tobacco (Djelic 2002: 241). In many cases, trusts combined productive and financial capital fractions, often also referred to as 'money trusts', composed of a network of interlocking directorates between banks and industry (Fennema 1982). The financial capital fraction that controlled these trusts generally enjoyed monopoly power over new technologies, particularly those of railroads and telegraphs, and moreover held close ties with political decision-makers (Wells 2002: 28). The emergence of large trusts eradicated smaller competitors or coerced suppliers and distributors to accept their conditions, and more generally dictated high prices for customers.

Farmers, small town-entrepreneurs and eventually also parts of the wider society, struck by poverty and unable to compete with the prices of the large trusts, came to protest against the practices of large trusts. This culminated in a broad-based popular protest movement against the concentration of economic power, demanding antitrust legislation (Fennema 1982: 4). At the heart of the debate was the question about the role of the state in relation to the emerging corporate market order. The size of private companies and the extent to which they had the right to organise the market without state intervention were central issues at stake. Against this background, Senator John Sherman drafted a law to prohibit large trusts, the famous Sherman Act, which was adopted by US Congress in 1890. Section 1 of the Sherman Act prohibited 'every contract, combination in the form of trust or otherwise, or conspiracy' that restrained interstate or foreign trade and Section 2 forbade 'attempts' to monopolise.

To date, the Sherman Act forms the most essential statutory basis for the US competition unit of regulation and is 'if not the most powerful instrument for economic policy in the United States, definitely the most characteristic' (Letwin 1981: 3). However, initially its success was rather limited. The strict prohibition of inter-firm collaboration induced companies to merge instead, which resulted in the oligopolisation and sometimes even monopolisation of entire industries. The takeover battle lasted from 1895 to the stock market crash of 1904. It entered history as the first and biggest merger wave, if measured relative to the size of the US economy, involving mainly direct competitors of the same industry (horizontal mergers) in sectors such as chemicals, food products, transportation equipment, machinery and bituminous coals (Djelic and Kleiner 2003: 3; Bittlingmayer 1985). In the context of poor economic performance and the difficulties of companies to achieve further economics of scale, the US authorities did little to stop corporate expansion through mergers. In 1909, the degree of economic concentration amounted to a situation in which the 100 largest US companies controlled nearly 18 per cent of the assets of all industrial corporations (Gaughan 2002: 25).

Against the backdrop of economic crisis in the US and protectionism in the world economy, antitrust sentiments revived once more. The Sherman Act was increasingly considered insufficient as a legal basis to tackle the concentration of capital into ever fewer hands. In 1914, under the tenure of President Woodrow Wilson (1913–21), US Congress adopted the Clayton Act, which significantly expanded the US competition unit of regulation. Similar to the Sherman Act, it entailed provisions to protect the interests of smaller and less powerful companies. Most importantly, Section 7 established a merger subunit, which specifically targeted mergers that 'substantially lessen competition'. This somewhat vague formulation did not prevent companies from growing in absolute size, but rather served as a basis for controlling concentrations in the context of the existing market structures. Thus, even though the Clayton Act was adopted with a view to curb the economic power of large companies, it did not prohibit corporate expansion. It prohibited instead exclusive agreements, tied-selling agreements (i.e. the practice of linking the selling of one product to another) and certain types of corporate interlocks between boards of directors (Fennema 1982: 20; Litan and Shapiro 2001). In addition to the Clayton Act, the Federal Trade Commission Act was adopted in 1914 to prohibit 'unfair methods of competition in or affecting commerce, and unfair or deceptive acts or practices in or affecting commerce'. This Act established the Federal Trade Commission as a second independent administrative body next to the Antitrust Division of the Justice Department, entrusted with the task to enforce the new law.

In the 1920s, the Department of Justice and the Federal Trade Commission adopted a lax attitude towards economic concentration, which at that time mostly concerned vertical mergers and mergers of companies from unrelated industries. In the context of an economic boom and enhanced liquidity of capital markets, the financial capital fraction was crucial in financing concentration activities through debt creation, which further spurred the rapid industrial expansion. In 1929, the US economy accounted for 42 per cent of the world's industrial output, followed by Germany, UK and France, whose economies together merely accounted for 28 per cent (Hobsbawm 1994: 97). The financial capital fraction was both the trigger factor for the second merger wave and eventually also for its halt, when the increasingly high returns on investments slowed down the real economy (Gaughan 2002: 28–30). This led to the Wall Street stock market crash of October 29 in 1929, the day that entered history as 'Black Thursday'.

During the early New Deal economic recovery programmes of the 1930s, the US authorities effectively shelved the vigorous enforcement of the competition rules as part of the wider protectionist measures to stimulate national economic survival. There were on average less than ten cases per year in this period (Gallo *et al.* 2000: 92). As part of the sweeping economic recession of the late 1930s, US antitrust authorities sought to avoid mass scale bankruptcies and the resulting social tensions from unemployment, and even gave their blessing to the formation of 'crisis' or 'depression' cartels some of which endured until the early 1940s (Motta 2004: 37; Baker 2003: 26).

2.2 Cartels and economic concentration in industrialising Europe

In the early twentieth century, cartels and monopolies constituted the prevalent form of industrial organisation in Europe. Cartels particularly controlled the markets for steel, iron, aluminium, chemicals, explosives, salt and cement (Fear 2006: 11). The propensity to form cartels varied between national economies and industrial sectors. Cartel formation had its heyday in the 1920s and 1930s, in the interwar period. The pinnacle of European cartel activity was concentrated in Germany. In 1905, roughly 400 cartels existed, including about 12,000 companies in Germany alone, and five years later, the number had almost doubled (Schröter 1996). This trend was reinforced when Germany was confronted with reparation payments as part of the Treaty of Versailles, and the overall financial instability of the early 1920s. The shattered public finances of the politically weak governments of the Weimar Republic (1919–1933), as well as the worldwide Great Depression of the 1930s further buttressed the formation of cartels in Germany (Borth *et al.* 1986: 167–8).

Against the backdrop of a political climate marked by social disruptions, economic chaos, mass unemployment and the pauperisation of large parts of society, cartels prospered. The fraction of industrial capital established close connections to financial capital, notably banks and other financial investors. Similar to the US trusts, banks occupied central positions in the supervisory boards of so-called joint stock companies, and also acted as the principal entrepreneurs of economic concentration and cartels meant to rationalise industrial structures and increase profitability (Edwards and Ogilvie 1996: 428, 430). In 1930, cartel activity in Germany reached a peak with 2,100 cartels (Fear 2006: 11). Most of these cartels lasted until the decartelisation efforts undertaken by the Allied Forces after 1945. Many of them exhibited a strong transnational dimension by transgressing national borders.[2] In fact, during the Second World War, more than 40 per cent of world trade was controlled by cartels (ibid.: 15).

A widespread popular antitrust movement, comparable to that in the US at the time of the Sherman Act in 1890, never materialised in the European context. The consolidation of cartels and large conglomerates very much marginalised the opposition of the German *Mittelstand*, consisting of smaller retailers, wholesalers and artisans. Nonetheless, in 1923 a decree against abuses of economic power was adopted which sought to counterbalance cartels and cartel-like organisations surfacing in the time of rising interwar inflation (Harding and Joshua 2003: 73). The view that cartels were an important stabilising factor in the German economy was however wide-spread. As a result, this meant that the decree did not prohibit cartels but rather made them subject to the surveillance of the state institutions (Deringer 2003). This first German encounter with some sort of competition rules was moreover only short-lived: it was abolished again as part of the broad-based hostility towards liberal markets, which arose during the worldwide economic depression in the aftermath of the Wall Street stock market crash (Djelic 2002). Nonetheless, Germany's ephemeral experience with competition laws triggered similar political discussions in other countries in the 1920s and 1930s, albeit without concrete political results (Gerber 1998: 7).

2.3 The political role of cartels in the rise of Nazi Germany

Cartels played a pivotal role in the rise of the fascist regime of National Socialism in Germany. With the advent of the National Socialists, a law was enacted in July 1933 declaring the formation of big industrial cartels compulsory. Moreover, a cartel tribunal, a sort of cartel supervisory institution within the Ministry of Economic Affairs, was entrusted with the task of supervising cartels (cf. Feldenkirchen 1992; Djelic 2002: 13). The adoption of Göring's Four Year Plan in 1936 further integrated cartels and monopolies into the totalitarian state apparatus. Mergers were promoted by means of fiscal incentives, which led to a considerable degree of economic concentration in the 1930s (Feldenkirchen 1992). A range of other measures reinforced this, such as complex forms of patent rights, interlocking directorates, exchange of shares and the pooling of profits. The resulting cartel-dominated and oligopolistic market-structures effectively eliminated competition from outside Germany and consisted of economic combinations that were 'not surpassed in any country, not even the United States' (Neumann 1942: 288). The CEOs of the most powerful companies administered the cartels in an autocratic style. This made it easier for the centralised Nazi state apparatus to communicate with similarly centralised cartels and monopolies (ibid.: 270). By awarding contracts of guaranteed procurement, the Nazi government helped industrial capitalists to secure economic profits. In turn they provided the Nazis with the indispensable production of military equipment, financial and hence also political support.

The enmeshment of the totalitarian state within the capitalist class exemplified a form of 'totalitarian monopoly capitalism', which combined the monopolistic economy with the command economy of the totalitarian state (cf. Neumann 1942). The symbiotic relationship between the state machinery and the fractions of industrial and financial capital also entailed the distribution of Jewish industries or industries of annexed territories to German companies (ibid.). Cartels such as IG Farben, the world's largest chemical company at the time, profited from forced labour camps and unrestrained experimentation on camp prisoners, as well as from supplying Auschwitz and other concentration camps with chemicals such as the notorious Cyclone B. The coal and steel syndicates constituted the core of the German war machinery. The highly vertically integrated Vereinigte Stahlwerke produced more crude steel than any other steel company in Europe. It was founded in 1926 by August Thyssen and later split into two conglomerates led by the sons Fritz and Herbert Thyssen. Fritz Thyssen, who was involved in financing the National Socialists, later titled his memoirs *I paid Hitler* (Thyssen 1941).

2.4 The influence of US antitrust architects on rebuilding post-war Germany

After the Second World War the Allied Military Government, with the US being the most dominant ally, sought to restructure the German economic and political system. At the Yalta Conference in February 1945, which divided Germany into four occupation zones, the US suggested a 'radical decartelisation' programme (Freyer 2006: 248). Only a few months later at the Potsdam Conference in July, the heads of the US, British and Soviet occupation zones agreed on a US initiative to dismantle the cartel-dense German economy and eliminate the excessive concentrations of economic powers 'at the earliest practicable date' (Article 12, Report on the Tripartite Conference of Berlin in Feldenkirchen 1992: 261). The staff of the US Decartelisation and Deconcentration Branch was drawn directly from the US Justice Department's Antitrust Division. When the US zone fused with the British zone in 1947, encompassing Germany's industrial heartland, the Ruhr Valley, the US Occupation Forces took the lead in the economic and political reconstruction of Germany.

The US occupation force adopted a statute that declared unlawful cartels and 'cartel-like agreements' such as syndicates, trusts and other monopolist arrangements (Djelic and Kleiner 2003: 4).[3] Likewise, additional legislation restricting the combination of commercial and investment banking was introduced with a view to disentangle corporate finance from the productive sector (Wells 2002: 153). Subsequently, more than 1,000 cartel agreements were dissolved, including cartel regimes such as IG Farben and Vereinigte Stahlwerke. At the Nuremberg Trials in 1947, leading industrial capitalists, including the managers of IG Farben, were sentenced for crimes against humanity and for holding close ties with the Nazi regime (Freyer 2006: 249). The cartel was dismantled into Hoechst, Bayer, and BASF.[4]

In marked contrast to the successful breakdown of big industrial cartels, the German economy was far from deconcentrated after the four years of Allied occupation. The famous Marshall Plan, building on the ideas of George C. Marshall, Chief Military Officer during the Second World War, changed the political course of the US in this respect. It replaced the 1944 Morgenthau Plan which in line with the preferences of the Soviet and the French governments, aimed at destroying the German manufacturing industry in its entirety and refocusing the economy on agricultural production only (Buxbaum 2006: 5). The Marshall Plan rather sought to facilitate the recovery of the German economy, and this also included the restoration of large German companies. A small but powerful group of US industrial capitalists lobbying in Washington supported this view. They wanted 'to ensure that German industrial assets would be available to support the recovery of capitalist Europe', in particular the Ruhr heavy industries (Van der Pijl 1984: 145).

Particularly Fordist-type, export-orientated companies producing cheap mass consumer goods, had a strong interest to offset their technologically far more advanced and more competitive products in post-war Europe. Fordism, named after Henry Ford's Motor Company, refers to the new capitalist system of industrial mass production of consumption commodities in the US after the First World War (see also Chapter 3). It became part of a growth model involving 'a virtuous circle of growth based on mass production, rising productivity based on economics of scale, rising incomes linked to productivity, increased mass demand due to rising wages, increased profits based on full utilisation of capacity and increased investment in improved mass production equipment and techniques' (Jessop 2002a: 56).

In the US, the competition unit of regulation contributed in important respects to facilitate Fordist growth. Economic concentration and centralisation was considered essential for the creation of efficiency in the industrial production process. Under the guidance of Thurman Arnold, the Department of Justice's Antitrust Division adopted a tolerant stance towards company size in the 1940s. A key purpose of antitrust control was to force companies to be 'efficient' in their production, particularly if so-called efficiency gains were not passed on to the consumers (Wells 2002: 41). This view was also reflected by the US Deconcentration Unit of the Allied Forces, who had considerable reservations regarding the need to deconcentrate the German industry. Composed of mostly economists, it executed its task with less vigour than the US Decartelisation Unit. Eventually, it even abolished the deconcentration activities altogether (Freyer 2006: 259; Wells 2002: 261).

As a result thereof, German industrial capital could rapidly re-concentrate again. The initial intention of the US was to focus on the largest firms only, including companies like Henschel & Sohn, Robert Bosch, Siemens & Halske and Metallgesellschaft (Wells 2002: 155). Eventually, Bosch and Siemens underwent only a marginal restructuring. The companies Hoechst, Bayer and BASF, which resulted from the deconcentrated IG Farben, rapidly re-concentrated again. Today, each of these companies is about 20 times larger than IG Farben. Similarly, after the dissolution of the Vereinigte Stahlwerke group that produced 40 per cent of the Reich's crude steel output in 1937, August Thyssen Hütte became the largest steel producer, accounting for 10 per cent of Germany's steel output (McLachlan and Swann 1967a: 197). Also the 'Big Three' of the banking sector, the Deutsche Bank, the Dresdner Bank and the Commerzbank, which controlled the financial system of Germany and held large stocks of leading German companies, were divided only into nine rather than thirteen different banks as initially envisaged (Berghahn 1986: 110). A number of mergers that took place in 1956 also led to the resurrection of the *Grossbanken* (Van der Pijl 1984: 164; see also Canelos and Silber 1970: 30–3).

The political elite of the US Occupation Forces, most notably Lucius D. Clay and his successor John J. McCloy, held close connections with US and certain German industrialists (Link 1978; Van der Pijl 1984). In 1946 and 1947, Clay invited representatives of US industrial capital to travel through the Western zones in order to 'gain a firsthand impression' of the state of the German economy and to establish closer ties with their German counterparts (Berghahn 1986: 82–3). Subsequently, in a 1947 Report on Germany, US industrial capitalists suggested the reinstatement of board members and directors of German companies to their posts (ibid.). This had the desired effect: in 1951, McCloy released Krupp from prison and reversed the confiscation of his property, deeming the prior judgment to be 'repugnant to American concepts of justice' (Van der Pijl 1984: 174). In 1952, he did the same with the IG Farben chief executive managers, who afterwards regained their high-ranking positions in German industry (Heall 2005). In an attempt to integrate the German industrial system into the realm of US economic domination, US industry representatives invited German industrial capitalists to inspect US factories and to take part in 'Training-within Industry' courses. The purpose was to teach Fordist production methods and Taylorist management strategies, as well as US advertising and marketing practices.

In reaction to the attempts of German industrial capitalists to reinstall cartels in the aftermath of the War, export-oriented US companies strenuously pressured for the establishment of a competition unit of regulation that abolished cartels and other restrictive private barriers inhibiting free market access (Djelic 2002: 21). When confronted with enormous devastation after the War, large parts of Germany's capitalist class however had no sympathy for the US project of outlawing cartels and for opening up German markets to foreign competition. Cartels continued to be considered essential for inducing technological progress. maintaining economic stability and in a wider sense, for curbing labour radicalism and class conflicts (Freyer 2006: 247). The *Bundesverband der Deutschen Industrie (BDI)*, the Federal Association of German Industry, encompassing 39 business associations with more than 100,000 member companies, started an aggressive propaganda campaign together with the Ruhr industrialists against the establishment of a competition unit of regulation (Djelic 1998: 231). Organised capital was not alone in its opposition. In the aftermath of the war, political sentiments were predominantly hostile towards the idea of introducing a US-style free market capitalism and the concept of free competition. Initially, the economic liberalism propagated by US authorities seemed to lose the battle against the socialist solutions of establishing a state-directed economy, as advocated by the Marxist-inspired Social Democratic Party and the Christian-inspired socialist parties based in Roman Catholic regions (Gerber 1998: 257).

In the changed spirit of the Marshall Plan, the US authorities made the enactment of competition rules a precondition for turning over sovereignty to Germany. Against the backdrop of political opposition however, the US Occupation Force authorities realised that they could not force the rules of capitalism upon Germany. The endeavour to establish a competition unit of regulation was doomed to failure without German cooperation. The German political decision-makers and the capitalist class needed to be convinced of the advantages of competition rules as part of a broader project of political re-education (Berghahn 1986: 103). The US government therefore required the German authorities to draft their own competition legislation. The preparatory stages were still initiated under the patronage of the US military government, who in 1946 commissioned a group of experts to come up with a draft. In the meantime, the interim competition rules of US military government remained in force.

2.5 The German cartel regulation and the question of ordoliberal influence

The rehabilitation of the German economy was accompanied by a long period of sustained growth and full employment, also known as the 'economic miracle'.

Whereas the average annual growth rate measured in GNP was 1.06 per cent in the period from 1914 to 1950, its annual average amounted to an astonishing 8.6 per cent in the 1950 to 1959 period (Dormois 2004: 12, 18). The miracle was fuelled by the introduction of Fordist production methods and significant state aid granted to industry. The political sphere was characterised by great stability after 1949, the year when the Federal Republic was founded. According to Davies (1996: 1074), 'West German politics were, frankly, unexciting' from this moment onward. The Christian–Democratic Union was in power for 17 years up to 1966 and envisaged a system of *soziale Marktwirtschaft*, a social market economy, combining free markets with a welfare state. This entailed a political focus on 'price stability, the creation of favourable conditions for production, a system of social security and international free trade', while 'the regulatory role of the state in this approach was and still is by and large restricted to securing general conditions' (Van der Wurff 1993: 164–65; see also Jessop and Sum 2006: 130–3).

The social market economy has often been mistakenly associated with 'ordoliberalism'. The ordoliberals were a small group of legal and economic theorists who met at the University of Freiburg in the 1920s and 1930s and who shared a clear vocation. As the term 'ordoliberalism' already suggests, they sought to establish *Ordnung* (order) after the political turmoil in the time of the Weimar Republic, the Great Depression and later, the excesses of the Nazi regime. The ordoliberal school of economic thought should, however, not be confounded with the elusive notion of social market economy. Rather, ordoliberalism needs to be understood as particular form of neoliberalism, which prescribed a specific type of liberal market economy, different from the narrow conceptions and basic institutions promoted by neoclassic liberalism. Ordoliberals criticised Adam Smith and other nineteenth century economic theorists for the *laissez-faire* idea of self-regulatory markets and for reducing the role of the state to a night-watchman function. In their view, it was not the invisible hand of the market but the visible hand of the state that had to act as guarantor of social justice and the humane functioning of market mechanisms.

Regulated competition constituted the centrepiece of *Ordnungspolitik*, the politics of order. Ordoliberals considered unconstrained private economic power a persistent threat to the creation of economic welfare, the cohesion of society and ultimately also democracy. As strong proponents of the German *Mittelstand*, ordoliberals believed that excessive economic power will always try to get hold of political power. According to Walter Eucken, one of the leading scholars of ordoliberalism, not only the abuses of economic power had to be prosecuted, but excessive economic power in itself (Eucken and Hensel 1952: 334). Consequently, many ordoliberals 'tended to view economic concentration with suspicion' and 'sought an economy composed to the extent possible of small and medium-sized firms and thus a society with a minimum of 'big business' (Gerber 1998: 240–1).

The political remedy against economic power concentration was to make market actors compete. As competition was not expected to evolve naturally, a politically independent state institution free from partisan influence had to be established and entrusted with the task to realise the ordoliberal proviso of 'complete competition' (*vollständiger Wettbewerb*), a notion referring to an ideal state of affairs in which no corporate entity had the power to coerce the conduct of other firms (Eucken 1938: Chapter III). The complementarities between ordo- and neoliberal type competition regulation are thus substantial. That is, in terms of content, a 'competition only' focus is prescribed and in terms of form, regulation enforced by politically independent institutions is advocated (see Chapter 1).

Ordoliberal ideas matched the outspoken liberal goals and denazification standards of the US. Consequently, with US political support, a range of eminent ordoliberals were placed in leadership positions or assigned the role of academic consultants in the economic policy planning of post-war Germany. As a result, ordoliberal ideas came to shape the broader ensemble of regulation. Also in the field of competition ordoliberal ideas can be detected. The German competition unit of regulation, which after years of negotiations replaced that of the Allied Forces, came into being with the *Gesetz gegen Wettbewerbsbeschränkungen*, the Federal Cartel Law, of 1957. As regards *content*, the combat of cartels was the main purpose of the newly established competition unit. As regards *form,* the politically independent *Bundeskartellamt* was provided with far-reaching administrative and discretionary powers to control and prosecute anticompetitive conduct, whereas the Ministry of Economic Affairs was merely allowed to supervise the *Bundeskartellamt.* In line with ordoliberal thinking, the *Bundeskartellamt* received exclusive powers to preserve competition. At the same time, ordoliberal ideas were however far from hegemonic in post-war Germany, and this affected the *Gesetz gegen Wettbewerbsbeschränkungen.* Its adoption was delayed for 10 years. The initial Josten Draft of 1949, designed according to ordoliberal standards and foreseeing a strong monopoly commission equipped with the right to deconcentrate large conglomerates and prosecute anticompetitive horizontal and vertical agreements under criminal law, ended up shelved without a parliamentary debate (Eickhof and Isele 2005: 93). More than 20 draft versions passed under review until competition rules could be adopted (Freyer 2006: 264).

It is noteworthy that the content of the *Gesetz gegen Wettbewerbsbeschränkungen* did not include provisions for merger control, although mergers clearly were an important mechanism leading to economic concentration. This was due to strong opposition by large sections of German industry and their partisan allies, especially the Christian-Democratic Union and its sister party the Christian-Social Union, which advocated a position informed by the national mercantilist discourse. The main argument against a merger control regulation was that 'many German firms had not yet reached their optimal size' (Gerber 1998: 302). Economic concentration was prioritised over free competition. Although ordoliberals in both the *Bundeskartellamt* and the Social Democratic Party pushed for merger control rules soon after the enactment of the *Gesetz gegen Wettbewerbsbeschränkungen* (Gerber 1998: 302–3), such rules became part of the German competition unit of regulation only in 1973. In other words, due to strong opposition, ordoliberals were not as successful as they might have wanted in their efforts to introduce strong competition rules at national level.

2.6 Competition regulation in France

According to estimates, the Second World War cost France approximately a quarter of its wealth: the infrastructure was seriously damaged, agricultural, and industrial production was very low compared to the pre-war levels and inflation high (Dormois 2004: 17). A path of state-led economic growth was chosen in order to bring the economy back on track. The French state already had a long tradition of economic interventions and now the state had to spur significant transformations in an economy characterised by many small and stagnant producers (Hall 1986: 139; Michalet 1974). The state took control over key sectors. The Bank of France and several private banks were nationalised, as were the coal, gas, railroad and electricity industries along with Air France and the largest insurance companies. A national planning board, the *Commissariat Général du Plan* was created and entrusted with the task to prepare plans to enhance the performance of French industry (Hall 1986: 140–1, 166–7). The planning board, which was led by Jean Monnet, considered industrial units in France too small by international comparison.[5] 'Modernization meant concentration within each sector of industry, larger production units and firms, the adoption of machines and technologies that would make mass production possible, and a rationalization of management and production methods' (Djelic 1998: 137). As later chapters will show, this positive attitude towards concentration of capital was to endure for many years in French economic and political circles.

The work of the planning board was mainly carried out in a number of Modernisation Commissions consisting of representatives of industrial capital and labour as well as experts and planning staff. From the outset however, trade unions were marginalised with the result that the two largest unions chose to boycott the proceedings for many years (Hall 1986: 158; see also Cox 1987: 229–30). According to Michalet (1974: 113), the Commissions 'contributed largely toward bringing together the state on the one hand and large enterprises on the other'. Whereas the state was mainly preoccupied with creating and sustaining a legal framework for companies to operate within the German model of capitalism, in the model that emerged in France, the state manifestly sought to steer the economy through economic planning, leading to particularly strong ties between industrial capitalists and the political system. The French route was successful. As Hobsbawm (1994: 274) comments, '[t]his adaptation of Soviet ideas to a capitalist mixed economy must have had some effect, since between 1950 and 1979, France, hitherto a by-word for economic retardation, caught up more successfully than any other of the chief industrial countries with US productivity'. The significance of the influx of American aid through the Marshall Plan should not be overlooked in this context. The *Trente Glorieuses*, the French version of the Golden Age, had begun, which led to an increase in the average annual growth rate measured in GNP from 1.15 per cent in the period 1914–1950 to 4.6 per cent in the 1950–1959 period (Dormois 2004: 12, 18).

It follows that the French approach to competition differed greatly from that in Germany. There was no tradition of competition regulation in France

(Venturini 1971: 9), where a national mercantilist discourse prevailed and mergers were not a specific object of regulation at this juncture. Nonetheless three articles dealing with the 'maintenance of free competition' (Article 59 *bis*, *ter* and *quater*) were included in the *Decree 53–704*, adopted in August 1953 to complement the *Price Control Ordinance* of 1945, which gave the government the power to freeze wages and control prices. The first prohibited agreements and concerted actions restricting 'the full exercise of competition'. At first glance, this could appear like an 'alien' neoliberal element in an ensemble of regulation that was predominantly informed by national mercantilist ideas. However, Article 59 *ter* exempted from prohibition those cases where it could be justified that the agreement had the effect of 'improving or extending the outlets of the production, or of assuring the development of economic progress by way of rationalization or specialization' (in Riesenfeld 1960: 595). Even though the *Decree* ruled that not all agreements between companies were acceptable, the inclusion of rather broadly formulated exemptions indicates that no radical departure from the national mercantilist path was chosen.

The reason for the introduction of these provisions can be ascribed to US pressures. In exchange for financial aid to the reconstruction of France, the US government pushed for antitrust measures to prevent distortions of free trade on national and global markets (cf. Pedersen 1996). According to Dumez and Jeunemaître (1996: 221), the French head of government only approved it 'on condition that "no one would ever hear about it", a political manoeuvre designed to pacify one of the parties in the governing coalition'. Consequently, the rules were never strictly enforced. Even though control over cartels and similar combinations increased, they still enjoyed 'a wide area of toleration and legitimate action' (Riesenfeld 1960: 587). Some commentators even wondered whether French competition regulation was not 'an exercise in futility' (Jenny and Weber 1975). Importantly, the provisions were not designed to target mergers. Such provisions only became part of French law in 1977.

2.7 Competition regulation in the UK

The UK has generally been regarded as the home ground of economic liberalism, with a minimum role reserved for the government, and a strong belief in the self-regulation of the market (Van Apeldoorn 2002: 72–3). Arguably, the era of the *Pax Britannica* from the first industrial revolution and/or the end of the Napoleonic Wars to the beginning of the First World War was associated with free trade and the freedom of finance. The British hegemony in this period was however also premised on active state interventions in the market, including for instance the encouragement of the development of joint-stock banks (Seabrooke 2006: 57–60). Britain's finance capital fraction known as 'the City', the world's financial centre at the time, promoted a general discourse of 'liberal internationalism' (Overbeek and Van der Pijl 1993: 7–9; see also Cox 1987: 123–47). Yet, similar to the models of capitalism emerging in Germany and France, in the UK a class compromise between industrial capital and labour also led to a combined market economy with a strong emphasis on a comprehensive welfare state. After winning the elections in July 1945 by a landslide, the new Labour government implemented a programme that was 'the most radical of any administration before or since' (Hall 1986: 70). Three elements were crucial: first, a comprehensive nationalisation, including the Bank of England, the railways, the iron, steel, coal, gas and electricity industries (ibid.: 70–6; see also Overbeek 1990: 114–19). Second, a commitment to introduce a welfare state including health care, social security and education for the population. Third, a goal to achieve full employment by means of Keynesian counter-cyclical demand management policies. Importantly, when the Conservatives took over from Labour in 1951 there was no dramatic policy shift, except that the nationalisation of the iron and steel industries was reversed. The Conservatives, who remained in power for 13 years, endorsed Keynesian economic policies and the continued development of the welfare state.[6]

In the regulatory field of competition, the UK was a pioneer. With the enactment of the 1948 *Monopolies and Restrictive Practices Enquiry and Control Act*, the British government was the first European country to establish a competition unit of regulation after the war (Utton 2000). Like the competition laws introduced in France and Germany, the Act was mainly a response to US political pressures. The UK was suffering from a considerable payment deficit and depended on Washington's commitment not to seek repayment for received military aid (Wells 2002: 109). As regards *content*, the Act allowed for investigation of industries where cartels and monopolies were suspected to operate against the 'public interest'. The latter was defined in terms of efficient production and distribution, an efficient organisation of industry, technological development as well as the expansion and opening of markets. As George (1990: 105) points out, there was however 'no mention of the word "competition" in the definition of the public interest'. Implicitly, cartels and monopolies were thereby not necessarily considered undesirable. Nonetheless, with the enactment of the *Restrictive Trade Practices Act* in 1956, the permissive stance towards cartels was reversed and a system of compulsory registration of 'restrictive practices' established.

As regards *form*, the 1948 Act established the Monopolies and Restrictive Practices Commission, which was authorised to carry out the investigations upon request by the government minister in charge of commerce and industry and obliged to report back to the minister. Ultimately, however, the Parliament decided on actions against anticompetitive practices. As Gerber comments, '[t]his arrangement left ultimate authority with the politicians and administrators, but placed responsibility for investigation on a separate commission that was given a measure of independence in performing its tasks' (1998: 216). This changed with the 1956 Act, which removed the responsibility for restrictive practices regulation from the Commission (now renamed the Monopolies Commission) and established two new institutions to deal with this. These were the Registrar of Restrictive Practices to which restrictive agreements had to be notified and the Restrictive Practices Court who was authorised to establish the legality of agreements (George 1990: 106).

Conclusion

The chapter explained the emergence of competition units of regulation in Germany, France and the UK in the late 1940s and 1950s. All three units came to embody elements associated with both the neoliberal and national mercantilist discourses. Whereas the neoliberal discourse entailed a pro-competition stance and the exclusion of political decision-makers from the regulatory processes, the national mercantilist discourse valued economic concentration above free competition and prescribed the involvement of political decision-makers in the regulatory processes.

Units of regulation protecting some level of 'free competition' appeared in Germany, which was due to the proponents of the neoliberal discourse, such as the US authorities and industrial capitalists, as well as the German ordoliberals. However, a purely neoliberal unit materialised nowhere. Instead, the aspirations to protect free competition were, in the cases of France and the UK, tempered with provisions that allowed for anticompetitive practices. In none of the three units of regulation were merger control rules introduced. This reflected the desire of the capitalist class and political decision-makers not to hinder significantly higher levels of intra-national economic concentration. As such, the content of the units needs to be understood in the light of both the neoliberal and the national mercantilist discourses. Regarding form, the units of regulation varied but had important features in common. In the German unit, the *Bundeskartellamt* was empowered to perform its regulation independently of political decision-makers. In the UK and France, political decision-makers were allowed to play a significantly bigger role. This reflected the fact that the proponents of the neoliberal discourse were stronger, relative to their 'national mercantilist' counterparts in Germany, than in the UK and France.

3 The origins of European competition regulation II

The supranational level

This chapter exposes the political struggles that led to the establishment of a European level competition unit of regulation. It explains why competition rules were included in the 1951 Treaty of Paris, which established the European Coal and Steel Community (ECSC) and in the 1957 Treaty of Rome, which led to the European Economic Community (referred to as the EC in the remainder). The chapter argues that, similar to the developments at national level, the supranational competition units were given shape on the basis of two discourses of regulation, namely the neoliberal and national mercantilist discourses. Section one discusses the adoption of the Schuman Declaration that preceded the ECSC Treaty, while sections two and three analyse the political controversies in the run-up to the ECSC Treaty and the content, form and scope of the resulting competition unit of regulation. Section four examines the political disputes that led to the establishment of the EC competition unit, while section five focuses on the content, form and scope it was eventually given. In section six, the adoption of Regulation 17/62 which further fleshed out the statutory rules for the enforcement of the Treaty's competition rules receives special attention.

3.1 The Schuman Declaration

On 9 May 1950 the Schuman Declaration, named after French Foreign Minister Robert Schuman, was announced. The Declaration, which was an important first step towards a united Europe, aimed at overcoming 'the age-old opposition of France and Germany' by means of a new supranational organisation that placed 'Franco-German production of coal and steel as a whole [...] under a common High Authority' (Schuman 1950). Schuman's idea to surrender the control over coal and steel to a supranational authority was unequivocally linked to the French experience with Nazi Germany. The potential resurgence of Germany as an economic and military power alarmed the French government, particularly when the US government proposed to rearm the Federal Republic as a result of the increased tensions with the Soviet Union in the context of the Korean War in 1950.

To understand the significance of the Schuman Declaration it is important to keep in mind that coal and steel were key production factors at that time, pivotal to the economic recovery of the Western European economies. As pointed out by Lovett (1996: 426), steel 'occupied a position of unchallenged supremacy', whereas coal provided European industries with three-quarters of its energy needs. France was the world's largest importer of coal and its ailing steel industry could not recover without access to new energy resources (Lynch 1984: 229–30). Germany in contrast was Europe's chief coal producer and its steel industry also enjoyed privileged access to coal, controlling more than half of Europe's coal resources overall (Berghahn 1986: 110).

The French government initially attempted to access the coal resources of the German Saar area and prevent economic recovery of the Ruhr, Germany's industrial heart, hosting the greatest concentration of economic power on the continent (Berghahn 1986: 112). The Ruhr area, however, formed part of the British occupation zone and was not subject to French influence. Once the governments of the UK and particularly the US agreed that the Ruhr's recovery was the key to the revitalisation of the European economies and 'gradually loosened the Ruhr's economic shackles', the French government could only watch from the sidelines (Dinan 1999: 20). With the Schuman Declaration, the French government sought to encapsulate the more dominant German economy in a framework of political control. The formation of a supranational organisation that ensured the abolition of national restrictions on imports and exports for coal and steel products seemed an attractive solution to ensure market access to German coal and steel sectors and importantly, to also secure the necessary support from other European governments whose economies also depended on German coal resources.

The negotiations on the creation of what became the ECSC started on 20 June 1950 in Paris, and involved officials of the six governments of France, Germany, the Benelux and Italy. The process of drafting the treaty basis, which took shape in the few months between summer and autumn of 1950, was characterised by fierce political controversies. Most notably, the disagreement on whether or not to include competition rules almost threatened the ratification of the entire ECSC Treaty. Although the Schuman Declaration did not foresee competition rules, it vaguely hinted at the need to rule out cartel practices by proclaiming that '[i]n contrast to international cartels, which tend to impose restrictive practices on distribution and the exploitation of national markets, and to maintain high profits, the organization will ensure the fusion of markets and the expansion of production' (Schuman 1950). In November 1950 Jean Monnet, who headed the French delegation, wrote to Schuman saying that 'substantive differences' existed with respect to the competition rules, adding that 'the provisions on cartels and industrial concentrations affect the very substance of the Schuman Plan' (Monnet 1950).

3.2 Establishing the ECSC competition unit of regulation

The most significant opposition to the establishment of a supranational competition unit of regulation came from leading industrial capitalists and related partisan interests in Germany, France, Italy and Belgium. This opposition was informed by a national mercantilist discourse (see Chapter 1). In France, protests against the

Schuman Declaration were massive. Notably, the less competitive French steel industry, which strongly relied on access to the precious Ruhr coal resources, opposed the idea of adopting strict cartel and merger rules that applied to all coal and steel industries in all member states. It had much to fear from competition rules, as strong cross-participation between companies and inter-locking directorates constituted the order of the day in France (Witschke 2001: 14–17, 27). Also in France cartels were widely considered necessary to stabilise the relation between capital and labour. In this spirit the French industry association *Conseil National du Patronat Français* suggested that, rather than establishing the need to compete, the ECSC could provide a framework in which national governments and producers' associations jointly fixed prices instead (ibid.: 7). At the same time, the French steel industry supported the idea of specific competition rules, which were aimed at the vertical disentanglement of German steel production, ending its privileged access to and/or ownership of coal mining industries (Karagiannis 2004: 12–13).[1] French industrialists held similar double standards in the area of economic concentration: 'What is wanted', Haas (1958: 185) commented, 'is freedom for French firms to merge as they please coupled with careful supervision over the parallel German process'. In a campaign led by the *Chambre Syndicale de la Sidérurgie Française*, the French steel industry mobilised the support from a broad range of other industries, mostly those of engineering and metal processing, against the inclusion of ECSC competition rules (Ehrmann 1954: 454–8; Berghahn 1986: 128; Haas 1958: 176–7).

In Italy, opposition also came from the steel associations who joined forces with the Federation of Industrialists. The Italian steel industry feared that the inclusion of competition rules in the ECSC Treaty could block the modernisation and concentration process that it had started in 1950–1951 (Haas 1958: 199–200). Likewise, in Belgium, the steel industry protested together with the coal industry and the *Société General de Belgique,* a major Belgian bank involved in the coal and steel sector (Witschke 2001: 14). In a joint position paper in December 1950 the coalition of Belgian capital fractions expressed concerns about the new organisation, which they saw as attempt to curtail 'the initiative and responsibility of firms', leading to 'a complete *dirigisme* of the High Authority equivalent in fact to a disguised nationalization' (in Milward 2000: 80).

In Germany, the capitalist class largely favoured the adoption of the ECSC Treaty as such. This was however mainly due to the fact that it was coupled with the abolition of the control exercised by the Allied Forces. Alarmed by the potential inclusion of a merger control regulation, the coal and steel industry lobbied the German government to resist the inclusion of such rules. The industries felt cornered by French competitors, who had concentrated on a massive scale in the years prior to the negotiations of the ECSC, in a time when German companies were subjected to the deconcentration efforts of the Allied Forces (see Chapter 2). They feared that ECSC merger control rules could thwart the German reconcentration process and insisted on a non-discrimination clause that did not differentiate between companies on the basis of nationality. Moreover, they wanted the High Authority to take the different economic positions of other companies into account when assessing mergers, while taking the size of the largest company as point of reference (Witschke 2001: 16). In a memorandum submitted to Bonn on 4 July 1950, the *Wirtschaftsvereinigung Eisen- und Stahlindustrie*, the trade association of the German steel industry expressed its worries about the far-reaching enforcement powers entrusted upon the proposed High Authority. Rather than having a centralised, supranational organ with wide-ranging powers for controlling the activities in the common market for coal and steel industry, it alternatively suggested administration of the industry privately. It proposed an 'international framework' governed by 'a directorium of industrialists of all participating countries', ensuring a 'certain coordination in the fields of production, sales or prices' (Memorandum cited in Berghahn 1986: 131–2). In other words, the *Wirtschaftsvereinigung* opted for an international coal and steel cartel instead.

The *Bundesverband der Deutschen Industrie (BDI)* also opposed the inclusion of competition provisions, but expected the negotiations to be unsuccessful on this issue anyway (Gehler and Gröben 2002: 12, 21). Upon realising that competition regulations could not easily be wiped off the negotiation table, the BDI joined forces with French industrial capitalists. The German-French industrial *rapprochement* resulted in a joint resolution against the inclusion of competition rules in the ECSC Treaty and in favour of protecting the tradition of national and international cartels. Eventually, this led to the formation of the *Council of the Federation of European Industries* in 1951, which encompassed the main employers' associations from France, Belgium, the Netherlands and Germany (Witschke 2001: 14). Somewhat ironically, as a side effect of these first transnational lobby efforts, old pre-war cartel ties across French and German borders were revitalised (Berghahn 1986: 114).

A number of political parties also expressed their reservations vis-à-vis the proposed ECSC competition provisions. In Germany, the position of the Social Democratic Party was rather hostile towards most aspects of the Treaty, including the cartel provisions. Likewise, the right-wing liberalist Free Democratic Party, a party associated with the views of heavy industry (Lovett 1996: 445), expressed concerns but decided to support the Treaty nonetheless. In France, partisan opposition mainly stemmed from the extreme left and right. While the communists were against any form of market integration as they expected negative consequences for the working class, the Gaullist *Rassemblement du Peuple Français* was not principally against European integration but still raised numerous objections, such as that the projected common market was primarily to the advantage of Germany, leading to increased French unemployment (Haas 1958: 114–5). In Italy, opposition also came from the extreme right and left, while the conservatives were worried about the effects of increased competition on Italian industries (ibid.: 140).

In short, the constellation of agents contesting the ECSC competition rules included a number of political parties and important members of the fraction of industrial capital in France, Germany, Belgium and Italy. None of these agents could directly influence the design of the competition rules but had to exercise power through the national governments. Although the reasons varied, what unified the opposition of French, Italian, Belgian and to some extent German organised capital was a shared concern about national industries being subjected to the need to compete. This opposition made it difficult to reach an agreement on the establishment of a European level competition unit that had the regulation of mergers, cartels and other anti-competitive agreements in the coal and steel sectors as its specific objects of regulation.

To be sure, there were also industries that wholeheartedly favoured the Treaty. Monnet mobilised countervailing forces in France and even managed to generate the political support of some coal and railroad industries (Ehrmann 1954: 473–4). He was also backed up by the manufacturing industry, who provided the necessary leverage against the joint forces of the heavy industries (Berghahn 1986: 131–2). The manufacturing industry was traditionally less cartelised and thus, more easily convinced about the endorsement of the principle of free competition in the ECSC Treaty. The French organisation of the metal manufacturing industry, the *Syndicat Général des Industries Mécaniques et Tranformatirces des Métaux* for example, hoped that competition led to lower domestic steel prices (Leucht 2009: 64). Similarly, industrial capital other than that of the steel and coal sector in the Netherlands and Luxembourg generally also favoured the Treaty for this reason.

The inclusion of competition rules was of great significance to the French government. At the Paris meeting in June 1950 where the negotiations between the six prospective ECSC members began, the French delegation suggested leaving the technical details of competition rules to the planned High Authority. The Dutch and Belgian negotiators however, refused to give the High Authority such free rein (Witschke 2003: 46). In a series of subsequent proposals the French delegation proposed to prohibit cartels on a *per se* basis similar to the antitrust provisions of the US Sherman Act. This implied that all restrictive business practices that hindered free competition, such as agreements on fixing prices, market distribution and production quotas were outlawed. The French government thereby advocated a competition unit in line with the neoliberal discourse, which went directly against the preferences of the cartel-minded domestic coal and steel industrialists.

Similarly, the German government accepted the establishment of an ECSC competition unit of regulation and thereby stood up to the opposition of organised capital. The German position was based on the ordoliberal/neoliberal pro-competition discourse, but also left room for deviation both in the fields of cartels and economic concentration. Walter Hallstein, who was nominated to negotiate on behalf of Germany upon the advice of one of the leading exponents of the Freiburg School Wilhelm Röpke, was a stark proponent of the neoliberal discourse and favoured the inclusion of competition rules in the new Treaty. He was however also 'prepared to think pragmatically' and less dogmatic than the founding fathers of the Freiburg School (Berghahn 1986: 120, 151). Much of his pragmatism was instigated by the fact that in the view of Ludwig Erhard, the Christian Democratic Minister of Economics, not every cartel was evil *per se*. Erhard demanded major revisions of the initial French proposal, which declared cartels categorically illegal (Hoeren 1999: 414; see also Monnet 1978: 351).

Moreover, Hallstein and his team were surrounded by a group of experienced and cartel-minded industrial capitalists including Max Boden, the director general of AEG Electrics and Max C. Müller, head of the Vereinigte Stahlwerke (Berghahn 1986: 120–1), who also strongly opposed a *per se* prohibition of cartels. In a sequence of counterproposals, the German delegation advocated an 'abuse principle' instead, according to which cartel practices were legal in principle and only prosecuted in the case of abuse. By only subjecting detected abuses to jurisdictional control, the German proposal would have resulted in a much more lenient system with regard to cartel prosecution (Witschke 2003: 58). Furthermore, in line with the interests of the German industry, Erhard contested the inclusion of supranational merger control rules (Hoeren 1999: 412–3). He was not willing to accept that German coal and steel companies had to be significantly smaller than their competitors in the newly established common market and feared that merger control rules inhibited the necessary post-war economic restructuring.

The US government played a crucial role in the negotiations. Certainly it is questionable whether Monnet's programme could have succeeded 'against the combined phalanx of European heavy industry if a "federator" […] had not existed on whom he could ultimately rely' (Berghahn 1986: 132). Even though US officials did not directly participate in the ECSC Treaty negotiations, a range of leading US industrial capitalists and US decision-makers such as Marshall Plan co-ordinator Paul Hoffmann, President Harry S. Truman and Secretary of State Dean Acheson kept themselves briefed about the proceedings during the drafting phase. Considering the longstanding cartel tradition in Europe, the US government was particularly concerned that the planned ECSC did not safeguard free competition. The inclusion of competition rules was regarded as a pivotal first step in the establishment of the same Fordist-type production and consumer market in Europe and in allowing US capital to expand across the Atlantic. The prospect of high prices for steel in Europe worried US industries, whose demand for raw materials increased rapidly during the Korean War (Berghahn 1986: 136). ECSC Treaty rules prohibiting any form of producer price agreements and guaranteeing free market access, reached high on the US agenda.

It should thus be no surprise that the US government, in a telegram to the Paris Embassy, considered the French draft proposal for competition rules based on a *per se* prohibition of cartels 'excellent' (Leucht 2009: 65). But when the US Secretary of State Dean Acheson was presented with the first draft on 7 May 1950, he noted that the ECSC was 'a clever cover for a gigantic European cartel for coal and steel producers' (Acheson 1969: 383–4). In fact, 'the more clearly it emerged that the discussions were being pushed into an unacceptable direction by a cartel-minded West European heavy industry, the more Washington began to intervene' (Berghahn 1986: 134). To make sure that US interests were safeguarded, the US government transferred US High Commissioner for Germany, John McCloy and two antitrust experts, Robert Bowie and George Ball to Paris to assist the drafting process. According to Gerber (1998: 338), 'the US role was concealed as much as possible for the fear that the project would be seen as controlled by the US and rejected by some participants on those grounds alone'.

Eventually, the Treaty's competition provisions were rewritten 'in a European idiom' by a member of the *Conseil d'Etat* in Paris (ibid.: 338–9).

US influence was however not all-determining. When confronted with the final text of the competition rules and the institutional outlook of the High Authority, the enthusiasm of the US government to support the ECSC considerably dampened. Even though the differences in content were negligible, the responsibilities attributed to the High Authority and the eventual enforcement mechanisms looked very different from that of the US Federal antitrust agencies.

3.3 The content, form and scope of the ECSC competition unit

On 14 April 1951, the Treaty drafters reached a political compromise with regard to the competition rules. Only a few days later, on 18 April, the ECSC Treaty was signed. National parliaments subsequently adopted the Treaty with rather large majorities, most notably due to the Christian Democrats, who were crucial in generating the necessary political support in Italy, France and Germany (Haas 1958: 124–51). The Treaty stipulated in Article 5 that the Community shall 'ensure the establishment, maintenance and observance of normal competitive conditions and exert direct influence upon production or upon the market only when circumstances so require'. The actual competition rules governing the coal and steel sectors were spelt out in Articles 65 and 66. The content, form and scope of the competition unit that was established with these rules were for the most part in line with the neoliberal discourse of competition regulation as advocated by the governments of France, the US, as well as Germany in spite of some of the reservations; yet, it also reflected some national mercantilist ideas that were advocated by national industrial capitalists. Thereby, the goal of preserving competition in the common market for coal and steel became blurred by other objectives.

In terms of *content*, the ECSC competition unit targeted concentrations, cartels and other restrictive business agreements. In line with the *per se* prohibition of the US Sherman Act and the French proposal, the first paragraph of Article 65 ruled that 'all agreements between undertakings, decisions by associations of undertakings all concerted practices tending directly or indirectly to prevent, restrict or distort normal competition within the common market (whether or not they affect trade between Member States) shall be prohibited'. Article 66 contained the rules for controlling transactions leading to a concentration, such as mergers and acquisitions and the prohibition of restrictive business practices, such as the abuse of a dominant position. It was the longest article in the entire Treaty. As noted by McLachlan and Swann (1967b: 44), its length was 'proportional to the significance that was attached to the control of economic power at the time when the Treaty was being negotiated'. The inclusion of rules prohibiting the abuse of dominant positions was a legal device without an equivalent in the US antitrust legislation, where only intentions to monopolise are ruled out. It reflected, albeit imperfectly, the ordoliberal distrust of 'bigness' entailing that companies should not grow too big in order to allow a vast number of competitors to compete on relatively equal terms.

In terms of *form*, the design of the High Authority, which was set up almost simultaneously with the *Bundeskartellamt* in Germany, echoed the ordoliberal notion of a strong state controlling the market. The High Authority was entrusted with the right to exempt horizontal cartel agreements from the existing prohibition in times of economic crisis, impose production quotas and specify conditions of sales (Article 58). Thereby, it could differentiate between harmful and harmless commercial agreements. This meant that even though cartels were ruled out on a *per se* basis, there was still a regulatory loophole for allowing them. Presumptively due to the influence of the French delegations, the High Authority could furthermore fix price margins (Article 61). This also fundamentally went against the idea of free and competitive markets as proclaimed by the US authorities. Moreover the High Authority was authorised to outlaw 'unreasonable' concentrations, intervene in already existing dominant positions of both private and public enterprises, declare a concentration unlawful, as well as 'order separation of the undertakings or assets improperly concentrated or cessation of joint control, and any other measures which it considers appropriate to return the undertakings or assets in question to independent operation and restore normal conditions of competition' (Article 66, §5). In case of disagreements, private parties could appeal to the Court of Justice; yet a US-type private enforcement system with wide-ranging claimant's rights and damage compensation was ruled out (Gerber 1998: 341). In terms of *scope*, the competition unit enjoyed far-reaching powers. As mentioned above, on the basis of Article 65, the High Authority was authorised to prohibit all types of agreements that prevented, restricted or distorted 'normal competition within the common market'. In the merger area, the Treaty granted exclusive jurisdiction to the High Authority over all mergers and acquisitions involving coal and steel companies.

The ECSC began operating in August 1952, with Monnet as the first President of the High Authority. In the following years, US influence vanished and the ECSC competition rules were hardly enforced. Anxious to keep the goodwill of industrial capitalists, the High Authority 'did not prohibit any concentrations, and its enforcement of other provisions was quite limited' (Gerber 1998: 342). There was no coherent and transparent enforcement strategy for Article 66 and mere company size was generally not considered a problem. Likewise, the High Authority failed to realise the decartelisation of the coal and steel sectors on the basis of Article 65 and even allowed the formation of a steel export cartel (Leucht and Seidel 2007). Of more than 80 registered syndicates, only three rather unimportant ones were dissolved, and of the more than 59 concentrations falling under Article 66, none was prohibited (Witschke 2001: 19; for details see also Schmitt 1964). Importantly, the High Authority did not take a hard line vis-à-vis the German coal and steel industries. It allowed that many of the 18 independent successor companies of the de-concentrated Vereinigte Stahlwerke rapidly re-concentrated again and re-established their links with the coal sector, or concluded vertical mergers (Witschke 2003: 115). For example, the German steel producers Mannesmann and Hoesch re-concentrated by 'restoring vertical integration with down and upstream companies', including coal producing companies (ibid.: 19). Similarly, the German coal syndicate Deutscher Kohlen Verkauf, which succeeded the Ruhr syndicate was not dismantled (Resch 2005: 16). In 1954, a French consortium supported by government loans took over the biggest German coal mine, the Harpener Bergbau AG (Witschke 2001: 21). The High Authority's friendly take on mergers also endured when the two large German steel companies, ATH and Phoenix–Rheinrohr merged in 1958, hereby creating by far the largest company in the community. Although it initially intended to impose conditions on the companies, the High Authority eventually felt compelled to 're-examine its previous thinking on the question of size' when confronted with a burst of resentment and thus approved the merger (McLachlan and Swann 1967b: 45). Overall, the High Authority evolved as one of the strongest advocates of larger groupings in the European steel industry, as long as 'the danger of monopoly was kept at bay' (1967b: 45). As a result, the European coal and steel market rapidly resumed an oligopolistic structure.

3.4 Establishing the EC competition unit of regulation

The decision to start negotiations on the creation of a common market including all industrial sectors of Germany, France, Italy and the Benelux countries was taken at a conference held in Messina from 1 to 3 June in 1955. In a resolution, the six governments declared that 'the establishment of a united Europe must be achieved through the development of common institutions, the progressive fusion of national economies, the creation of a common market and the gradual harmonization of their social policies' (Messina Declaration 1955). Crucially, 'rules assuring the free play of competition', 'particularly in such a way as to exclude all preferences of a national basis' had to be included (ibid.). In other words, the envisaged common market had to guarantee free market access to all companies and outlaw discrimination on grounds of nationality.

Under the chairmanship of the Belgian Foreign Minister Paul-Henri Spaak, a committee of representatives from the various governments, assisted by experts, was set up to prepare a draft treaty (Laurent 1970). The Foreign Ministers accepted the draft version with only small modifications at a conference in Venice in May 1956. In the 10 months that followed, the precise wording of the various articles was negotiated. Much emphasis was given to the role of competition rules. The draft stressed in paragraph 55 that provisions were needed to 'counteract the formation of monopolies within the Common Market' (in Goyder 1993: 24–5). The underpinning rationale was that 'national markets offered the opportunity of attaining optimum dimensions only to firms enjoying a de facto monopoly', while in a common market, mass production could be reconciled with the absence of monopoly (Moschonas 1996: 33).

Similar to the ECSC negotiations, the neoliberal and national mercantilist discourses informed the negotiations over the establishment of an EC competition unit of regulation. According to the neoliberal discourse, supranational regulatory institutions had to enforce strict competition rules. In contrast, the national mercantilist discourse gave primacy to national level enforcement institutions. Compared to the ECSC negotiations however, the strength of the constellation of agents advocating positions grounded in the neoliberal discourse had weakened significantly when the EC Treaty was negotiated. The reasons for this lie in the fact that by the time the EC Treaty was negotiated, US influence in Western Europe had decreased significantly. Moreover the French government, who strongly pushed for the inclusion of competition rules in the ECSC Treaty in order to prevent the re-concentration and re-cartelisation of the German heavy industry, saw no reason to expose all economic sectors to EC competition regulation. This difference was due to the radically diverging contexts in which the two treaties were negotiated. The threat of war was less imminent and European economies were booming for some years (Bayliss and El-Agraa 1990: 141). As a consequence, the position of the French negotiators came to be underpinned by the national mercantilist discourse, while including also some centre-left elements. The French Socialist Prime Minister, Guy Mollet (1956–1957) opposed the idea of a law-based market economy in which competition rules constituted the centrepiece for steering economic integration and suggested a common market steered by an economic planning authority instead. He and his delegation favoured the 'harmonisation of social regulations and fiscal burdens as a precondition for the integration of industrial markets' (Scharpf 2002: 646). The French Ministry of Economics cooperated closely with organised French capital, which resulted in a position according to which EC competition rules had to prohibit only the most protectionist agreements, while tolerating most of the others (Warlouzet 2005: 66). Subsequently, the Commission's role had to be limited to merely coordinate the compatibility of national competition rules (ibid.).

In the absence of the US–French alliance in favour of strong competition rules, the German Adenauer government was the only remaining advocate of a position grounded in the neoliberal discourse. Particularly, adherents of ordoliberalism emerged as enthusiastic proponents for an 'ordered' market economy in which competition provisions played the primary structuring device for organising societal welfare in an integrated Europe. Walter Hallstein, the principal negotiator on behalf of the German government and the first President of the European Commission which he headed for nine years, referred extensively to ordoliberal concepts in his writings and speeches, both during the formation of the EC and his Presidency (Gerber 1998: 263). His friend Hans von der Gröben, a lawyer by origin who became the first Competition Commissioner, played a pivotal role in the detailed formulation of competition rules. He was later also called 'Jean Monnet of Germany' as he drafted much of the Spaak Report (Von der Gröben 1965a; Gehler and Von der Gröben 2002: 8). In the view of Von der Gröben (1962: 16), strong EC competition regulation rather than central planning had to provide the key steering instrument for economic integration.

The question of whether the EC competition unit had to apply the *prohibition* or the *abuse* principle raised political controversies once more. Compared to the positions taken in the ECSC negotiations, this time the German and French negotiators changed camps (Hoeren 1999: 414). The German government vehemently advocated the establishment of a competition unit that prohibited all cooperative agreements affecting trade in the common market, albeit with the possibility of granting exemptions. This implied that an authorisation system had to be established, requiring the *ex ante* notification of all intercompany agreements. Following the ordoliberal spirit of a continuously policed competition order, a strong competition authority, independent of governmental and thus partisan influence, had to review these notifications and take decisions. The French delegates proposed an abuse system instead, according to which only predefined abuses of business practices were subject to judicial control. Rather than installing a mechanism of prior notification for all intercompany agreements, the *ex post* abuse control system would have been more lenient and in line with the national mercantilist position of the French government.

The reason why the French and German delegates reversed roles is linked to the changed macroeconomic context. In the drafting phase of the ECSC Treaty, the French delegation favoured the inclusion of competition rules as part of the broader geopolitical goal of weakening the German coal and steel industry and creating market access for the French industries to these sectors. Once competition rules had to be applied consistently to all industries in all six member states, prohibiting cartels on a *per se* basis no longer seemed attractive. Rather, cartel-like cooperative intercompany agreements were considered vital for French industries to face foreign competition. The German delegates in contrast, feared that the protectionist stance of France foreclosed market access for German companies (Warlouzet 2005: 66–7). The German export-oriented industry in manufactured goods particularly depended on free access to new markets and, thus, free competition. Whereas the Italian government agreed with the French position, the governments of the Benelux supported the German proposal. Eventually this secured the 'ordoliberals' the necessary leverage power to equip the Commission with decisive powers to regulate competition.

Von der Gröben noted at a later stage that the proposal for competition rules was taken up as he and his advisory committees composed of members of the *Bundeskartellamt* designed it (Von der Gröben 1963: 18–9; Gehler and Von der Gröben 2002: 56). However, he did so in alliance with the Frenchman Pierre Uri from the French Planning Commission, one of Monnet's high-ranking associates.[2] Importantly, in the drafting phase of the EC competition rules, the presence of national organised capital was less marked than during the ECSC negotiations. The creation of a common market and the new opportunities to expand and to achieve economies of scale was in the interests of large corporations. Moreover, the lax enforcement record of the High Authority in applying Articles 65 and 66 to the coal and steel sector gave the impression that there was little to fear from the inclusion of competition rules at this juncture. The process of re-concentration of the Ruhr giants proceeded unconstrained and industrial capitalists, including the Ruhr industry and organised capital such as the BDI, were no longer worried about strict competition rules (Karagiannis 2004: 24–5). Instead, other parts of the Treaty raised more concerns (see Kniazhinsky 1984: 126–40). Nonetheless, many industrial capitalists and government officials alike opposed the inclusion of merger control rules. The German Ministry of Economics was no exception in this respect. It considered merger rules a discriminating measure for the industry (Witschke 2001: 6).

3.5 The content, form and scope of the EC competition unit

The EC Treaty, which was signed on 27 March 1957, came into effect on 1 January 1958 and established, at least in principle, a common market allowing for the free movement of goods, capital, services and people. It abolished trade-related quotas and tariffs among the six member states and foresaw the establishment of a customs union with a common external tariff and a joint foreign trade policy, next to a common agriculture policy with also common transport and, at the margins, social policies. The ECSC's institutional framework was maintained, yet the High Authority was renamed the European Commission (henceforth the Commission), the Common Assembly the European Parliament (henceforth the Parliament) and the Court of Justice the European Court of Justice (henceforth the Court). The advisory committee of the High Authority was labelled the European Economic and Social Committee, while the Council of Ministers (henceforth the Council) was given more political weight vis-à-vis the supranational institutions (Dinan 1999: 31–3; Mazey 1996: 30).

The concept of 'competition' came to occupy a central position in the EC Treaty. The opening articles stipulated that the EC should promote 'a high degree of competitiveness' (Article 2) and establish 'a system ensuring that competition in the internal market is not distorted' (Article 3f). The actual competition provisions were contained in Article 85, Article 86 and the Articles 90 to 94, which after the renumbering through the Treaty of Amsterdam and later the Treaty of Lisbon became Articles 101, 102 and 106 to 109 (for the sake of simplicity, the article numbers of the Lisbon Treaty will be used henceforth). Herewith, a competition unit of regulation comprising four subunits was installed. In terms of *content*, the objects of regulation of these subunits comprised cartels and restrictive business practices, the abuse of dominant positions, public enterprises and state aid. In other words, two subunits of regulation aimed at controlling the behaviour of companies, whereas the two other subunits aimed at preventing undue state intervention in the market place.

Articles 101 and 102 came to form the centrepiece of the competition provisions. Article 101(1) prohibited anticompetitive agreements and practices, notably cartels and other collusive business behaviour, particularly 'all agreements between undertakings, decision by associations of undertakings and concerted practices which may affect trade between Member States and which have as their object or effect the prevention, restriction or distortion of competition within the common market'. Such restrictive intercompany agreements can include price or quota fixing, market-sharing and market-allocation agreements between direct competitors, generally referred to as horizontal agreements, as well as agreements between companies involved in the different stages of the production and distribution process, generally referred to as vertical agreements.

Article 101(3) provided the basis for exemptions for certain forms of anticompetitive agreements, which contributed 'to improving the production or distribution of goods or to promoting technical or economic progress, while allowing consumers a fair share of the resulting benefit'. Article 102 came to prohibit 'any abuse by one or more enterprises of a dominant position within the common market or in a substantial part of it in so far as it may affect trade between Member States'. Abusive dominant behaviour can include unilateral or bilateral conduct that purports to disadvantage other market players, such as applying dissimilar conditions to equivalent transactions with other trading partners, discriminatory purchases or prices or tied-selling agreements, as well limiting production in order to create scarcity in a market, which in turn allows prices to be raised (McGowan 1996: 14).

There seems to be a wide-spread consensus in the academic literature that EC competition rules were strongly influenced by ordoliberal thinking (Gillingham 2003: 249; Giocoli 2009: 1, 30; see also Maher 2000; Möschel 2001; Hildebrand 2002; Buxbaum 2006). Arguably, the EC competition rules were designed in the ordoliberal spirit of fostering competition and as such, they constituted 'a firm attempt to create a neoclassical liberal economic structure based on as close an approximation as possible to the "ideal type" of perfect competition' (Allen 1977: 94). Nonetheless, both Articles 101 and 102 failed to reflect a wholehearted commitment to ordoliberalism, let alone the ideal of perfect competition. This can be seen first by the fact that mergers and acquisitions were not mentioned with a single word, even though they provided an important mechanism through which competition can be undermined. Additionally Article 102, which is sometimes mistakenly also referred to as the anti-monopoly law of the EC, did not provide a judicial basis to fight monopolies or oligopolies. Rather than prohibiting dominant positions, it only ruled out the *abuse* thereof, thereby potentially allowing for significant degrees of concentration. Also, Article 101(3) established a legal possibility for exempting certain intercompany agreements from prohibition, which in principle provided a loophole for the toleration of cartels and other restrictive business practices inhibiting the free play of competition. As McLachlan and Swann (1967b: 49) bluntly put it: 'Clearly the Treaty cannot be regarded as in any way an obstacle to concentration. On the contrary, by providing what is virtually a *carte-blanche*, it seems to permit the creation of market power even in situations where no real technical arguments could be urged in its support'.

The reason why EC competition rules only reflected ordoliberal ideas to a certain extent is due to the fact that ordoliberalism was not a hegemonic discourse at EC level. Articles 101 and 102 need to be understood as a compromise between advocates of positions based on the incompatible discourses of national mercantilism and neoliberalism. Even though EC competition rules came to serve the overarching purpose of free competition in line with the neoliberal discourse, it also reflected the view of the French government and the important fractions of the capitalist class who opposed strict a competition regulation. This is why, in the words of one scholar, '[i]t is difficult to see exactly what the objectives of competition policy were for those who drafted the Treaty of Rome' (Motta 2004: 14). The vagueness of the provisions reflects the diverging objectives of its architects.

Whereas Article 101 and 102 were directed at private companies, Article 106 addressed state-owned companies that were granted special or exclusive rights by member governments, such the public utility sector, which at the time included energy, transport, telecommunication and water. Section 3 ruled that the Commission could bind member states by directives and decisions in individual cases without the prior approval of the Council of Ministers. Thereby, the Commission had the power to require the de-monopolisation or privatisation of public companies. Moreover, Article 107 to 109 prohibited state aid by national or sub-national authorities that may distort competition and intra-community trade. The EC state aid rules had no equivalent in the ECSC Treaty, nor in US antitrust legislation. The remaining Articles 103, 104 and 105 further specified the Commission's competences in the application of EC competition law vis-à-vis the Council, as well as member state competition authorities.

Regarding *form* and *scope* of the EC competition unit of regulation, there is no doubt that the architects of the EC Treaty envisioned the Commission to play a key role in the enforcement. Yet the Treaty is also rather vague in this respect (see also Goyder 1993: 28–29). Following Bulmer (1994: 427), whereas the ECSC Treaty was a *traité-loi*, specifying to a large extent the regulatory content, the EC Treaty was a *traité-cadre*, which merely set out a broader legal framework that needed secondary legislation or jurisprudence from the Court in order to have any effects. Exemplary in this regard is the fact that no procedural enforcement framework for the application of Article 101 and 102 was included in the EC Treaty. Due to enduring opposition by the French government in the run-up to the Treaty, no agreement on how to enforce the competition rules could be reached. Instead the Commission, notably the Directorate General (DG) within the Commission, which later became the DG Competition,[3] was entrusted with the mandate to make a proposal for a statutory provision that gave effect to Articles 101 and 102. It had to do so within three years after the Treaty entered into force, after which the proposal had to be adopted unanimously by the Council. This ultimately resulted in the adoption of Regulation 17/62.

3.6 The adoption of Regulation 17/62

In the first years of its existence the DG Competition, under the leadership of Commissioner Von der Gröben, was busy preparing what later became Regulation 17/62, widely known as Regulation 17. The preparations to flesh out the rules of enforcement took place on the basis of a number of meetings and conferences with member state representatives and experts (Goyder 1993: 35). Arved Deringer, a German competition expert from the private sector who at the time served as a *rapporteur* at the Parliament, took a leading role in modelling the new regulation. Inspired by the German competition unit of regulation, particularly the ordoliberal idea of a strong state supervising the market, he suggested to equip the DG Competition with far-reaching executive competences (Deringer 2003). The resulting draft regulation had first to be accepted by the College of Commissioners and then passed on to the European Economic and Social Committee and the Parliament. The Council negotiations took place in November and December in 1961 and were later described by Von der Gröben (1987: 108) as 'extremely tense'. Disagreement flared up between the governments of France and Luxembourg on the one hand and the governments of Germany, the Netherlands, Belgium and the Commission on the other. In line with the national mercantilist discourse of competition regulation, the French and Luxembourg governments preferred a model where the Council and the Commission took joint decisions in order to prevent the Commission from undermining domestic industrial policies. The other member state governments supported the neoliberal idea of granting the Commission a significant degree of autonomy and equipping it with significant powers to shape the evolution of competition regulation in the EC setting.

The proposed Regulation 17 was unanimously adopted by the Council in early 1962 and came into force on 13 March of the same year. The reason why most notably the French government voted in favour was due to a package deal. Regulation 17 was adopted on 14 January – only shortly after the difficult CAP negotiations were concluded (Von der Gröben 1987: 108, 110; Warlouzet 2005: 67). Important with regard to the French approval, was the fact that a number of economic sectors were constitutionally exempted from the EC competition rules: the agricultural sector (falling under the CAP), the defence industry, the transport sector and nuclear energy (Neven *et al.* 1998: 5), while the coal and steel sector continued to be regulated separately under the ECSC until it was fully incorporated into the EC Treaty in 2002.

The adoption of Regulation 17 was vital for the future development of the EC competition unit of regulation. For more than 40 years, it provided the procedural and interpretative framework for the application of Articles 101 and 102. With Regulation 17, the form and scope of the EC competition unit of regulation was clarified considerably. The Commission was authorised to act as a supranational competition authority, entrusted with considerable powers. It could investigate competition cases either on its own initiative, or on the request of a member state, a third state, a company or consumers. It held the right to 'undertake all necessary investigations into undertakings', including '(a) to examine the books and other business records; (b) to take copies of or extracts from the books and business records; (c) to ask for oral explanations on the spot; (d) to enter any premises; land and means of transport of undertakings' (Article 14(1)). It was also given the power to impose fines of up to ten per cent of the company's annual turnover (Article 15). Moreover, Regulation 17 created a notification system under which existing and new agreements, decisions and practices of the kind described in the Treaty's Article 101(1) had to be notified to the Commission. Moreover, only the Commission was authorised to exempt agreements from prohibition under Article 101(3) (see European Council 1962, Articles 4, 5, 6 and 8 on notification requirements and the criteria for exemption). Even though the Commission was required to consult with the 'competent authorities of the Member States' (Article 10(2)) and to hear the views of the 'Advisory Committee on Restrictive Practices and Monopolies' consisting of officials from the member states (Article 10), these views were not binding. Except from being '[s]ubject to review of its decision by the Court of Justice' (Article 9, paragraph 1), the Commission could take decisions without the Council and the Parliament having a say, meaning that it was not subjected to democratic control. In short, Regulation 17 was noteworthy as it 'represented a drastic reversal in the traditional relationship between the Commission and the member states' (Kon 1980: 156). By creating a system in which the enforcement 'prerogatives were centred in the Commission and the role of national legal systems was marginalised' (Gerber 1998: 349), Regulation 17 clearly reflected the neoliberal discourse underpinning the position advocated by the German government.

Conclusion

With the enactment of the ECSC Treaty, the first pan-European level competition unit of regulation came into being. The drafting process of the ECSC took place against the backdrop of the presence and assistance of the pro-competition oriented US government, which epitomised the rising hegemonic weight of the US economy in the world. Notwithstanding, the political project of establishing a competition culture similar to that of the US faced considerable difficulties in gaining a foothold in Europe. The opposition of important industrial capitalists and their partisan alignments was massive, but could not block the inclusion of competition rules in the ECSC Treaty in the end. Rather than a wholesale Americanisation, the particular configuration of adherents to positions informed by the neoliberal and national mercantilist discourses gave shape to the content, form and scope of the ECSC competition unit.

The EC Treaty, which was adopted a few years later, constituted the next step towards the establishment of a European level competition unit of regulation. By subjecting almost all economic sectors to competition rules, this treaty was much wider in scope than its predecessor. Yet, as argued by Cini and McGowan (1998: 17), the EC competition provisions ended up being 'a much watered-down version of the ECSC rules'. Unlike the ECSC Treaty, merger rules were not included. At this juncture, the European economic integration project developed without direct US involvement or help. Whereas cartel-minded industrial capitalists formed crucial forces of the political struggle in the run up of the ECSC, only few members of the capitalist class were concerned about the inclusion of competition rules in the EC Treaty. Indeed, it was widely assumed that competition regulation was not going to be important and this also explains why Regulation 17 authorised the DG Competition with wide-ranging enforcement powers.

4 European competition regulation in the era of embedded liberalism

This chapter explains the development of European competition units of regulation in the 1960s and 1970s. It argues that national and EC level competition regulation formed part of the institutionalised nexus of the broader post-war hegemonic order of state-organised capitalism known as 'embedded liberalism', and the responses to the 'American challenge'. Although European competition units continued to be shaped by the neoliberal and national mercantilist discourses, elements of centre-left and Euro-mercantilist discourses were incorporated into the formation of competition rules and their enforcement. The resulting regulation of competition was politically legitimised with references to social inclusion, full employment goals and inter-class solidarity, thereby reflecting the wider class compromise between organised labour and industrial capital fractions of the mixed economies of Europe. The first two sections outline the broader socioeconomic context. The third section focuses on the development of national competition regulation, particularly regarding the content and form of the merger subunits of regulation that appeared in the UK, Germany and France in this period. Section four and five examine the development and enforcement of EC competition regulation during this phase and section six explains the failure to reach agreement in the 1970s on an EC level merger control regulation.

4.1 The era of the embedded liberalism compromise

The end of the Second World War signalled the beginning of a new era in the global economic order. As outlined in Chapter 2, the US assumed leadership of the capitalist world and adopted a strategy to (re)create an open world economy and transform the capitalist world, not least the Atlantic realm, into a zone of economic growth, stability and international cooperation. The Marshall Plan formed part of an attempt 'to kick-start the transformation towards Fordism' in Europe (Van der Pijl 2006: 38) and to incorporate Western European industrialised states in this open world economy.

What later was termed 'embedded liberalism' (Ruggie 1982) embraced a socioeconomic order of state organised capitalism, which gave primacy to active state interventions and social protection over the invisible hand of the market, the national territorial state over the international level and industrial capital over money capital (see also Overbeek and Van der Pijl 1993: 6, 11–14; Rupert 2007: 160–1). The broad-based commitment to an open and competitive world economy was accommodated by domestic systems of government-steered market intervention. Even though different models of capitalism evolved in Europe after the War (cf. Coates 2000; Hall and Soskice 2001), on the whole, the period was characterised by Fordism at the level of the organisation of economic production, Keynesian-inspired macroeconomic and social policies at the level of society and state, and the *Pax Americana* at the level of the overall organisation of the capitalist world system (Overbeek 1990: 87).

Fordism was premised on the idea that companies expand by increasing their productivity and investing in new technologies. This presupposed the complementary development of a mass consumer society in Europe. Typically, Fordist companies exploited economies of scale and scope through the large-scale production of cheap standardised consumer goods, combined with a rigid division and fragmentation of work tasks. Production was centralised in one location and the different stages of the manufacturing and distribution process were vertically integrated. This meant that a few dominant companies commonly assembled the finished products from their manufacturing subsidiaries (cf. Knudsen 1996; Jessop and Sum 2006: 124–5). High levels of vertical integration freed companies from their dependence on suppliers and distributors, and allowed for tight organisational hierarchies and meticulous Taylorist managerial control. Key to the competitive edge were efficiency gains from the use of unskilled or semi-skilled labour carrying out single or a limited number of tasks at assembly lines, as well as enhanced mechanisation in the production process. At the same time, higher wages for labour served to increase the demand for mass consumer goods such as cars, washing machines, radios, vacuum cleaners, and refrigerators.

This Fordist growth model was stabilised by Keynesian-type domestic welfare states, building on the male breadwinner wage idea, and a high degree of technocratic government-steered market intervention. Governments were committed to full employment and modest inflation rates, a strategy that was coupled with rigid capital controls regulating financial in and outflows. Importantly, Keynesian welfare states were the contingent outcome of political struggles and as such did *not* emerge in order to make Fordism function. Organised labour demanded higher wages and social security rights whilst political decision-makers and the capitalist class, particularly fractions of nationally oriented industrial capital, sought to minimise working class support for communism (Lipietz 1992: 5–8; Klein 2007: 251–3). Once the Keynesian welfare state proved capable of facilitating Fordist growth, it gradually attracted the necessary support of not only social democratic and but also conservative circles (Lipietz 1992: 12). Another defining feature of the new order was that it 'combined aspects of expanding production with a measure of re-liberalization in the international sphere' (Overbeek and Van der Pijl 1993: 6). The increasing openness of national markets to foreign trade was sustained through the elimination of trade barriers of the General Agreement of Trade and Tariffs in the late 1950s and early 1960s, and the stepwise liberalisation of capital controls supported by the Bretton Woods system of fixed exchange rates.

The heyday of 'embedded liberalism' stretched from the 1950s to the early 1970s. In this period, which was later referred to as the 'Golden Age', the European economies, or rather the world of developed capitalism, experienced an exceptional economic boom. The output of manufacturers quadrupled on a world scale and trade in manufactured goods increased tenfold (Hobsbawm 1994: 258–61). Industrial capital generally financed its investment through internal funds and was relatively independent from the control of financial capital (Foster and Magdoff 2009: 72). In the early 1970s, the Golden Age ended and was succeeded by a leaden age of deep economic crisis. For various economic, political and social reasons, the world economy entered a recession. This was reflected most prominently after 1973 by sharp decreases in output, productivity and export growth, increasing unemployment and inflation in all industrial countries (see Glyn *et al.* 1990: 43–7). This also marked the end of the embedded liberalism era. Initially, political reactions to the crisis consisted of intensifying the features of national Keynesian welfare states, rather than transforming them radically (Jessop 2002a: 90). Such a crisis management was above all in the interest of those segments of industrial capital hit by economic recession, most notably old industries of steel, shipbuilding, chemistry and textiles, as well as the sugar industry. In the face of growing unemployment rates, however, this strategy also received the political support of labour (Dolan 1983; Kenworthy 2008).

4.2 Responding to the American Challenge

The 1957 Treaty of Rome arguably contained 'little, if anything at all, of what is commonly understood as Keynesianism or associated with so-called Fordism' (Bonefeld 2002: 118). But even though the EC member governments did not attempt to install a supranational version of the Keynesian welfare state, the creation of a large free market for the trade of goods and services produced by nationally based companies was part of a broader strategy to stabilise and facilitate capital accumulation at national level, which was in line with the Fordist growth model. Moreover, the creation of the common market was intended from the outset as a political response to the challenges posed by the US hegemony in the emerging world order, most notably the dominance and technological superiority of US industrial capital in the market for high-value goods. US companies generally enjoyed a structural advantage over European companies. The large homogeneous home market, supported by a single currency, one language and a rather business-friendly competition unit of regulation, allowed US companies to reap the benefits of economies of scale and scope production, expand through mergers and compete in global markets. Enhanced transatlantic trade and investments resulted in a situation in which the largest US companies located more than half of their total assets abroad and generated most of their profits across the Atlantic (Woods 2001: 284). In 1960, 27 of the 30 largest industrial companies worldwide originated from the US (Adams and Brock 1990: 175).

Compared to their US counterparts, European companies were rather small. The European marketplace continued to be highly fragmented along national borders, also after the creation of the EC. Cultural-linguistic barriers, but also the institutional landscape of varying national ensembles of regulation, imposed structural constraints on corporate growth and cross-border mergers. Thus, by gradually opening national market barriers, the EC member governments sought to establish analogous market conditions to those of the US. As Walter Hallstein, the first President of the Commission, noted, the goal of 'the transformation of the market relations in the European Community as a whole was to build a new giant big enough in a world of giant powers' (in Freyer 2006: 282). The project of market integration at first took shape through the subsequent abolition of trade-related quotas and tariffs among the six member states.

The process of breaking down trade barriers was combined with the establishment of a customs union and a common external tariff on 1 July 1968. As this move disadvantaged export-oriented US capital, many US companies sought to set up a commercial base in the EC prior to that date, mostly through mergers and acquisitions. A range of transatlantic mergers transformed a number of European companies, such as Philips and Siemens, into virtual trading companies for US producers (Hager 1987: 59). The dominant presence of US companies in Europe and their leadership in the information technology sector, including the emerging computer industry, increasingly exposed the competitive disadvantage of the relatively smaller, domestic market oriented European companies. This evoked the picture of a growing submergence of Europe to US economic hegemony, particularly in France, where politicians feared that 'US transnationals would be a Trojan horse undermining French economic sovereignty' (Gill and Law 1989: 485; see also McLachlan and Swann 1967a: 237).

When the French journalist Jean-Jacques Servan-Schreiber published his bestselling and widely discussed book *Le defi américain,* the American Challenge, in 1967, the picture of US companies being the main beneficiaries of the common market was reinforced among political decision-makers and organised capital alike. According to Servan-Schreiber, Europe was the target of an economic invasion by American companies, who outclassed European industry in sectors of vital importance such as chemicals and electronics. As European companies did not have the necessary size to face US competition, he warned that Europe was about to 'become an annex of the United States' (Servan-Schreiber 1968: 139). An important reason why European companies were small was that the vast majority of mergers were still *intra*-national. In a memorandum called 'Industrial Policy in the Community' of 1970, the Commission enumerated 1861 mergers between firms in the same country for the period 1961–1969, and only 257 mergers that had taken place between firms in different member states (European Commission 1970a: 92). As a scholar commented, '[t]he record of fusion of enterprises across national frontiers must be accounted one of the failures of the EEC' (Harrison 1974: 190).

Another reason why many European companies could not effectively compete with their US rivals was that they were simply not used to being exposed to a US-type competition culture. In a declaration in 1967, the European business association UNICE noted that certain American firms were 'badly informed about the price mechanisms used in the European market – mechanisms which the various Continental rivals respect'. It added that European companies had 'set up rules' which 'proved beneficial to all' while still safeguarding competition. The conclusion was that American firms suffered from a lack of knowledge of European methods, the potential consequence being 'a price war that would cause serious difficulties in the market' (in Servan-Schreiber 1968: 17). A range of European governments embraced the concerns of domestic organised capital about the lagging competitiveness and the growing technological gap. In line with the national mercantilist discourse of regulation, national governments opted for the strategy of creating 'national champions', in both the private and public sector. Far-reaching industrial policies were adopted across Europe, meant to boost industries considered 'strategic'. These measures generally included protectionist non-tariff policies, such as guaranteed preferential public procurement contracts, tax rebates for some industries, national standard setting and the stimulation of mergers among national companies, as well as (research) subsidies and investment in technical education (Sauter 1997: 81; Ruigrok and Van Tulder 1995: 106).

National governments also implemented proactive programmes encouraging concentration activities among domestic companies as a catalyst for technological advancement. Corporate size was deemed vital for achieving competitiveness and gaining market shares in the global economy. In 1968 for example, British Prime Minister Wilson announced the intention to fundamentally rethink the British hostility to monopolies and restructure British industries 'on a scale and at a speed such as we have not seen in this century' (Adams and Brock 1990: 177). Available data show that these policies bore fruit: significant concentrations took place in countries such as Germany, France and the UK towards the end of the 1960s and in the early 1970s (Cable 1979; Suleiman 1975: 27; Hattersley 1978: 16). Eventually, the political responses to the American challenge and the concomitant project of European economic integration, prepared the ground for the later emergence of large transnational companies (see Chapter 5).

Initiatives to counter the American challenge were also taken at EC level, albeit to a smaller extent. From 1963 to 1969, the project of European integration was crisis-ridden, which considerably slowed down the pace of market creation. The French President General Charles de Gaulle, lending his name to the political ideology of 'Gaullism', envisaged that the French state had to play an important role in world politics, independent from foreign (economic) powers. De Gaulle strongly opposed European 'federalism' and vetoed British membership of the EC twice in the course of the 1960s. He feared that the British entry would threaten the EC's common agricultural policy in the name of free trade, and that the EC would 'become a colossal Atlantic community under American dominance and direction' (De Gaulle in Dinan 1999: 52). When Commission President Walter Hallstein brought forth a range of ambitious proposals for further economic integration, the French subversion culminated in the famous 'empty chair crisis', in which De Gaulle, together with other French representatives, absented the Council meetings from 30 June 1965 until 29 January 1966.

With the resignation of De Gaulle, a short-lived new phase of optimism with respect to the European integration project began. The accession negotiations with the UK, Ireland and Denmark in the years from 1970 to 1972 and their eventual membership in 1973, generated a renewed integration momentum. At a summit in Paris in October 1972, the political leaders of the enlarged EC proclaimed 'their intention of converting their entire relationship into a European Union before the end of this decade' (EC Summit 1972). In line with the Euro-mercantilist discourse, a supranational industrial policy was proposed to establish 'a single industrial base for the community as a whole' and to ensure that 'mergers affecting firms established in the Community' were 'in harmony with the economic and social aims of the Community' (EC Summit 1972, Point 7).

As will be outlined below, this reinvigorated pro-integration spirit created a window of opportunity for the Commission to propose a merger control regulation in 1973. This moment of Euro-optimism was however of an ephemeral nature. In 1973, the Golden Age of the developed capitalist world ended, followed by years of economic crisis. At the Copenhagen summit in December 1973, deep divisions and disinclinations with regard to the Paris summit conclusions surfaced. Although minor steps towards enhanced integration were taken in the 1970s, national mercantilist responses to the economic crisis and the American challenge prevailed over joint EC solutions.

4.3 National competition regulation and the introduction of merger control

In the literature, the 1960s and 1970s tend to be portrayed as a period in which competition regulation in Europe was ineffective and failing to live up to the standards of today's enforcement practices (cf. Wilks and McGowan 1996; Goyder 2003: 31). This impression is generally due to the fact that competition rules were enforced in a very generous, business-friendly manner: not many agreements were prohibited, even in the case of plain distortions of competition. Certainly, the regulation of competition was a relatively new phenomenon in Europe and sophisticated economic analyses similar to those used in contemporary regulatory processes were absent. Nevertheless, it is inadequate to describe the enforcement practices of the 1960s and 1970s as primitive, immature or ineffective. Instead, the content, form and scope of competition regulation took shape in the context of the rise and incipient fall of embedded liberalism and the responses to the American challenge. That is, the ideas underpinning the broader social order, which resulted from the class compromise between organised labour and industrial capital, were also reflected in the way competition was regulated.

In the 1960s and 1970s, proponents of positions grounded in the national mercantilist and neoliberal discourses continued to shape the content, form and scope of the European competition units of regulation. However, a third unit-specific discourse of regulation made its entry, which was a testimony to the broadened circle of agents that took an interest in this area. Whereas initially mainly political decision-makers, state bureaucrats, and nationally oriented organised capital were involved, subsequently organised labour and centre-left parties also started to articulate a position on competition regulation. This position was informed by the centre-left discourse of regulation, and defended the interests of labour by prescribing competition units that took full employment and labour rights into account (see also Chapter 1). It enjoyed popular support and was crucial for shaping European competition regulation in the era of embedded liberalism, particularly the merger control subunits that were established at national level in response to increasing levels of economic concentration in certain industrial sectors.

The UK was the first European state to establish a merger control subunit. Initially proposed by the Conservative government, the Monopolies and Mergers Act was passed in 1965 under the Labour government with the support of the Conservatives, and the Trade Union Congress, while capital organised in the Confederation of British Industries vehemently opposed it (Wilks 1999: 195–204). In 1973 the Act was replaced by the Fair Trading Act, which remained virtually unchanged until 2002 (see Chapter 6). As regards *content*, mergers had to be regulated by 'public interest' criteria, rather than merely anti-competitive effects. Compared to the 1948 Monopolies and Restrictive Practices Act (see Chapter 2), the coverage of the public interest criteria was expanded in line with the neoliberal discourse and also came to include a notion 'of maintaining and promoting effective competition' (in Paines and Reynolds 1988: 216). At the same time, the need to maintain and promote 'the balanced distribution of industry and employment in the United Kingdom' was added as a criterion (ibid.), which reflects a centre-left element. As regards *form*, a political decision-maker, namely the Secretary of State for Trade and Industry, was empowered to take the final decisions in merger cases, and a new institution, the Office of Fair Trading was equipped with the task to screen all mergers beforehand. The Secretary of State decided whether a merger needed a more detailed scrutiny by the Monopolies and Mergers Commission and whether its recommendations had to be followed.

Merger control was also made part of the German competition unit of regulation in 1973. This was largely due to the political efforts of the Social Democratic Party who governed in a coalition with the Free Democrats. As regards *content*, the *Bundeskartellamt* was entrusted with the power to investigate and regulate mergers with annual turnovers greater than DM 50 million, requiring a notification of all mergers meeting a certain turnover threshold. In line with the neoliberal discourse, a pure competition criterion guided the decision-making: mergers leading to or strengthening a position of market dominance were prohibited, unless the involved companies showed that the merger resulted in improved competitive conditions (Schwartz 1993: 629). As regards *form*, the subunit did not completely live up to ordoliberal, and thus neoliberal ideals. The *Bundeskartellamt* was independent from political interference in its control of mergers, on the basis of the criteria outlined in Section 24(3) of the *Gesetz gegen Wettbewerbsbeschränkungen*. However, the Minister of Economics could overrule merger decisions 'when in the specific case the restraint of competition is more than offset by the general economic advantages of the merger or when an overwhelming public interest justifies the merger' (in Baur 1980: 459). The Minister had to take into account the report from the *Monopolkommission*, who published opinions and reports on developments regarding the climate of competition; yet eventually, the self-chosen criteria were critical (Smith 1994: 438–42). Entrusting a political institution with such far-reaching discretionary power to judge mergers clearly went against the prescriptions of the neoliberal discourse.

In 1977, merger control rules were also adopted in France. Similar to Germany and the UK, this step constituted a political response to the high degree of economic concentrations in some sectors, which resulted from the proactive French industrial policy in the 1960s and 1970s. Importantly, the prospect of an EC level merger regulation (see below) spurred the adoption of national merger regulation. French planning institutions feared that the Commission would ban mergers between large French companies, hereby undermining French industrial policy. Hence, 'although public-policy-makers in charge of French industrial policy still believed in the positive effect of concentration and mergers, they were led to favour the adoption of some kind of merger control at the French level [...] as a way to defeat the European merger-control project' (Jenny 1990: 151). As regards *content,* horizontal and non-horizontal mergers with market shares exceeding 40 and 25 per cent respectively, had to be examined by the *Commission de la Concurrence*, a new regulatory institution. As regards *form,* there was no mandatory merger notification system and a government agency, forming part of the Price Control Ordinance department, was responsible for the actual enforcement of the rules.

From the outset the *Commission* opted for a lax enforcement attitude. Between 1977 and 1986, it only examined eight mergers, and when the merger between Ashland Chemical France and Cabot Corporation was prohibited, the French Administrative Supreme Court reversed the decision with reference to alleged procedural mistakes (Voillemot and Michel 1988: 33). As cartel rules were also not strictly enforced, commentators wondered whether French competition regulation was not 'an exercise in futility' (see Jenny and Weber 1975). Also in Germany and the UK, the vast majority of mergers were permitted. Following a report on merger activity in the UK in the early 1960s, less than 3 per cent of the mergers were scrutinised in greater detail, and 'only 13 were found to be against the public interest and a further 15 were abandoned', which amounted to a prohibition of less than 2 per cent of the mergers falling within the legislation (Hattersley 1978: 17). In Germany, between 1973 and 1975, only 4 of the 582 notified mergers were banned (Schwartz 1993: 629). Comparably, in the period between 1974 to 1989, only 90 of the 10,849 notified mergers were prohibited, of which nearly all were appealed, half of them successfully so

(Smith 1994: 442). On a number of occasions in the 1970s, the Minister of Economics overruled *Bundeskartellamt* decisions and approved large mergers, for instance with reference to employment considerations, the preservation of petroleum supplies, or the attainment of international competitiveness in specific sectors (see Baur 1980: 460). The German stance toward cartels was similarly permissive. The *Bundeskartellamt* granted numerous exemptions, resulting in the presence of more than 200 'legal' cartels in Germany in 1973 (Smith 1994: 437; see also Cable 1979: 2, 24).

To recapitulate, the merger subunits of regulation appearing in the 1970s in France, Germany and the UK embodied elements from different discourses of regulation. The neoliberal discourse was most influential in Germany, where the politically independent *Bundeskartellamt* regulated mergers on the basis of a pure competition criterion. Yet, in line with the centre-left discourse, all three national subunits of regulation provided the necessary room for taking employment considerations and other decisional yardsticks into account. Hereby the regulation of economic concentration was made compatible with the commitment to full employment underpinning the Keynesian welfare state. Moreover, in line with national mercantilist ideas, all three national subunits were designed to ensure capital accumulation, and thus the emergence of big companies – even if this undermined competition. This was considered important not only in relation to the Fordist growth model, in which mass production was a crucial feature, but also in relation to the American challenge. In sum, the content and form of national merger subunits displayed the key characteristics of the broader ensemble(s) of regulation.

4.4 The development and enforcement of EC competition policy in the 1960s

In the first four years after the establishment of the EC, Competition Commissioner Hans von der Gröben and his DG Competition focused on the creation of a regulatory framework for the application of Article 101 and 102, prohibiting cartels and other restrictive business practices and the abuse of dominant market positions. The adoption of Regulation 17 in 1962 (see Chapter 3) required companies located in the common market to notify all existing and planned commercial intercompany agreements before 1 November 1962 to the Commission. This requirement immediately raised the opposition of organised European capital, rendering their relationship with the DG rather conflict-ridden. Despite the geographical divisions of national business associations and the absence of joint lobbying efforts against the inclusion of competition provisions into the Rome Treaty, organised European capital saw its economic freedom constrained and urged the Commission to take a soft line (Warlouzet 2005). UNICE even declared competition policy one of the most important subject matters in the 1960s (ibid.). In order to reconcile organised capital with competition regulation, Commissioner Von der Gröben started a promotional tour, in which he visited a broad range of national business associations, particularly those in Germany (cf. Von der Gröben 1964).

Immediately after the enactment of Regulation 17, the centralised prenotification regime was fraught with immense difficulties. An abundance of notified agreements arrived in Brussels, amounting in a serious deadlock right from the start. Prior to 1 February 1963, approximately 34,500 notifications, requests and complaints of bilateral intercompany agreements were registered and 920 multilateral agreements notified (European Council 1963: 585). In 1964, this number climbed up to 37,000 notifications (Slot 2004: 468), overburdening the DG Competition to an extent that it was not even worth getting started with the review process. The first decision was taken in 1964 and years later, in 1968, it had taken only five decisions (Warlouzet forthcoming). At this juncture, the DG Competition was equipped with only 78 officials who lacked previous national experience with enforcing competition rules and clear enforcement strategies (Wilks and McGowan 1996: 231). The Commission urged the Council to expand the staff of the DG Competition (Von der Gröben 1965b: 11); yet against the backdrop of the empty chair crisis, this plea remained unsuccessful.

Nonetheless, the notification impasse led to a much more far-reaching decision: the introduction of so-called 'block exemption regulations'. Rather than reviewing each notified case individually, exemptions 'en bloc' categorically excluded whole groups of intercompany agreements from the notification requirements that fell under the loosely defined conditions spelled out in Article 101(3). In 1965, the Council enacted the first block exemption regulation, which excluded certain vertical agreements and other concerted practices from Article 101 (see Council Regulation No. 19/65). As the number of notifications remained high, only two years later in March 1967, the Council delegated the Commission the power to issue its own block exemption regulations. In other words, the Commission was empowered to enact legislation that excluded whole classes of commercial intercompany agreements without the consent of the Council, in addition to exempting intercompany agreements on a case-by-case basis. This made it possible for the DG Competition not only to investigate and prosecute anticompetitive conduct, but also to codify existing competition rules further and hence, steer them in the desired direction.

The chosen direction of the enforcement towards the end of the 1960s and throughout most of the 1970s was informed by the Euro-mercantilist discourse. As part of a proactive industrial policy, EC competition regulation served as a regulatory vehicle to boost the competitiveness of European capital in the global economy. In order to catch up with the American challenge, the Commission sought to spur economic integration through the creation of cross-border commercial interdependencies. In 1967 it adopted block exemptions for exclusive selling and purchasing contracts between companies belonging to at least two member states (European Commission 1972: 99). Through the block exemption regime, it officially authorised cartel-like commercial cross-border agreements. This led to a number of enduring and successful cross-border alliances, including government-sponsored production cartels. Illustrative examples are Transall, Concorde and Airbus, the European Space Agency, and the TGV (Train à Grande Vitesse) (cf. Hayward 1995). To be sure, the Commission did not artificially stimulate cooperative intercompany agreements. It remained largely passive instead, leaving the decision to cooperate to the entrepreneurs, or sought to coordinate the national planning and control of these consortia (Von der Gröben 1963: 6).

Throughout the 1960s the Commission was very reluctant to interfere with national industrial policies directed at the creation of national champions. It did not apply Articles 106 and 107 to tackle the preferential treatment of state-owned companies, or the state aid granted to private companies (Cini and McGowan 1998: 22). Nonetheless, in an attempt to supersede the member states' aspirations to create national champions, the Commission actively sought to foster European champions instead, and thereby improve the overall competitiveness of the European economy vis-à-vis that of the US, and increasingly also Japan. In the so-called Colonna-Memorandum of 1970, the Commission encouraged companies to organise intercompany collaboration and mergers on a European scale. By promoting new 'sunrise' industries in the high-technology sector and to restructure obsolete industries it hoped to push forward economic integration (Geroski 1989: 27, 28). The Commission became more activist in pursuing industrial goals and attempted to bring more coherence to national industrial policies. Although the EC did not directly finance European champions, the Commission adopted an overtly lenient approach towards economic concentration by deliberately not enforcing Article 102 in the first decades. The need for large competitive companies was more pressing than worries about market dominance. Economic concentration in technology sectors with a high R&D intensity were considered particularly important for the emergence of successful European champions (Von der Gröben 1965b: 4, 13).

The Commission also strongly encouraged intercompany cooperation between small and medium-sized enterprise (SMEs) as a means to counterbalance the promotion of successful European champions in the EC. Commissioner Von der Gröben (1963: 6) declared that 'cooperation between SMEs of different Member States was not only irrelevant in terms of EC cartel law, but actually politically much desired'. In 1970, SMEs were in principle categorically exempted from EC competition rules with the adoption of the *De Minimis* Notice (European Commission 1970b). Although this might seem unspectacular at a first glance, more than 90 per cent of the companies operating in the common market in the 1960s and 1970s fell under this rule (Bright 1996: 440–1). With regard to the agreements requiring EC scrutiny, the Commission allowed the vast majority of the notified deals, either straight away or by granting exemptions under Article 101(3). Almost a third of all cases received exemption, less than 15 per cent of the cases were held to infringe Article 101 and Article 102 of the Treaty and, until 1970, no fines were imposed.[1]

Notwithstanding, it would be incorrect to conclude from the Commission's overall pro-cooperation and pro-concentration stance of the 1960s that the competition provisions were simply not enforced for a decade. Rather, the centre of gravity of the enforcement lay elsewhere. The prosecution of vertical agreements between companies stood in the limelight of the Commission's attention.

Vertical agreements are those taking place between companies involved in the different stages in the production chain, such as agreements on supplier-distribution networks, resale price maintenance, tied selling, specialisation, marketing, and (patent) licensing schemes, or private standard setting agreements. Such agreements were widespread in Europe and also generally considered legitimate by both companies and national public regulators. Vertical agreements also formed the bulk of notifications received by the DG Competition during the first five years (European Commission 1980: 15). Many concerned exclusive selling and re-selling agreements, which could have the effect of price discrimination and refusal to deal, and hence, distortion of trade between member states (OECD 2005). Often, such agreements were managed through national trading associations (Harding and Joshua 2003: 119).

Illustrative is the Commission's prohibition of the exclusive distributorship agreement between the German company Grundig and the French company Consten in September 1964, only two years after the adoption of Regulation 17. In a so-called 'closed circuit' vertical agreement, the companies agreed not to make use of each other's distributor network. Consten was the exclusive distributor of Grundig consumer electronics in France and was not allowed to resell these products to other member states, while Grundig agreed not to supply its products to any other distributor than Consten. When the companies appealed together with the Italian and West German government, the Court reaffirmed the Commission's decision (Schinkel *et al.* 2004: 4). The Grundig-Consten ruling became a landmark case. The Commission's strategy of breaking down private, vertical market barriers served the purpose of market integration and the enmeshment of cross-border corporate activities. It signalled to European industries that intra-brand competition could no longer be avoided. The Commission and the Court thereby acted as principal forces of economic integration at a time in which the overall regulatory process seemed to be stagnating.

4.5 EC Competition regulation and crisis management in the 1970s

In the 1970s, national crisis management strategies impacted on the enforcement of EC competition rules. After the brief moment of Euro-optimism in the early years of the decade and an overall commitment to a proactive EC industrial policy, member states turned their back on the EC once the prolonged economic recession materialised. They opted instead for strategies informed by the national mercantilist discourse of regulation. Urged by domestic industrial capitalists facing economic decline, European governments sought to offset the effects of foreign competition through measures of 'new protectionism' at national level, leading to an 'ever-rising tide of restrictive agreements, concentrations and protectionist national subsidies' (Cini and McGowan 1998: 27).

Reacting to the national mercantilist responses to the American challenge and the economic recession of the early 1970s, the Commission sought to adapt EC competition regulation and industrial policies with national industrial policies yet without losing the overarching goal of market integration. In practice, this meant that the Commission continued to largely ignore the aid granted by EC member states to national 'champions' and other domestic industries, leaving Article 107 virtually unenforced. Next to direct financial aid to the private sector, state aid practices included subsidised loans, tax concessions, guaranteed procurement, financial guarantees and export assistance. In the 1970s, when state aid granted to crisis-stricken industrial sectors and companies proliferated, the Commission prohibited only 21 instances (Allen 1983: 217).

The pre-notification and exemption regime provided a convenient and flexible tool to deal with the pressing problems of the European crisis-hit economy. Old industries of steel, shipbuilding, chemistry and textiles, as well as the sugar industry, gratefully took advantage of the Commission's permissive attitude. Rather than outcompeting each other, companies suffering from chronic excess production in combination with under-consumption, could engage in joint ventures and make use of production quotas to deal with disparities between existing production capacities and actual demand (European Commission 1981a). The Commission became more interventionist from 1974 onwards, most notably in the steel sector, where it enjoyed far-reaching powers under the ECSC Treaty. In the Davignon Plan of 1977, the Commission imposed a range of voluntary and mandatory minimum prices and production quotas, as well as voluntary export restrictions on the steel sector and controlled national subsidies to assist closures and investment decisions of European companies (Geroski 1989: 27). In the sector of synthetic fibres, the Commission orchestrated a provisional market-sharing cartel in June 1978, imposing strict capacity reductions (ibid.: 28). Overall, reduced competition in the short-run was expected to spur the recovery of the affected industries and ultimately benefit the competitiveness of the European economy in the long run. Similar to national crisis management, EC crisis management was largely in the interests of capital. The Commission was fully aware that these practices were incompatible with EC competition rules. It hence informed organised capital that the various protectionist measures could not be taken as a commitment to similar protectionist measures in the future (cf. European Commission 1977).

To enhance the legitimacy of the EC competition unit of regulation in the course of the 1970s, the Commission adapted its strategies to the broader class compromise underlying embedded liberalism. The Euro-mercantilist discourse of regulation was synthesised with elements associated with the centre-left discourse, notably considerations of employment effects. In the First Annual Report of 1972, it was not the preservation of competition, but the fight of inflation, unemployment, underutilisation and underpayment of workers that were declared central policy goals (European Commission 1972: 12). Although the overarching purpose of competition regulation was still 'the creation and proper operation of the common market', the Commission acknowledged that the dynamics of the competitive process created 'intolerable social tensions' (ibid.: 17). EC competition regulation was seen as an instrument to create 'an environment in which European industry can grow and develop in the most efficient manner and at the same time take account of social goals' (ibid.: 18). As part of the underpinning class compromise, the Commission linked its stance towards state aid and crisis cartels to social policy considerations and assured that it would not 'lose sight of the social and human factors involved, which may justify aid beyond what is required by strictly economic reasoning' (European Commission 1972: 18). In the Sixth Annual Report on Competition, it proclaimed that it was 'firmly in favour of aid which solves long-term social problems' (European Commission 1977: 10). Employment considerations surfaced also in its justification of crisis cartels – an approach that was further reinforced in the case of *Metro SB-Grossmärkte GmbH & Co. KG vs Commission* in 1977, where the Court ruled that exemptions to intercompany agreements could be granted under Article 101(3) when they had a beneficial impact on employment, particularly in times of unfavourable market conditions (Monti 2007: 96).

On a more general note, the Court assisted the DG Competition to incrementally expand its powers on a case-by-case basis. In the 1970s, in a long string of rulings 'the frontiers of competition law were pushed forward and its detailed application was clarified' (Cini and McGowan 1998: 29). Both the DG Competition and the Court were however overburdened with the high number of notifications and appeals, as a result of which the Commission earned itself the reputation of being ineffective and incompetent, over-centralised and over-ambitious (ibid.).

4.6 The 1973 proposal for an EC merger regulation

From the mid 1960s onwards, the DG Competition sought to expand its powers by acquiring the right to vet mergers. The Court's ruling in 1972 in the famous Continental Can case made it possible for the Commission to intervene *post hoc* in certain economic concentrations on the basis of Article 102. The Court interpreted 'the competition provisions so as to give the Commission the greatest possible scope for intervention' (Wyatt and Dashwood 1980: 281). Even though the Commission began to apply Article 102 with new vigour, and the Court eventually reconfirmed its ruling in nine other cases in the early 1970s, Article 102 was not deemed an effective instrument to regulate mergers as the DG Competition could intervene only after a merger took place.

Against the background of the Continental Can ruling and the member states' short-lived aspirations to create a strong EC industrial policy in the early 1970s, the Commission made its first proposal for a merger control regulation in July 1973 (European Commission 1973). As regards *content*, the proposed EC merger control subunit could have blocked all mergers of a certain size, provided that they hindered competition. However, at the same time the proposal also exempted concentrations which were 'indispensable to the attainment of an objective which is given priority treatment in the common interest of the Community' (European Commission 1973: Article 1(3)). As such, it embodied the contradictory aims of ensuring competition, whilst also allowing for the emergence of companies large enough to compete on global markets. As regards *form*, intended mergers had to be notified three months in advance. The Commission, in turn, had to decide within this period whether the merger was problematic, and whether it needed an additional nine months of investigations. The circumstantial grounds for exemptions were deliberately not further clarified. The reason for this was that the Commission wanted to preserve the 'future flexibility for possibly changing Community needs' (European Commission 1974: 16). Thereby, the proposal would have equipped the Commission with significant discretionary powers to pursue EC level industrial policy goals. As regards *scope,* the prospective EC merger control subunit targeted combinations with a yearly turnover of ECU 1,000 million. At the same time, the proposal exempted smaller firms with a yearly turnover of less than ECU 200 million. In sum, the proposal mainly reflected the Euro-mercantilist discourse of regulation, inasmuch as it provided the Commission with significant discretionary powers to foster European champions.

As we have seen in previous sections however, member state governments and industrial capital adhered to positions informed by the national mercantilist discourse at this juncture. Notably, the governments of France, Italy, Ireland and the UK preferred national industrial policies to create national champions and were unwilling to transfer new competences to the supranational level that could constrain such policies (Allen 1977: 107; Woolcock 1989: 12). Organised European capital largely supported this position. The Confederation of British Industry lacked confidence in the DG Competition and proposed 'that investigations of mergers by the Community should be conducted by a body independent of the Commission' (House of Lords 1974: 2). A similar view was expressed by the International Chamber of Commerce, UNICE and the *Conseil National du Patronat Français*, the largest French employers organisation, which opposed any form of EC merger control exceeding the scope of Article 102 (The Economist 1973: 53; see also UNICE 1974).

The German government fundamentally opposed the Commission's proposal. In the Council negotiations, it was the strongest advocate of an EC merger subunit modelled according to the neoliberal discourse of regulation. EC merger control had to be based on objective criteria and transparent procedures in order to protect competition in the common market. In other words, according to the German government, the Commission should have no room for discretion to promote certain industrial sectors or companies above others. This was also the basis upon which the *Bundeskartellamt* was empowered to control mergers at national level. In contrast, the proponents of a position informed by the centre-left discourse advocated taking the effects on unemployment and the rights of workers into consideration in the regulation of mergers. Next to national organised labour, a majority in the Parliament subscribed to this position (cf. European Parliament 1974). Also a range of governments took a national mercantilist stance and sympathised with this position, especially the British government after Labour won the elections in 1974.

The Council negotiations endured for years. Following the Commission's Sixth Report on Competition Policy of 1976, a range of issues caused divisions, such as 'the principle of premerger control and the legal basis of the proposed regulation, the field of application, the possibility of derogations from any prohibition, the notification of planned mergers and the decision-making procedure' (European Commission 1977: 21). According to Allen (1983: 229), the proposed merger regulation 'lacked any real support as the economic climate progressively worsened and interest in competition declined'. In the end, the advocates of the national mercantilist positions prevailed: no agreement could be reached and European merger control remained national in scope. Eventually, it took 16 years of arduous negotiations until the EC level merger regulation finally could be adopted in 1989.

Conclusion

In the 1960s and 1970s, the European competition units of regulation evolved against the backdrop of the rise and incipient fall of the broader 'embedded liberalism' order and its underlying class comprise between industrial capital and organised labour. Various mixed national economies sought to accommodate domestic markets with the exposure to an open and competitive world economy through government-steered, Keynesian-type socioeconomic market intervention units. In this era, the initial neoliberal and national mercantilist script of the European competition units of regulation coalesced with elements grounded in the centre-left and Euro-mercantilist discourses of regulation. This had a crucial impact on the overall content, form and scope of the competition units.

Regarding *content*, the preservation and generation of competition was not the only objective. In accordance with the class compromise underlying the wider social order, social and industrial policy considerations were also taken into account. Although EC competition regulation was genuinely market opening in nature, it also entailed a rather tolerant stance towards mergers and various (cross-border) intercompany agreements. This was considered a necessity in the face of the American challenge. But more generally the understanding that the prohibition of cartels was detrimental to the overall economic development constituted one of the vestiges of the deep-rooted tradition of cartels and monopolies in Europe. Particularly, once the economic crisis of the 1970s set in, declining companies and industries were permitted to engage in 'crisis cartels', or to receive state aid.

Regarding *form*, democratically accountable national decision-makers were allowed to play a key role in the national regulatory processes, notably in the subunit of merger control. Likewise, the Commission managed to obtain significant discretionary powers, especially with the adoption of Regulation 17 and the subsequent introduction of the block exemption system. Finally, as regards *scope,* the national and EC competition units largely functioned independently from each other. The national units were generally more dominant. This could be witnessed in the merger control area where national subunits appeared in France, the UK and Germany, whilst no agreement on an EC level merger control regulation could be reached.

5 The neoliberalisation of European competition regulation

In the course of the 1980s the neoliberal discourse of regulation increasingly came to prevail in Europe, echoing what is commonly called the Reagan Revolution or Reaganomics in the US and Thatcherism in the UK, as well as the dictatorial regime of Pinochet in Chile. In this period, the content, form and scope of European competition units of regulation underwent a gradual and also contested process of transformation. This chapter illuminates the nature and causes of this process. Section one deals with the crisis of the social order of embedded liberalism. Section two provides an account of the gradual and partial neoliberalisation of national competition units. Section three explores the transition phase of EC competition regulation in the early 1980s, whilst section four and five expose the political role played by transnational capital in the re-launch of the European integration process in the mid-1980s and the neoliberalisation of the EC competition unit. The last two sections address the adoption of the merger control regulation in 1989.

5.1 The crisis of embedded liberalism and the ascendancy of neoliberalism

In the early 1970s the Golden Age came to an end. The post-war economic boom that resulted from Fordist mass production and Taylorist management strategies could no longer be sustained by further investments in new productive capacities. After 1973 economic stagnation started to surface and the world economy entered a deep crisis, which manifested in sharp decreases in output, productivity and export growth in combination with increasing unemployment and inflation in the industrialised part of the world (Glyn *et al.* 1990: 43–7). In reaction to the crisis, many Fordist companies expanded into foreign markets with a view to achieve further economies of scale. This gradually led to the emergence of transnational corporations (Jessop 2002a: 81). Growing world trade, enhanced cross-border capital flows and the transnationalisation of production increasingly challenged the Fordist growth model. The two 'oil shocks' of the 1970s and the massive budget deficits that resulted from the generous benefits paid to the high number of unemployed further aggravated the crisis. By the end of the 1960s, labour was increasingly discontent about the inhuman traits of the Taylorist separation of work between those who design and those who perform tasks, and demanded more job satisfaction (Lipietz 1992: 12–7).

The economic crisis impacted negatively on the lives of millions of people. Yet a crisis is never an entirely objective phenomenon, nor are the political responses given beforehand. Rather, the nature of a crisis and the suggested remedies are discursively mediated, sustained by underlying social power relations. Thus, '[i]n periods of social restructuring there is an intersection of diverse economic, political and sociocultural narratives that seek to give meaning to current problems by construing them in terms of past failures and future possibilities' (Jessop 2002a: 92). Ultimately, the 'narrative' based on neoliberal ideas of regulation prevailed. There are three, to some extent overlapping, moments in the ascendency of the neoliberal discourse to distinguish (Overbeek 2000: 248–9): a *deconstructive moment* in which the market-correcting institutions of the post-war era of European capitalism were fiercely criticised; a *constructive moment* in which the general neoliberal discourse of regulation gave rise to a series of strategies aiming at transforming different aspects of the post-1970s unit(s) of regulation; and finally, a *moment of consolidation* stretching from the early 1990s to the present in which neoliberalism became the hegemonic discourse of regulation in most parts of the capitalist world.

In the late 1970s and early 1980s, as part of the deconstructive moment, the era of embedded liberalism increasingly came to be discredited by labels such as the 'European Disease' and 'Eurosclerosis' (cf. Giersch 1985). In addition to referring to the lethargic stupor of the European integration project in the 1970s, it also entailed a fundamental critique of Keynesian welfare states, selective market intervention and pro-industrial policies. At this stage however, neoliberal ideas were not having a great impact on the responses to the crisis in Europe – except in the UK, where the Conservative Thatcher government came to power in May 1979. Initially, most governments responded to the crisis of embedded liberalism by intensifying the features of the Keynesian type welfare state (Jessop 2002a: 90). When the desired results failed to materialise, governments started to reform the existing ensembles of regulation in the hope to restore economic growth.

Neoliberal ideas had of course been around for quite some time at this juncture. As accounted for in previous chapters, they had *inter alia* contributed to shape the European competition units of regulation. However, in the era of embedded liberalism neoliberal features were generally combined with elements associated with the Euro-/national mercantilist and centre-left discourses of regulation, reflecting the broader class compromise of the epoch. Only gradually, political and corporate elites in Europe accepted neoliberalism as the primary discourse to inform reforms. This neoliberalisation process took shape simultaneously at national and transnational level. An early example of the neoliberal market remedy to cure 'sick' economies was the OECD's 1977 'McCracken Report' which recommended the pursuance of 'non-inflationary growth through tight monetary policy, prudent fiscal policy, reforms to make markets function better (especially labour markets) and further trade liberalization' (Ougaard 2004: 90).

In its constructive moment, neoliberal unit-specific discourses of regulation underpinned the strategies for reforming the existing ensemble(s) of regulation. In terms of *content*, the aim was to disembed capital from a great part of the web of social, political and regulatory constraints, while in terms of *form*, the separation of key market institutions from democratic accountability stood central (Harvey 2005: 11, 66). As regards *scope*, the aim was to transnationalise regulation by either removing regulatory powers from the national level or subsuming national regulatory institutions under transnational institutions. Together, these strategies sought to stabilise and promote the transition towards 'post-Fordism', referring to more flexible production techniques and the transnationalisation of production (Jessop and Sum 2006). Indeed, the ascendency of neoliberalism was closely related to the disruption of the class compromise between organised labour and nationally oriented industrial capital: it was premised on a shift in favour of capital, most notably transnational capital, in the underlying power balance. In the words of Van Apeldoorn (2002: 55), 'the hegemonic project of neo-liberalism can be argued to be about re-establishing the hegemony of capital over labour after, under the previous regime, the growing power of the latter had threatened to undermine capitalist accumulation'.

Importantly, the neoliberalisation of national ensembles of regulation was not a straightforward linear process. It rather colluded with existing institutional environments and took the shape of an open-ended trial-and-error search for regulatory solutions, leading to different pathways and modalities in different geographical realms. As noted by Brenner *et al.* (2010b: 3–4, emphasis in the original), on the variegated character of neoliberalisation processes, such 'regulatory experiments have unfolded in a sporadic, yet wave-like, non-linear sequence, generating important *cumulative* impacts or sedimented patternings upon the uneven institutional landscapes of world capitalism'. Some EC member states went much farther and faster than others in reforming existing ensembles according to the neoliberal script in the 1980s. The break with Keynesian welfare state was sharpest under Thatcher in the UK, where the government privatised large parts of the public sector and succeeded in significantly weakening the power of labour unions. This was part of its commitment to restore what it perceived as the 'over-governed, over-regulated and over-taxed' economy of the 1970s (Coates 2000: 193).

In France, the socialist government under the presidency of Francois Mitterrand, who took office in 1981, also adopted a neoliberal policy programme. As observed by Gourevitch (1986: 185), '[t]he ending of over two decades of right-center rule occurred just as the international economy was entering the worst depression since 1929'. After some unsuccessful attempts to restore the economy by means of state aid, the large-scale nationalisation of some industries and social policies, the government eventually opted for new solutions in 1983. Jacques Delors, then Minister of Finance, introduced a plan which was aimed at reducing inflation and regaining global competitiveness – at the cost of high unemployment (Dormois 2004: 24). When the French government managed to stay within the European Monetary System, it started to embrace the European integration project more wholeheartedly and the *dirigiste* industrial policies of the 1960s and 1970s were to some extent 'rolled back' (Schwartz 1993: 634).

In Germany in 1982 the Christian Democratic Kohl Government replaced the Social Democratic Government, which had been in power for 16 years. This signalled a partial re-orientation of German politics in a more neoliberal direction. However, instead of breaking radically with the inherited units of regulation, some of them were gradually reworked (Jessop and Sum 2006: 145).[1] The government promoted free markets, deregulation, flexible labour markets, free capital flows, tax reductions and the reduction of the power of labour unions (Van der Wurff 1993: 176). This did not, however, amount to a frontal attack on the unions similar to the one launched by Thatcher. Rather than trying to exclude unions from influence, the strategy was to tie them into the flexibilisation process (Jessop and Sum 2006: 139).

5.2 The transformation of national competition regulation in the 1980s

As part of these broader tendencies in the national ensembles of regulation, the competition units in the three core EC member states were increasingly framed according to the neoliberal discourse. In Thatcher's UK the competition unit did not undergo a major reform. Nevertheless, some changes were introduced. For instance, the investigation of firms' anticompetitive practices was streamlined with the 1980 *Competition Act* and the 1989 *Companies Act* significantly increased the negotiation power of the Office of Fair Trading vis-à-vis companies seeking merger clearance (Kryda 2002: 255; Utton 2000: 276). The most significant development in this period was that merger control became 'exploited to redirect attention in an increasingly economics-oriented direction' (Scott *et al.* 2006: 7). Despite the continued existence of the public interest criterion, more and more mergers were regulated exclusively on the basis of their alleged effect on competition. This was especially the case after the issuance of the so-called 'Tebbit Guidelines' in 1984, which in a legally non-binding way established competition as the primary criterion in merger inquiries (Wilks 1999: 221–3). Thereby, the wider neoliberal shift became reflected in the regulation of mergers.

In France, the 1986 *Ordinance* designed to liberalise the French economy introduced some changes in the existing competition unit of regulation (Garnier and Asselineau 1991: 44). Important in this regard was the replacement of the *Commission de la Concurrence* by the *Conseil de la Concurrence,* a quasi-judicial institution, independent of the Ministry of Economics, which was authorised to function as the main enforcer of French competition rules. Thereby, political discretion was substituted by judicial oversight over the interpretation and enforcement (Souam 1998: 209). At the same time, in the subunit of merger control, the Minister of Economics retained the decision-making powers established by the 1977 law (Dumez and Jeunemaître 1996: 226).

In the German competition unit, next to cartels, mergers became ever more central objects of regulation in the 1980s. Despite the opposition of organised

German capital, the *Gesetz gegen Wettbewerbsbeschränkung* was revised in 1980 in order to enable the politically independent *Bundeskartellamt* to deal more effectively with conglomerate and vertical mergers (see Smith 1994: 446). In the Kohl era, merger control was less politicised, even though the Minister of Economics remained the highest instance of appeal. While the decisions of the *Bundeskartellamt* were overruled on some occasions in the 1970s, this became a rare phenomenon in the 1980s with only two instances (in the 1990s there was none) (Bundeskartellamt 2009).[2] This retrenchment of a democratically accountable politician reflects the intensification of the neoliberal features of the German merger subunit.

5.3 EC competition regulation in the transition phase

In the field of EC competition regulation, the deconstructive moment in the ascendancy of neoliberalism in the early 1980s paralleled the continuation of the crisis management of the 1970s and the Euro-mercantilist strategy of fortifying the competitiveness of European companies in the global market. The lenient course in favour of restructuring 'sick' industries through state aid and crisis cartels did not abruptly end. Frans Andriessen, who took office as Competition Commissioner in 1981, strongly believed in the virtues of competition. Yet he also noted that 'competition should not be an objective in itself, but constitute an instrument to create a market structure within which effective competition can take place' (Andriessen 1983a: 5). Elsewhere he confirmed that 'the promotion of the harmonious development of economic activities throughout the community' had not lost its relevance (ibid. 1981: 5). At this juncture, the Commission therefore continued to frame its overall policy mission in terms of creating an environment in which European industry could grow and develop, while at the same time taking social goals into account.

Notwithstanding this, a more stringent enforcement philosophy made its inroads at EC level. Even though state aid was still considered perfectly legitimate in some cases, in others it was compared to 'woodworms eating away the carcass of the ship of integration' (Andriessen 1982: 6). In contrast to the tolerant approach of the 1970s, the Commission also announced its intention to act with more firmness in cartel cases (ibid. 1981: 2). Industries facing prolonged economic downturn were despicably called 'sunset industries' or 'lame ducks', while crisis cartels and branch-wide agreements sheltering indigenous companies from foreign competition were discursively constructed as 'anomalies' and as examples of a 'frozen economy' (ibid. 1982b). Subsequently, the DG Competition actively encouraged and monitored 'restructuring plans' meant to rationalise industries and ensured that the 'healing process' was not delayed or obstructed (European Commission 1981a). In practice, these programmes often implied the downsizing of employment and the strict prohibition of price and market sharing agreements.

The new rigour in the enforcement of competition laws was first felt in the ailing European steel industry. Under the alleged reason of revitalising the industry, the Commission demanded a radical restructuring by 1985, which included the termination of quota levels and a limitation of state aid. In the case of the highly indebted steel group Saarstahl, the Commission rejected Bonn's request to permit any further government grants unless a radical 'restructuring' took place (The Financial Times 1982: 2). National mercantilist minded organised capital and political decision-makers from some member states, particularly from France, preferred more relaxed EC competition rules in times of economic downturn and thus vehemently opposed the DG's new approach in the enforcement of competition laws (Andriessen 1983a: 13). Those in favour of protectionist measures against foreign competition were beginning to lose political ground at EC level however.

The Commission's 1985 block exemption regulation on the selective distribution regime in the car industry aptly illustrates how on the one hand, protectionist practices were still going strong and considered legitimate, while on the other hand, the scope for governments to protect their national champions from outside competition was diminishing. Member state governments shielded their car manufacturing industries from increased competition from US, Japan and later Korea, rendering this sector one of the best protected in Europe (cf. Seidenfuss and Kathawala 2005). In response to the intense lobbying of national car producers and member state governments, the Commission endorsed the view that the car sector needed special protection. However, the block exemption regulation adopted for the industry was a double-edged sword. Although the regulation contained strong protectionist elements, allowing European car manufacturers to install exclusive and separate dealer distribution arrangements to reduce the exposure of brand names and hence (foreign) competition, it also initiated a transition to a more competition orientated system. First, the Commission imposed an expiring date of 10 years, and second, the condition that the EC manufacturer's pre-tax car prices were not allowed to differ more than 12 per cent in the long-term and not more than 18 per cent for periods of less than a year. As the lowest price became the new benchmark, the Commission hoped to stimulate price competition (cf. Akbar 2003). Thereby, one of the best protected industrial sectors was gradually exposed to the forces of free competition.

5.4 Transnational capital and the re-launch of the European integration project

The paralysis of the integration project of the late 1970s continued into the early 1980s. Only in the mid-1980s it gained renewed momentum. Jacques Delors, the new President of the Commission in 1985, made the promotion of the single market his main project. In the same year Lord Arthur Cockfield, the Internal Market Commissioner, presented the famous White Paper, which identified 300 obstacles that needed to be removed in order to arrive at a truly integrated internal market and suggested the year 1992 for its completion (European Commission 1985a). In 1986 the Single European Act was adopted, which revised important parts of decision-making of the EC Treaty.

Organised transnational industrial capital evolved as a crucial driving force behind the re-launch of the European integration process in the 1980s. The European Roundtable of Industrialists (ERT) became a highly important elite platform for the emerging transnational capitalist class (cf. Van Apeldoorn 2000). Hosting the captains of industry, the top executives from Europe's largest industrial companies, the ERT was formed in 1983 in order to push for a European level initiative bringing the economic crisis to a halt. Wisse Dekker, CEO of Philips, one of the main initiators declared: 'If we wait for our governments to do anything, we will be waiting for a long time. You can't get all tied up with politics. Industry has to take the initiative. There is no other way' (in Gutteridge 2000: 16).

The ERT developed general strategies for improving the overall business climate in Europe, but did this from the vantage point of transnational and primarily industrial capital. According to Van Apeldoorn (2002: 118–23), from the outset a fractional class struggle took place *within* the ERT. In its first five years, a Europeanist fraction advocating a position originating in the Euro-mercantilist discourse of regulation dominated a globalist fraction. The Europeanist fraction supported the creation of a European home market shielded from outside competition, most notably from US and Japanese companies and pushed for EC level policies supporting the emergence of globally competitive European champions. In contrast, the globalist fraction sought to supersede regulatory market constraints on capital mobility and capital accumulation beyond the European integration project and to impose the neoliberal free market idea on a worldwide scale through institutions that limited the discretionary power of states within their national markets.

The Europeanist fraction began pushing for a European solution to the crisis in the immediate wake of the Roundtable's creation. The above-mentioned 1985 White Paper was strongly inspired by plans for a single market drafted by Wisse Dekker in 1983. A crucial reason why the European Council endorsed and subsequently implemented the White Paper were the proactive efforts of Roundtable members (Cowles 1995: 514–6; Van Apeldoorn 2002: 130). Notwithstanding, the direction of the internal market turned out to be different than envisaged by the Europeanist fraction. This was because it was not supplemented with the kind of industrial policies such companies 'had hoped would nurture the growth of European champions and protect them against global competition' (Van Apeldoorn 2002: 130–1). Euro-mercantilist ideas of regulation seeking protectionist market intervention at EC level were increasingly on the defensive in the late 1980s, and within the ERT, where the strengthened globalist fraction gave primacy to a neoliberal outlook (ibid.: 87–8).

From the start the ERT took an interest in EC competition regulation. At the 1983 European Management Forum Symposium in Davos, Wisse Dekker suggested a fundamental rewriting of the EC's competition rules, prompting the Commission to reconsider the basis upon which it took decisions and relax the stringency of competition rules (Andriessen 1983b: 2). This early attempt by the ERT to influence the future course of EC competition regulation was successful to some extent. Competition Commissioner Andriessen introduced a new post called *Conseiller-Auditeur*, entrusted with the task to make sure that the DG Competition heard a company's defence and guaranteed 'fairness and balance' in the investigation process of anticompetitive conduct. This provided business representatives with a direct avenue to express their interests. In a later interview, Andriessen validated this move by arguing that the previous administrations had operated in an ivory tower without understanding the needs of business. To remedy the situation, Andriessen cooperated more intensively with organised capital, as well as with the legal community (Interview with Andriessen 2006).

5.5 The neoliberal turn in EC competition regulation

In 1985, when Delors became President of the Commission, Irishman Peter Sutherland, a neoliberal hardliner who staunchly believed in free competition, replaced Andriessen. Sutherland asked Delors for the job 'because of its economic importance and because a close reading of the Treaty of Rome had shown him that, in theory, the commission had more power in this field than in any other' (Ross 1995: 160). Young and charismatic, he was eager to turn these powers into practice and soon became known for his aggressive style in combating anticompetitive conduct. His ideological position resonated well with the growing dominance of the neoliberal discourse in the Community.

Despite the receptiveness of the political and economic elites to neoliberal ideas, Euro- and national mercantilist positions were not completely abandoned yet. The Commission was internally divided on ideological grounds. The strong presidency of Jacques Delors to some extent counterbalanced the neoliberal course that started to take shape from the mid-1980s onwards. Nurtured in the French *dirigiste* tradition of active government intervention, he fiercely criticised the neoliberal free-market approach. He hoped to breathe new life into proactive and sector-based EC industrial policies alongside policies aiming at more social equality in the Community (Wilks and McGowan 1996: 256). Commissioner Sutherland in contrast, devoted his tenure from 1985–1989 to challenging national governments before the Court for state aid granted to national industries. According to estimates, EC governments supported industry with 93 billion euro in 1986, an amount almost three times as large as the EC's entire budget (The Economist 1988: 68). Whereas the DG Competition had often not interfered in the past, most forms of state aid were now perceived as a member state trade barrier and thus declared incompatible with the single market. By further specifying the conditions for state aid, the Commission narrowed the leeway for public market intervention and acquired an enhanced grip on the course of the member states' national industrial policies. Moreover, Sutherland adopted a 'naming and shaming' strategy in which the size of state aid granted by each member state government appeared in periodic surveys (Wilks 2005a: 124). Italy, Greece and Ireland were marked as the 'bad guys' on almost all fronts. Italy exhibited a level of state aid about five times as high as France, the UK or Germany, which the Commission considered unacceptable (The Financial Times 1989).

Next to fighting state aid, the Commission also started to tackle state monopolies by means of so-called privatisation directives on the basis of Article 106(3), a hitherto virtually unused provision, which allowed it to issue directives in the field of public enterprises and monopolies without the further approval of the Council. Such directives concerned utility sectors such as telecommunication networks, the aviation sector, rail transport, postal services, electricity, natural gas and water (Pollack 1998: 230–1). Sutherland fully realised that the Commission entered a field which used to be the prerequisite of the member states and that this was as close as he could 'get to touching the nerve of national sovereignty' (The Financial Times 1987: 18). By the application of Article 106, the Commission steadfastly opened up previously closed sectors to competition.

Furthermore, in line with the approach introduced already under Commissioner Andriessen, cartels were prosecuted with an unprecedented stringency from the mid-1980 onwards, marking a sharp contrast with the previous lenient stance. In 1987, on its own initiative, the Commission started up cartel investigations in 42 cases, which led to a total of 166 pending cases (European Commission 1988: 55–6). The imposed fines for breaching EC competition laws reached unparalleled levels. For example, a price-fixing and market-sharing cartel involving 15 chemical companies involved in polypropylene manufacturing was fined ECU 60 million in 1986 (European Commission 1986). Overall, the era of structural crisis cartels seemed definitively over. Commercial intercompany agreements were only exempted in cases of strong evidence that the agreement furthered technical progress in the field of R&D, the transfer of technologies, innovation and economic integration across borders.

To recapitulate, the re-launch of European integration, the ascendancy of neoliberalism and the transnationalisation of capitalism generated a spirit in which the competition unit became increasingly prevalent in the broader EC ensemble of regulation. As McGowan and Wilks (1995: 151) observed, the DG Competition transformed from 'an uninspiring and fringe directorate into one of the most prominent and important'. After a transition phase under Commissioner Andriessen, the broader macroeconomic welfare vision of EC competition regulation, which had survived until the end of the 1970s and early 1980s, gave way to more market-based and short-term oriented considerations. Under the incumbency of Commissioner Peter Sutherland (1985–1989), competition regulation was subordinated to the sole purpose of establishing rigorous competition, thereby becoming a major regulatory instrument to warrant a genuinely free-market economy.

5.6 Transnational capital and the question of EC merger control

With the renewed impetus to create 'an ever closer union', the Commission attempted to obtain merger controlling powers and issued an amended proposal for a regulation in December 1981. No agreement over the content, form and scope could be reached however. Divisions between advocates of positions informed by the national mercantilist and neoliberal discourses of regulation remained fundamental. The proponents of the national mercantilist position insisted on exemption rules on the basis of industrial, regional and social policy considerations, as well as the right of member states to overrule the Commission in merger cases. In contrast, the proponents of the neoliberal position favoured pure competition criteria and the Commission as the sole instance to regulate mergers (see European Commission 1981b: 3). A majority in the Parliament, as well as the Economic and Social Committee, supported the proposal but proposed a series of amendments informed by the centre-left unit-specific discourse, such as the inclusion of social policy goals (cf. EESC 1982). Organised European capital vehemently opposed the idea of a supranational merger control regulation. In a position paper in June 1982, UNICE noted that its objections to the draft remained 'fundamental': the decision-making criteria were unclear, the proposed system too bureaucratic and overlaps between national and EC level control likely (UNICE 1982: 1–2). The proposal was without a chance at this stage and when the Commission drew up a new proposal in February 1984, history repeated itself: the Council could not reach agreement (European Commission 1984).

Competition Commissioner Sutherland and also Leon Brittan, who replaced him in early 1989, nonetheless continued the endeavour to convince the member states of reaching an agreement on a merger control regulation with undiminished zeal. From the outset, the adoption of a merger control regulation was a top priority of Sutherland. To put pressure on the member states he adopted a more proactive and aggressive strategy than that followed hitherto. He warned that if the Council did not reach an 'adequate agreement' quickly, the Commission would simply start to review mergers under existing competition law, that is Articles 101 and 102, with a view to stimulate an 'interest in looking at a regulation as such' (Interview with Sutherland 2006). In his words, '[t]he issue is not whether Europe has a merger policy but what type it has' (The Economist 1988: 68). In November 1986, the Council once more turned down the Commission proposal which contained some rather minor amendments compared to the 1981 proposal. Similar to earlier proposals, organised capital opposed an EC merger subunit of regulation, believing that DG Competition would make life even harder for companies involved in cross-border mergers.

Sutherland realised that without the necessary support of European capital, member states would continue to block the expansion of Commission powers in this field. Consequently, he 'spent a lot of time speaking to the corporate world at conferences, and individuals in powerful companies, the European Roundtable of Industrialists and so on, to make the point that the control of mergers at a national level ultimately meant the division of the internal market often on the basis of less than objective criteria and political influence and interference' (Interview with Sutherland 2006). To take away their biggest concern he assured that '[w]e're not taking the line that bringing the big together is bad' (The Financial Times 1985: 3).

The controversial Court ruling in the Philip Morris case played into the hands of Sutherland. Two tobacco companies, BAT Industries and R.J. Reynolds complained to the Commission about an agreement between two of their rivals, namely Philip Morris and Rembrandt Group, who transferred the control of over half of the shares in Rothman Tobacco Holdings (one of the Rembrandt Group's subsidiaries) to Phillip Morris and entrusted it with the right to veto a possible future sale of Rothman's shares. Phillip Morris appealed to the Court when the DG Competition concluded that the agreement had to be changed. The Court took the opportunity to comment on the applicability of Article 101 to mergers. Contrary to common perception, it ruled that Article 101, prohibiting cartels and other anticompetitive business practices, was also applicable to 'agreements between two or more companies that allowed one of the companies to obtain legal or de facto control over the other', thereby providing the Commission with a 'backdoor route' to deal with mergers (Pollack 1998: 233–4).

The consequence of the Philip Morris ruling was that a system with multiple controls of certain mergers arose – that is, a simultaneous regulation by both national authorities and the DG Competition. This created legal uncertainty and additional costs. Companies intending to merge started to notify mergers to the DG Competition even though they were under no obligation to do so (Bulmer 1994). Meanwhile Sutherland was determined to show the world that his threats of using Articles 101 and 102 to regulate mergers were serious. In March 1988, he forced British Airways to give up some of the routes it had acquired when taking over British Caledonian, despite the fact that the deal had been approved by the British competition authorities (Grant 1994: 161; The Economist 1988: 67).

Against this background, the owners and managers of companies started to orient themselves beyond national markets. They more and more came to prefer a pan-European merger regulation as a potentially desirable alternative (Interview with Davignon 2006). This was also related to the changing nature of economic concentrations through mergers. Previously, mergers were predominantly an intra-national phenomenon. From the mid-1980s onwards, companies from different EC states, and also from beyond, increasingly started to merge. According to Commission statistics, the number of intra-national level mergers increased from 101 in 1983/1984, to 145 in 1985/1986 and 214 in 1987/1988, to 241 in 1989/1990, while in the same period, EC level mergers increased from 29 to 52, and 111 to 257 and mergers involving companies from beyond the EC from 25 to 30 and then from 58 to 124 (European Commission 1985b, 1988, 1989, 1992). The bulk of merger activity was inherently linked to the context of the 1992 programme, which aimed at completing the internal market by 1 January 1993. The fundamental reconfiguration of several national markets into one giant common market created the prerequisites to transnationalise, to expand in size with increased velocity and, hence, to be more globally competitive. It also forced many industries to restructure their production and seek synergy effects, such as economies of scale and scope through mergers.

The enhanced cross-border nature of mergers triggered the wish for an EC merger control subunit. Many ERT members, such as British American Tobacco Industries, Nestlé, Unilever, Hoechst, Phillips, Thomson, Fiat, Olivetti and Daimler-Benz were involved in the merger mania of the late 1980s (Gray and

McDermott 1989: 10–16). The Roundtable emerged as one of the most important supporters, even though it initially feared that the Commission's proposal for a merger control regulation was insufficient to support 'corporate restructuring' in the common market (ERT 1988a). It strongly pushed for the introduction of a so-called 'one-stop-shop' rule, which entrusted the Commission with the exclusive control of 'Community-dimension' mergers, thereby ruling out overlapping and potentially contradictive merger reviews by national competition authorities (ERT 1988b). Moreover, it advocated that '[t]he criteria for judging merger proposals should be clear and workable and the administrative procedures permit rapid decisions' (ibid.). In line with the neoliberal discourse, the ERT discarded the notion of leaving room for regulatory discretion and political intervention. The outspoken preference for 'clear' competition criteria indicates that the globalist fraction and its neoliberal orientation within the ERT gradually came to prevail over the more protectionist Europeanist fraction.

Towards the end of the 1980s, corporate support for a pan-European merger control regulation also included UNICE and its member federations (cf. UNICE 1987). The introduction of a 'one-stop-shop' rule, together with the competition criterion as the exclusive basis upon which the Commission could regulate mergers, was considered particularly important by the Confederation of British Industry, as well as the UK-based Institute of Directors, representing several thousand company directors (CBI 1988: pt. 9; IoD 1988 pt. 28). Despite the neoliberal inclination of the representatives of British capital, the two main capital fractions, industrial and financial capital, were not unified in their position. The corporate governance regime of the liberal model of capitalism and the traditional strong shareholder value culture of the Anglo-Saxon world rendered companies in the UK much more vulnerable to hostile takeovers than their rivals on the Continent. Notably in the coordinated market economies of Germany and France, stable ownership and control structures shielded companies from foreign hostile takeover bids. The market for corporate control was relatively weaker, due to the presence of large block holders, relatively limited rights for minority shareholders, overall lower rates of return and a system in which *Hausbanken* formed stable sources of long-term funds for industries (cf. Hassel and Beyer 2001).

With the enhanced pace of cross-border merger activity, many managers of companies operating in sectors particularly vulnerable to hostile takeovers by foreigners supported 'the retention in the merger Regulation of national public interest, as a means of blocking bids where reciprocity conditions are not met' (Woolcock 1989: 26). As rumour had it, the 'aggressive takeovers by French nationalised companies proved especially irritating to the British' (The Financial Times 1991: 14). This gave rise to two conflicting positions in Britain's capitalist class. Industrial capitalists subscribed to the national mercantilist view that, unless the other EC member states transformed their systems according to the British model, measures had to be implemented to make it more difficult for foreigners to take over companies in the UK. As pointed out by Woolcock (1989: 27), this went 'against the interest of the British financial community in maintaining an open environment for investment' with the result that 'British business as a whole is split on the issue'.

5.7 The adoption of the 1989 merger control regulation

Pressures on member state governments to reach agreement on an EC merger control regulation were mounting towards the end on the 1980s. Eventually, 16 years after the first proposal, Regulation 4064/89 was adopted on 21 December 1989. The regulation was strongly informed by the neoliberal discourse of regulation. In terms of *content*, little room was left for criteria other than competition. As Commissioner Brittan (2000: 3) noted, it 'gives clear primacy to the competition criterion, with only the smallest nod in the direction of anything else'. In terms of *form*, democratically accountable decision-makers were granted merely a non-binding advisory role, and in terms of *scope*, the regulation established the desired 'one-stop-shop' rule which moved the powers to control large mergers from the national to the supranational level.

The content and scope of the prospective merger control subunit were heavily disputed and the draft regulation went through several changes in order to accommodate the twelve member state governments and organised capital alike. As regards *content*, the Commission was eventually not allowed to pursue social or industrial policy goals. Brittan, who replaced Sutherland as Commissioner in early 1989 and who also gained the reputation of 'a bulldog of a politician inside the Commission' and a 'genuine neo-liberal to whom a fully open market was the only industrial policy' (Ross 1995: 130), favoured a pure competition regulation. His amended proposal of March 1989 left out notions that allowed taking industrial and social policy criteria into account (Interview with Brittan 2006). This contrasts with the other competition rules of the Rome Treaty, of which many required testing a case against the particular notion of whether 'Community interest' was harmed.

Article 2(3) of the 1989 Regulation reads that '[a] concentration which creates or strengthens a dominant position as a result of which effective competition would be significantly impeded in the common market or in a substantial part of it shall be declared incompatible with the common market'. Similarly, Article 2(1) reads that the Commission shall take into account 'the interests of the intermediate and ultimate consumers, and the development of technical and economic progress provided that it is to consumers' advantage *and does not form an obstacle to competition*' (emphasis added). This move away from the Euro-mercantilist formulation was not only consistent with Brittan's personal ideological preference, but also necessary to accommodate the German and British governments who opposed the expansion of the Commission's powers (Interview with Faull 2006).

The German government had defended a neoliberal formulation with an exclusive focus on competition as a decision-making criterion since the 1970s and thus sought to limit the Commission's right to make discretionary assessments. Similarly, when the British Conservative government was willing to discuss EC merger control in 1987 (The Times 1987; DTI 1988), in line with the interests of British financial capitalists in particular, it wanted to avoid including a notion remotely similar to the British 'public interest' criterion at EC level. Together with the German government it pushed for competition as the only decision-making criterion (House of Lords 1989: 78).

In contrast the French and Italian governments actively pursued industrial policies, but abandoned the national mercantilist position in favour of a Euro-mercantilist position that supported the creation of European champions and a strong national presence in such firms (Armstrong and Bulmer 1998: 100). This u-turn was related to the explosive rise in cross-border mergers and to the fact that they were under severe pressures from organised capital desiring the introduction of EC merger control. Although still far away from the neoliberal camp, the French and Italian governments started to genuinely favour an EC merger control regulation over the status quo, even if there were no loopholes for industrial policy considerations included. This made it possible to reach an agreement on a merger control regulation that was neoliberal in content.

With regard to the *scope* of the EC merger subunit of regulation, namely the turnover thresholds defining the division of labour between the EC and national authorities, opinions continued to diverge markedly. Whereas the German and British governments wanted to limit Commission's powers to the control of mergers with an aggregate global turnover above ECU 10 billion, leaving all other combinations to the member states (Woolcock *et al.* 1991: 17), the French government suggested thresholds around ECU 5 billion, whilst the Italian government and those of the Benelux and Denmark preferred an even lower threshold of ECU 1 billion (Europe Daily Bulletin 1988). Higher turnover thresholds obviously limited the Commission's reach to very large mergers only. Smaller member state governments favoured the Commission having a larger say in the merger area and thus opted for lower turnover thresholds.

The final regulation entailed a compromise, stipulating that the Commission had exclusive competence over deals involving companies with a combined worldwide turnover of what today is equivalent to 5 billion euro, or then each with more than 250 million euro in sales in Europe, unless they each realised more than two thirds of their European turnover in one and the same country (Article 1(2)). With a threshold 25(!) times higher than that originally proposed by the Commission in 1973, the scope of the EC merger control regulation was eventually much more limited than initially envisaged. The final regulation did however not entail a clear division of competencies between the Commission and national authorities. Even though the German government supported the establishment of an EC merger subunit, together with the *Bundeskartellamt*, it pushed for the inclusion of the so-called 'German clause' in Article 9(3) of the regulation, allowing national competition authorities to block a Community-level merger under exceptional circumstances, that is, if a merger was of great significance to a national market. In addition, due to pressure from the Dutch government, the so-called 'Dutch clause' was included in Article 22(3), allowing the member states to request the Commission to also review mergers with no

Community dimension and, thus, compensate those member states with a preference for lower thresholds. Organised European capital strongly disliked these clauses, in particular the German clause, as it considerably weakened the much cherished 'one-stop-shop' rule and introduced the possibility for a double control (cf. UNICE 1989).

Conclusion

This chapter has shown how and why the neoliberal discourse of regulation increasingly came to prevail among Europe's political decision-makers and the transnational capitalist class in the course of the 1980s. The rise of neoliberalism was premised on the transnationalisation of capitalism and made possible by a shift in the underlying power balance in favour of capital – most notably transnational capital. The resulting transformation of the broader ensembles of regulation was gradual and partial. It neither took place overnight, nor was it uncontested. This was also the case in the national and EC competition units of regulation. Rather than radically breaking with the past lenient course, which sought to restructure 'sick' industries through state aid and the toleration of crisis cartels, engendering the preservation of both companies and jobs, neoliberal ideas institutionalised in uneven and non-linear ways. Nonetheless, a steady neoliberalisation of both the French, German and British competition units took shape in the course of the decade, materialising in the reduced involvement of politicians in regulatory processes and an informal removal of non-competition criteria from competition regulation, especially in the merger control subunits.

The EC competition unit also underwent a significant neoliberalisation in the course of the 1980s. This happened after a phase of transition in the early 1980s. In the wake of the re-launch of the wider European integration process, a development that was strongly promoted by the transnational capitalists organised in the ERT, the neoliberal discourse increasingly came to overshadow the other discourses that underpinned the DG Competition's regulatory practices in the past. After the mid-1980s, the cartel and state aid subunits were subjected to a 'competition only' vision, which left no room for industrial and social policy considerations. Likewise, the merger control regulation of 1989 entailed an entirely neoliberal text. It gave rise to merger control based on a pure competition criterion (content). There was no possibility for the involvement of a democratically accountable institution or person in the regulatory processes (form) and significant regulatory powers were moved from national to EC level (scope).

6 Consolidating neoliberalism

European competition regulation from the 1990s onwards

Capitalist production and accumulation transnationalised at an unprecedented pace throughout the 1990s. This fundamental transformation of the context in which competition rules were enforced took shape through a massive increase of cross-border mergers and intercompany agreements, which in turn were facilitated through various neoliberal forms of regulation. The neoliberal counter-project to the social order of embedded liberalism and concomitantly to centre-left, national and Euro-mercantilist ideas and practices gained the discursive upper hand both in the competition units and in the broader ensembles of regulation in the course of the 1990s. It served to promote the superiority of free market forces and competition-driven mechanisms above state-regulated social and economic organisation. Section one looks into the changes of capitalism and capitalist power relations since the 1990s, whilst section two discusses the consolidation of neoliberalism as a general hegemonic discourse. Section three explains how the neoliberal discourse became hegemonic in the EC competition unit of regulation, while section four and five deal with the Commission's cartel and state aid prosecution, privatisation directives and merger control. Section six addresses the wider repercussions of EC level neoliberal practices on national level regulatory developments.

6.1 The transnationalisation of capitalism

The ascendency of the neoliberal discourse of regulation was dialectically related to the emergence of transnational accumulation structures, which profoundly altered the production process, capitalist power relations and in a wider sense, the global capitalist system itself. Albeit far from being a uniform process, ensembles of neoliberal regulation facilitated the 'expansion of market relations and the freedom of capital to maximise its accumulation potential' (Overbeek 2002). Transnational corporations (TNCs) became an increasingly widespread phenomenon. The number of TNCs steadily increased from 7,000 in 1970 to 37,000 in 1993, 53,000 in 1998, and exceeding 60,000 in 2000, with 690,000 affiliates/subsidiaries (UNCTAD 2000: 8–10). The combined impact of new technologies, the improvement of transport and possibilities of communication on the one hand, with ongoing trade liberalisation, ever more mobile and unrestricted capital flows, as well as processes of deregulation and public utility sector privatisation on the other hand, account for their growing prominence. Most of the TNCs originated in a few advanced industrial countries of the OECD, most notably the US, UK, Germany, France and Japan. They operate in 'the world economy's most dynamic sectors', such as the food industry, the sectors of electronic products, chemicals, automobiles, drugs, machinery, banking and telecommunications (Went 2002: 100).

The growing presence of TNCs incrementally changed the nature of capitalism and capitalist power relations. To grasp the depth of capitalist restructuring in Europe, a comparison to the situation in the 1960s and 1970s is indicative. Back then relatively small European companies, operating in predominantly national markets, faced the 'American challenge' and sought shelter from outside competition through protectionist arrangements at national and EC level (see Chapter 4). Today, many of the largest TNCs in the world are European, setting the pace of competition in the global market place. The aggregate annual income of the largest TNCs surpasses the level of GDP of most countries in the world. TNCs are estimated to account for approximately two-thirds of world trade, and one third of global trade is generally assumed to be linked to intra-firm trade only, also referred to as foreign affiliate sales (UNCTAD 1996: 104). As the different stages in the production and distribution chain are completed by companies and subsidiaries located in different regions of the world, vertical intra-firm trade has increasingly replaced traditional horizontal trade in finished products (ibid.). This change was not only of a quantitative nature in the form of extensive cross-border trade and capital flows, but also entailed a shift in gravity from productive to finance capital. Today, the actual trade of physical commodities accounts for only one per cent of total trade (Harris 2006: 59). Instead, trade in financial products and currencies have increased. After the collapse of the Bretton Woods System in 1971, and especially from the 1980s and onwards, the integration of finance capital has intensified significantly. The magnitude of speculation and the proliferation of financial instruments such as stocks, futures, options, derivatives and currency has grown out of proportion with regard to the underlying 'real' economy.

What came to be known as 'financialisation' in the process capital accumulation is also reflected in the massive rise in foreign direct investment (FDI), which often takes the form of mergers and acquisitions of foreign companies or parts of them, rather than Greenfield investments through new assets creation by foreign investors in their host country, such as physical plants and machinery and eventually also jobs. During the 1990s, the share of merger activity of total FDI flows was estimated to account for 87 per cent (UNCTAD 2000: 10). Financial capital started to play a key role in financing mergers, which led to a massive wave of economic concentration throughout the 1990s. The magnitude of this merger wave was without historical precedent, peaking in a total of 31,019 mergers in 2000, the highest number ever (The Washington Post 2006). Traditionally, economic concentration involved bigger companies 'eating' smaller ones. This merger wave consisted of 'mega-mergers' instead, defined as transactions exceeding

US$ 1 billion, involving companies of equal size, including successful global players, touching on virtually every industry. The number of such mega mergers rose from 45 in 1996 to 109 in 1999, reaching 175 in 2000 (Evenett 2003: 31). The conspicuous examples of the mergers between Vodafone and Airtouch-Mannesmann, and the AOL-Time Warner merger in 2000 concerned transactions of respectively US$ 190 and 166 billion, comparable to the GDP of a middle-sized European country like Portugal (Budzinski 2002: 2). More than 70 per cent of all mergers were horizontal in nature, involving companies from the same industrial sector; yet vertical concentrations involving companies along the production chain were also on the increase (UNCTAD 2000: 10).

Financial capital was the driving motor of what has been identified as the 'marketisation of corporate control' throughout the 1990s (Horn 2009), referring to the situation in which corporations were being traded similarly to other commodities in the market with the purpose to achieve large capital gains in the future. The traditional role of finance capital as a helpful servant to production waned. Rather than financing new productive capacities, financial investment institutions were seeking short-term capital gains in equity markets through leveraged buyouts and predatory bidding for shares. As a result, merger activity correlated with the booming stock markets, with the bulk taking place against the background of raising stock prices signalling higher than normal profits (Mueller 1997: 664). UNCTAD statistics also confirm this picture: from 1980 to 1999, the vast majority of transactions were acquisitions by means of either the purchase of the majority of shares or assets of a corporation and less than three per cent of the total number of cross-border mergers were 'true' mergers, if defined in terms of a mutual consent of executive directors. Moreover, only a third were full acquisitions and in 5 per cent of the cases, the acquisitions were of a hostile nature, when shareholders acquired the stocks of companies against the wish of company boards (UNCTAD 2000: 10).

Alongside investment banks, new financial players such as private equity companies and hedge funds entered the takeover battles, seeking to profit from the speculative arbitrages that resulted from buying and re-selling corporations and/or corporate assets. In the business of leveraged buyouts, financial institutions became massive borrowers themselves, financing frenzy merger activities through the accumulation of an enormous debt 'with little to no stimulatory effect on production' and job creation (Foster and Magdoff 2009: 45). The growing weight of financial capital had major ramifications for labour in the form of enhanced pressures on cutting back jobs and keeping real wages stagnant (ibid.: 74).

Although mergers and acquisitions by private investment firms slowed down after 2000 as a consequence of the bursting of the dot.com bubble and a more general hangover of bad debt, the year 2006 nonetheless set a new record of merger activity, topping the previous record of 2001, if measured in terms of aggregated volume. Eight of the ten world-wide largest deals ever were concluded in this year. The biggest transactions were the acquisition of Bell-South by AT&T (US$ 83 billion) and the mergers between E.ON and Endesa

(US $ 66 billion), Suez and Gaz de France (US$ 43 billion), and Mittal and Arcelor (US$ 39 billion) (International Business Times 2006). Low interest rates for lending money and the event of the growing presence of private equity houses and hedge funds provoked an upsurge of market concentration. In 2007, global mergers and acquisitions continued to reach new heights, despite a significant fall in the volume and number in the second half of the year. The total value reached an astonishing US$ 4.74 trillion in 2007 (The Financial Times 2007b). With the advent of the global economic crisis and the resulting liquidity shortage, the global merger volume dropped by one third after 2008 (Reuters 2008). Yet it remains to be seen whether this slowdown will precipitate a drastic halt. As predicted by analysts, falling stock prices may trigger hostile takeovers in the form of unsolicited bids by corporations with strong balance sheets. Likewise, partial acquisitions in the form of buyouts might become more frequent.

The rhythm of economic concentration is far from stable. The contemporary reduced merger activity should not distract from the fact that, in the past decade, acts of economic concentration proceeded at an unparalleled scale, reaching highly 'daring and complex transaction combinations' (Draghi 2003: 10–11). These included tender offers to the shareholders of a target company, proxy fights by the acquisition of shareholder's voting rights or different forms of leveraged buyouts. Importantly, mergers and acquisitions were not the only gauge for the concentration of economic power. Together with a pronounced transnationalisation of interlocking of positions, various forms of commercial intercompany agreements and strategic alliances, such as partnerships, joint ventures, business consortia and alike proliferated too in the course of the 1990s (Goddard 2003: 438). Such forms of economic integration were often more commonplace than mergers and highly complex in nature. The actual degree of corporate enmeshment through such agreements often remains opaque and the boundaries with so-called structural joint ventures and mergers blurred. Most intercompany agreements and intra-company trade lines generally tend not to be public, and fall under the confidentiality of the involved companies. As a direct result of the complexity and intertwining of economic interests that accompanies economic globalisation, discrete enterprises with clearly separable interests have become increasingly difficult to identify. To recapitulate, the structures of capitalism have undergone important processes of transnationalisation since the 1990s, which in turn profoundly altered the relationships of power between productive and financial capital, as well as between capital and labour.

6.2 The neoliberal hegemony of the 1990s

As outlined in Chapter 5, the ascendancy of neoliberalism in the 1980s encompassed moments of deconstruction and construction. In its third moment, which stretched from the early 1990s to the present, the neoliberal discourse of regulation consolidated in most parts of the capitalist world. It became deeply engrained in perceptions of social reality, social practices, policy solutions and regulatory and institutional adjustments. As such, this discourse was not visibly dominant, but 'obscured by achieving an appearance of acquiescence to this whole as if it were the natural order of things' (Cox 1994: 366). At the most general level, the entrenchment of neoliberal policies and strategies around the world led to 'market-based, market-oriented or market-disciplinary responses to regulatory problems', intensified 'commodification in all realms of social life' and 'mobilized speculative financial instruments to open up new arenas for capitalist profit-making' (Brenner *et al.* 2010a: 2). Neoliberalism, however, never became manifest in a pure fashion. Important differences in the neoliberal organisation of capitalist markets endured at different places and levels of regulation, which was due to variations in the contestation by various social groups, regulatory experimentation and inherited institutional landscapes. Nonetheless, since the mid-1980s, a large majority of those occupying positions of power in both national and transnational institutions have implicitly or explicitly endorsed neoliberal ideas (cf. Harvey 2005; Mirowski and Plewhe 2009).

At EC level, neoliberal ideas became hegemonic in the course of the 1990s, giving rise to a wide-ranging array of concrete policies which, in essence, promoted the superiority of free market forces and competition-driven mechanisms above a state-regulated social and economic organisation. The economic integration project was decisively shaped according to the neoliberal discourse since the 1990s. With the adoption of the 1992 Maastricht Treaty leading to the establishment of the European Union (EU), the initial Rome Treaty was revised in important respects towards a more neoliberal content. In addition to consolidating the four freedoms of movement, it set out a timetable for the completion of the Economic and Monetary Union (EMU). In line with prevailing monetarist ideas the European System of Central Banks imposed the goal of price stability maintenance on national central banks and the newly created European Central Bank was entrusted with a degree of institutional independence, unparalleled to that of any other central bank (cf. Verdun 1999). Ensuring low inflation, even at the cost of high unemployment, formed its primary task. This development was closely related to the general shift in the balance of power between capital and labour. Low inflation rates first and foremost served the interests of the owners of capital. Concurrently, the Stability and Growth Pact put a tight straitjacket on member states' fiscal policies, thereby obstructing Keynesian-type macroeconomic steering of aggregate demand.

The organised transnational capitalists who had played a decisive role in the European integration process in the 1980s continued to do so in the 1990s, thereby consecrating an 'ever-closer Union' in the neoliberal spirit. The ERT voiced its discontent with EC institutions in a series of reports, reform proposals, position papers and newspaper interviews. Most notably, in the early 1990s when Europe was overshadowed by a small economic recession and European companies were losing market shares in the world export of manufactured goods, especially in the export of high technology products, the ERT deplored the lack of competitiveness in the European economy. This was further enhanced with the conclusion of the Uruguay GATT Trade Round, which lowered the average weighted import duty on industrial goods between the EU, the US and Japan to below 4 per cent, which ensured an increased degree of import competition from the industrial giants of the US and Japan (European Commission 1995: 3). In the view of the ERT, the EU had failed 'to keep pace with the liberalisation which has transformed the global economy over the past 10 years' (Helmut Maucher, CEO of Nestlé in The Financial Times 1996a). Next to calling for more 'flexible' labour markets and limited social and environmental policies, it articulated a neoliberal 'competitiveness discourse', meant to ensure the Darwinian logic of 'the survival of the fittest', rather than protectionist solutions (Van Apeldoorn 2002: 172).

The goal of competitiveness became a catchword, enjoying primacy above all other policy goals (ERT 1996a). Boosted by deepening integration and confident in making use of its powers, the Commission was utterly receptive to the ERT's initiatives and surfaced as a major protagonist in orchestrating the neoliberal restructuring of the common market. The salience of the Commission as a pivotal regulator grew with the increase of its workload. As the guardian of the treaties, it kept close track of the progress of the single market project and did not shy away from reproaching national governments for the lax implementation of EU rules. It proclaimed that the common market should become 'synonymous with rationalised production and stronger competition' (European Commission 1988: 14).

The overall commitment to competitiveness culminated in the so-called Lisbon Strategy in March 2000, aiming at making Europe by 2010 'the most competitive and the most dynamic knowledge-based economy in the world' (European Council 2000). More investment in R&D but also reforms of the social security systems and labour market policies, implemented by means of benchmarking, were considered essential in this regard. Albeit social cohesion and a good environment were also mentioned as goals, the strategy established a clear hierarchy with enhanced competitiveness being the top priority. Thereby the Commission echoed the ERT's Competitiveness Working Group, which was very much involved in the preparation of the Lisbon Summit (Janssen 2000). Organised transnational capital, including the ERT and UNICE, strongly embraced the Lisbon Strategy and frequently voiced dissatisfaction with the lack of ability or will of the member states to implement it.

The political momentum of a thorough neoliberalisation of EU policies was mirrored at member state level. In the UK, the Labour Party of the Tony Blair government, re-branded as 'New Labour', adopted so-called 'Third Way' policies which continued the radical neoliberal course followed by Conservative governments since the late 1970s. As Jessop (2006: 9) pointed out, successive New Labour governments 'have deliberately, persistently, and wilfully driven forward the neo-liberal transformation of Britain rather than halting or reversing it'. Similarly, in Germany, important steps towards a neoliberalisation of the 'social market economy' during the 1990s were taken. The privatisation and deregulation of public services of the Kohl government in the 1990s were continued by the social-democratic government of Gerhard Schröder (1998–2005), notably in the form of neoliberal pension reforms (Schmidt 2002: 72–4; see also Ryner 2003). Also the subsequent French governments following up the socialist Mitterrand government adopted a more market-based model of capitalism with less interventionist industrial policies, privatised many industries and deregulated labour and financial markets (Prasad 2005: 358). Yet in France, neither the political decision-makers nor the majority of the population embraced neoliberal ideas wholeheartedly. As a result, the shift away from the French model of capitalism never fully materialised and budget cuts in social regulations faced staunch resistance from the 1990s onwards (Schmidt 2002: 84–7; Clift 2003).

6.3 Transnational capital and the 'ayatollahs' of neoliberal competition regulation

The overall consolidation of the neoliberal discourse of regulation spurred the salience of the competition unit of regulation as a mechanism of dismantling intra-European market barriers. The broader claim of organised transnational capital for more competitiveness was sustained by a notion of 'market justice', according to which anticompetitive practices were considered 'unfair' to others. It was believed that the number of those winning from the removal of private market barriers and enhanced exposure to market competition was offsetting the damage suffered by those losing from it. Corresponding with the interests of the transnational capitalist class, the Commission was committed to the view that fierce competition constituted a catalysing force for the allocation of production factors in the most efficient and profitable way and therefore, for increased social wealth. Competition Commissioner Karel van Miert, a Flemish socialist, who initially promised to 'broaden the scope of competition policy' and adjust it to economic, political, social and environmental goals (The Financial Times 1993a: 1), eventually also joined the ranks of the neoliberal hardliners in the College of Commissioners (see also Cini and McGowan 1998: 43). His successors, Mario Monti, an economist by profession and later Neelie Kroes, were both neoliberals who firmly believed in the virtues of competition and never made a secret of their contempt of protectionism (Kroes 2007). Likewise Joaquín Almunia, who was appointed Competition Commissioner in 2009, at the time of writing, seems eager to continue down the neoliberal path (e.g. Almunia 2010).

The neoliberal discourse did not go uncontested within the Commission in the 1990s. The views of the DG Competition regularly clashed with that of the DG of Industrial Policy. Martin Bangemann, former Commissioner in charge of the latter, went as far as to opine that the 'academics' in the DG Competition 'have no idea of the reality of economic life' (The Financial Times 1992a). Also officials from the Regional Policy DG regularly complained about the views held by competition officials (Menon and Hayward 1996). The neoliberal hardliners were nicknamed 'ayatollahs' or 'gurus', as a way to refer to their 'arrogance and unshakable faith in their beliefs' in the rationality of the market (The Financial Times 2002a). As pointed out by Cini (2000: 85), the neoliberal rhetoric of DG Competition officials almost went as far as 'delineating good from evil and right from wrong' in 'a biblical sense', while adopting a 'missionary zeal' to spread its values 'not only within the EU but also globally'.

The process of neoliberalisation received strong support by the ERT and organised transnational capital more generally. In various position papers they made clear what content, form and scope of the EC competition unit they desired. As regards *content*, transnational capitalists largely favoured freeing the forces of free competition (for an elaborate discussion, see the ERT memorandum 'Freedom to Compete' of 1994). Sheltering uncompetitive or smaller companies from competition by protectionist regulatory practices or tolerating cartels was considered market-distorting. The ERT therefore also advocated a 'passive' facilitation of cross-border mergers through the invisible hand of the market, rather than the adoption of interventionist industrial policies targeting national and European champions in particular industrial sectors. Governments should not actively try to create 'European Champions', but should also not block their development (ERT 1993: 25). In the wake of the Lisbon Strategy, the Roundtable called for a fundamental reform of EC competition policy, arguing that the strategy 'cannot be pursued, let alone realised, unless competition has space to flourish' (ERT 2000: 1). It urged the Commission to apply less strict 'market definitions' as globalisation forced 'EU companies to grow in size both organically and through acquisitions/mergers in order to achieve new efficiencies' (ibid.: 1–2).

The desired *form* of the EC competition unit was defined in terms of 'speed, transparency and predictability' (ERT 1993: 25). The request for speedy procedures also surfaced with respect to the enforcement of Article 101 type agreements, which had to be notified to the Commission prior to their conclusion. UNICE pushed for a far-reaching reform of the administration of the notification procedure and the scope of Article 101 (UNICE 1995). Furthermore, there was a broad-based consensus among organised capital that the inclusion of political decision-makers slowed down the regulatory process, which made it less transparent and thus unpredictable. As regards *scope*, the ERT suggested limiting or even eliminating the regulation of competition by national authorities. Instead, a 'one-stop-shop' within the common market had to be established, according to which any competition issue was 'judged once and for all' in 'a single European competition policy system with a common philosophy and no possibility of conflicting jurisdictions' (ERT 1993: 25).

ERT members enjoyed particularly easy access to Competition Commissioners such as Peter Sutherland, who himself became a member of the ERT in 1997 as Chairman of BP and Leon Brittan who, after his subsequent position as Commissioner of External Affairs in 1999, became Vice Chairman of the US investment bank Warburg Dillon Reed, a subsidiary of Swiss megabank UBS. The Commission's accessibility for the ERT and organised capital more generally did not change under the subsequent Competition Commissioners. According to a study by Neven *et al.* (1998: 137–8) on the contact between company representatives and Commission officials, only a small share (13 per cent) proceeded by written or phone contact. The vast majority met with high-level staff of the different units within DG Competition. Generally, the larger the company the more high-level the contact. In the run up to formal decisions in competition cases, person-to-person contact became more frequent (ibid.). In the words of a member of the ERT – the Commission and its DG Competition 'is extremely open to the business community' (Janssen 2000).

6.4 Cartel prosecution, privatisation and state aid in neoliberal times

With the consolidation of the treaty texts through the 1991 Maastricht Treaty, the Community's overall objective of guaranteeing 'balanced trade' and 'fair competition' as spelled out in the preamble was replaced with 'balanced trade' and 'free competition'. Except from this seemingly trivial, but in fact telling, change, neither the SEA, the 1991 Maastricht Treaty, or the 1997 Amsterdam Treaty introduced major substantive changes in the competition field. The neoliberal discourse of regulation nonetheless became hegemonic in all EC competition subunits. It consolidated above all in the way in which the Commission interpreted and enforced the rules, and in the adopted enforcement-related regulatory instruments. This can be seen in the subunits of cartel prosecution, the prosecution of state aid and abuses of dominant positions, as well as in the application of privatisation directives.

As outlined in the previous chapter the Commission became more proactive and aggressive in busting cartels already in the mid-1980s. Taking inspiration from the US competition units, it issued a Leniency Notice in 1996 (later revised in 2002 and 2006). This Notice granted immunity from prosecution to those who first confess to having participated in collusive or other types of unlawful agreements. On the basis of game theoretical logics, most notably the assumptions of the prisoners' dilemma, leniency schemes were not only expected to create an incentive for cartel members to disclose information in order to reduce enforcement costs, but also a situation of mutual distrust among companies and to destabilise illegal cartel practices altogether. The introduction of this scheme was coupled with significantly increased fines. Aggregate fines for breaching cartel rules dropped from € 344,282,550 in the years from 1990 to 1994, to € 270,963,500 from 1995 to 1999 but then rose to € 3,166,247,910 from 2000 to 2004 (European Commission 2010b). From 2005 to the end of 2009, the Commission imposed a total of € 9,422,440,500 – more than double the total amount imposed between 1990 and 2003 (ibid.). The highest ever fine amounting to € 1.38 billion, was imposed on a cartel fixing the price of car windows in 2008 (European Commission 2010b).

The increase in aggregate fines was certainly due to the overall size of the companies involved and to the growing number of cartels prosecuted. This increase partly resulted from the leniency schemes that induced a number of 'carteleers' to report about their cartel practices (Brenner 2009). Yet without doubt, cartels were punished much harder in the neoliberal era compared to the era of embedded liberalism, where the toleration of certain cartels formed part of the overall proactive macroeconomic steering. As McGowan notes, '[b]y today's standards the initial fines seem ridiculously light as a deterrent' (2007b: 6). Interestingly, a number of ERT companies have received gigantic cartel fines in recent years. The list includes companies such as Saint Gobain, E.ON, GDF Suez, ThyssenKrupp and Siemens. Seen in this light, the Roundtable's consistent calls for 'freedom to compete' involve a great deal of hypocrisy. Apparently, certain companies find it difficult to practise what they preach.

The record fine of € 497 million imposed on Microsoft in 2004 by the Commission attracted more public attention than any other competition case. The Commission ruled on the basis of Article 102 that the company had abused its dominant position when refusing to provide suppliers of server operating systems with interoperability information and when tying its Media Player with its Windows operating system. The fine might sound astronomical, yet several commentators raised doubts about its actual impact on a company with more than € 50 billion in cash reserves (Johnson and Turner 2006: 119). Nevertheless, the case demonstrates the Commission's willingness to apply the competition rules, no matter how controversial the issue and how big the company. The Microsoft record fine was topped in 2009, when a fine of € 1.06 billion was levied on Intel for abusing its dominant position in the market for computer chips.

Further to consolidating a neoliberal vision in the cartel subunit of regulation, the Commission also intensified its efforts to 'liberalise', that is to privatise key utility and infrastructure sectors such as telecommunications, energy, post and transport in which state owned companies often enjoyed a monopoly status. In the era of embedded liberalism, public monopolies were exempted from the necessity to compete due to public interest considerations (Wilks 2005a: 125–6). Organised transnational capital strongly pushed the Commission to expose these sectors to the logics of free market competition. Next to offering prospects of corporate expansion in new lucrative sectors, privatisation was believed to create more efficient and cheaper goods and services. The ERT therefore disparaged the allegedly high-cost, inefficient, bureaucratic, and highly overstaffed public monopolies (The Financial Times 1996a: 16). In response, the DG Competition continued to endorse privatisation directives under Article 106(3) (see also Chapter 5).

In a 'radical set of judgments in the 1990s' the Court interpreted Article 106(1) in a manner that legitimated the Commission's liberalisation strategy (Monti 2007: 448). The Court encouraged not only the Commission but also private litigants to pursue member states, in the hope that private enforcement induced 'a catalyst towards EC-wide liberalisation' (ibid.: 451). Privatisation received every emphasis when the Commission took over the role of guiding the Central and Eastern European Countries through the transition to free-market capitalism in the 1990s. Alongside the institution of market freedom and ownership rights, it promoted competition regulation as a key instrument for introducing the logic of open competition to previously government-controlled economies, where monopolies and centralised price-fixing constituted the norm (European Commission 1995).

Likewise, the Commission became increasingly active in the field of state aid. By further specifying the conditions for member states granting state aid, the Commission narrowed the leeway for public market interventions and thereby acquired an enhanced grip on the course of national industrial policies. It launched the 'State Aid Scoreboard' in 2001, a benchmarking instrument to measure the progress of the Lisbon agenda. Commissioner Monti believed that this would reinforce 'the process of peer pressure' and lead 'to a vigorous debate on State aid in Member States' (European Commission 2001a). Similarly, Commissioner Kroes made clear from the outset of her tenure that she would make state aid control a top priority. Under the guise of promoting 'growth, jobs and cohesion', the Commission introduced the so-called State Aid Action Plan, obliging member states to recover illegal aid from past beneficiaries (European Commission 2005a). In 2004, 25 per cent of 'illegal and incompatible aid' was recovered and in 2006 this rose to 71 per cent (or € 6 billion) (European Commission 2007a). In 2007, the Commission took 608 decisions on unlawful aid in the period of 2000–2006. Germany topped the list (148 cases), followed by Italy (105), Spain (70) and France (63) (European Commission 2007b: 12–13). If measured in terms of subsidy level per capita, 'Germany emerges as one of the worst culprits and the neoliberal UK one of the most reluctant to award subsidies' (Wilks 2005a: 125). By aggressively tackling state aid, the Commission launched a major assault on one of the last vestiges of the mixed economies of the embedded liberalism era.

6.5 Neoliberal enforcement practices in EC merger control

The 1989 merger control regulation entered into force on 21 September 1990. A separate department within the DG Competition, the so-called Merger Task Force, was created to especially deal with 'Community dimension' mergers. The merger review process was composed of two phases, starting with an investigation phase of a month (phase one), after which the Commission could ban or clear a merger with or without attached conditions, or then assess the situation with greater scrutiny for another four months (phase two), after which it had to come up with a final verdict. The Commission had to take into account the opinion of the Advisory Committee, consisting of member state representatives. This opinion was non-binding however, which made the Commission in effect both investigator, prosecutor and judge in the regulation of mergers. In the case of disagreements the involved companies and third parties could only appeal at the Courts.

The merger control regulation required the Commission to assess mergers on the basis of the 'market dominance' test. Following Article 2(3) a concentration 'which creates or strengthens a dominant position as a result of which effective competition would be significantly impeded in the common market or in a substantial part of it shall be declared incompatible with the common market'. In other words, the yardstick for a prohibition was firstly that a given merger created or strengthened a dominant position, and secondly, that it 'significantly impeded' competition (Weitbrecht 2005: 67–8). The decisional ground for judging a merger was the resulting market shares relative to other companies. Assessing dominance in the relevant product markets was a controversial matter as it was often notoriously difficult to clearly establish the delimitation of one product market from another, leaving much room for interpretation to the Commission. This can also be seen from the fact that over time, both the Commission and the Courts interpreted dominant market positions differently (Schmitz 2002: 558).

Judging from the actual enforcement practice since 1990, the EC merger subunit genuinely served to facilitate economic concentrations and not to block them. In the years from 1990 to 1992, the Commission hardly ever came across anticompetitive mergers. More than 100 of the 134 notified mergers were permitted in phase one, namely within one month. Ten of the notified mergers underwent the more detailed four month phase two investigation. Of these only one was prohibited, namely the proposed merger between the Canadian aircraft manufacturer De Havilland and ATR, a consortium of the French company Aerospatiale and the Italian state aerospace group Alenia. The blocking of this industrial concentration led to considerable political disputes, notably between the Commission and the French and Italian governments, but also within the College of Commissioners. The companies, together with the Franco-Italian government alliance, lobbied the Commission to allow the merger. It would have made them market leaders in the regional turbo-propeller commuter aircraft market, and helped them survive the economic slump caused by the reduced military spending since the end of the Cold War (The Financial Times 1991). The Commission was split into a Euro-mercantilist camp and a neoliberal camp. Industrial Policy Commissioner Bangemann, as well as the Commission's President Jacques Delors, played the 'Eurochampion' card and criticised the Competition DG and the supportive Internal Market DG for radically breaking with the tradition of industrial and employment reasoning in competition cases. In the end, the neoliberal camp won and the College prohibited the takeover with nine votes to seven, while Delors abstained from the vote (Ross 1995: 178). Commissioner van Miert (1998: 4–6) declared later that 'the concept of national champions was dead' and that industrial intervention was an 'old-fashioned policy'. Not to expose companies to full competition, in his view, was 'a false economy' (ibid.).

The Commission's ban came as a shock to the owners and managers of transnational capital, who feared that future economic concentrations would also be blocked on the basis of narrowly defined product markets within the EC. The globalist fraction within the ERT wanted to 'punch their weight in a globalised economy' and repeatedly urged the Commission to judge competition against a global perspective, that is, to view the world market as the relevant market for judging mergers (ERT 1993; 2004). The overwhelming majority of ERT member companies were involved in mergers of a 'Community dimension' at some point in the 1990s. These included Alcatel, BASF, Bertelsmann, BP, E.ON, Nestlé, Nokia, Shell, and Vodafone to mention but a few. Although the Commission cleared the bulk of mergers involving ERT companies, it also prohibited a few, namely Deutsche Telekom, Volvo, ENI and on two occasions, Bertelsmann. Thereby it demonstrated its operational autonomy from transnational capital. This should however not conceal the fact that, overall, the Commission took a business friendly stance and strongly encouraged companies and their legal advisors to discuss their proposals 'early and often' (The Financial Times 1992b: 10). Organised transnational capital did not orchestrate the overall development of the EC competition unit of regulation from the 1990s onwards. The Commission itself evolved as a faithful advocate of modelling the various subunits according to the neoliberal discourse.

Since the inception of the merger control subunit, mergers with a 'Community dimension' were generally not prohibited. The Commission unconditionally approved the vast majority of the notified mergers (87 per cent), the bulk of which in phase one, and imposed conditions in only 288 cases (European Commission 2010c). Just 20 out of 4,376, or 0.45 per cent of mergers notified in the period of 1990 to the end of May 2010 were blocked (ibid.). In 132 cases the merger was withdrawn, 'often because the modifications needed to satisfy the Commission were unacceptable and because of prohibition fears' (Morgan 2001: 459). To recapitulate, EC merger control subunit of regulation served to facilitate the concentration of capital. It considerably eased cross-border transactions by providing companies with a regulatory alternative to the involvement of multiple national authorities. For this reason, organised transnational capital strongly supported the merger control regulation and took a keen interest in influencing the future course of this subunit when it was revised in 2003 (see Chapter 7).

6.6 National competition regulation

The consolidation of the neoliberal discourse from the 1990s onwards was not only restricted to the EC competition unit of regulation. The broader evolution of the content, form and scope of the national competition units in the UK, Germany and France also followed the pathway of neoliberalisation, albeit to varying degrees and without synchronisation. The neoliberal restructuring at national level was mainly reflected in a narrowing of the criteria underpinning competition regulation (content), a reduced involvement of political decision-makers in the regulatory processes (form) and a gradual, yet systematic, subordination of national competition units to the EC unit (scope).

In the UK, the 1998 *Competition Act* and the 2002 *Enterprise Act* marked 'a fundamental shift in the core characteristics of the traditional UK policy' (Eyre and Lodge 2000: 69). A new 'substantial lessening of competition', or SLC-test in short, was introduced in the merger control subunit, which made competition the sole criterion in merger decisions. As pointed out by Vickers (2004: 456), this had already been the criterion used in British merger regulation for a long time and the reform merely 'crystallised in law how practice had developed'. Nonetheless, the formal institutionalisation of the competition only vision, rather than the reliance on public interest criteria, is a 'tell-tale sign of a change in outlook' (Arestis and Sawyer 2005: 204). With the Enterprise Act, the involvement of political decision-makers was significantly limited, which meant that the Trade and Industry Secretary could no longer intervene in merger cases, apart from exceptional cases related to national security (Scott *et al.* 2006: 8). The

Competition Act entailed a 'Europeanisation' of the British competition unit through the incorporation of EC competition rules, namely Articles 101 and 102 (Eyre and Lodge 2000: 69–71; Utton 2000: 281). Moreover, it entrusted the British competition authorities with similar investigative powers to those of the Commission (Cini 2006; Kryda 2002: 256).

The German competition unit of regulation was also gradually 'Europeanised'. In the course of the 1990s, the BDI pushed for the harmonisation of German with European competition rules in order to minimise the administrative burden of compliance with different competition units (Eyre and Lodge 2000: 72). In 1999, the *Gesetz gegen Wettbewerbsbeschränkungen* was reformed and adapted to EC competition law, for instance by adjusting the merger control subunit to that of the EC. In 2005, another adjustment included 'the abolition of the obligation to notify and seek approval of agreements between undertakings and the adjustment to European provisions of substantive exemption requirements for horizontal and vertical agreements' (Bundeskartellamt 2005; see also Wise 2005a). Like EC Regulation 1/2003 (see Chapter 7), it sought to enhance private antitrust litigation by allowing private parties to sue for damage compensation under Articles 101 and 102.

Likewise, the French competition unit of regulation was reformed and aligned with the EC competition unit. In 1992, the *Conseil* was empowered to apply the EC Treaty's Articles 101 and 102 (with the exception of granting exemptions under Article 101(3)). In 2001, the 'modernisation' introduced a clemency procedure similar to the Commission's leniency scheme and authorised the *Conseil* to levy higher fines, which also paralleled the developments at EC level. Only one year later, new merger control rules came into force which, similar to the EC merger regulation, required companies above a certain turnover threshold to notify intended mergers in advance (Wise 2005b). In November 2008 the *Autorité de la concurrence* was established to control mergers in France, comprising a centralisation of 'most of the powers and resources previously shared between the Ministry of Economy and the Council' (Noguès 2009). Yet neither the content nor the form of the newly established merger control regime reflected a full conversion to neoliberal ideas and, thus, a thorough Europeanisation. Even though the involvement of the Minister in particular merger cases was significantly reduced with the 2008 reform, it still preserved a number of competences for the Minister. Public interest criteria, such as employment and industrial policy goals, were not ruled out.

Similar processes of Europeanisation in competition units also took place elsewhere. According to McGowan (2005: 988), 8 of the then-existent 15 national competition authorities were in a position to apply Article 101 directly by the end of 1998. With the 2004 modernisation (see Chapter 7), which paralleled the welcoming of 10 new member states, Article 101 in its entirety was declared directly applicable, involving national competition authorities in the enforcement of EC competition. Together with the additional steps taken to streamline enforcement practices, the alignment of national competition regulations with that of the EC heralded a slow but steady process of 'European integration through the backdoor' (see Wigger and Nölke 2007).

Conclusion

The neoliberal discourse of regulation entered a phase of consolidation throughout the 1990s until present, complementarily generating a thorough neoliberalisation of EC and national competition units. These developments need to be understood in the context of the larger transformation of capitalist organisation in Europe and the liberalising global economy. The accelerated pace of the common market project, enacted by the Single European Act in 1987 and the creation of the EU in the early 1990s, was constitutive for corporations to grow in size, mobilise financial capital more easily and henceforth, to invest in new spheres of production on a global scale. This chapter has demonstrated that together with the enhanced pace of global competition, the EC competition unit of regulation essentially facilitated these processes. Overall, more narrow and more rigorous definitions of competition were employed, which became manifest in the more stringent cartel prosecution, the prohibition of state aid and the endorsement of privatisation directives, which brought the era of public monopolies to an end. The subsequent privatisation of state-run industries and the market-oriented re-regulation at supranational level, offered new prospects for transnational corporations to adapt to the challenges posed by global competition. This brought about a considerable increase in economic cross-border transactions in the 1990s, such as mergers and acquisitions, strategic alliances and other forms of commercial intercompany agreements.

The consolidation of the neoliberalisation of EC competition rules and its philosophy of unfettered competition did not proceed without political contestation. Industrial sectors that were afraid to branch out from the enhanced competition sought to revive the protectionist Euro-mercantilist discourse. Yet the contenders from the less competitive industries could not match the power of the private-public alliance between transnational capital and the European Commission. Likewise, there was no coordinated response of those bearing the largest part of the social costs of the further consolidation of the neoliberal restructuring, namely labour.

7 EC competition regulation at the dawn of the century

Modernisation, contestation and crisis

This chapter explains the politics that has driven and shaped the developments in the field of EC competition regulation since the dawn of the 21st century. It analyses the nature and reasons for the 2004 'modernisation' and examines the scale and impact of the growing contestation to the neoliberal type of competition regulation before and during the global economic crisis. The chapter argues that the reform further consolidated the neoliberal course towards a more marked-based and free competition oriented European capitalism, and that so far the crisis responses did not deviate from this. Section one discusses the central elements of the modernisation in the cartel subunit of regulation and ponders on the consequences of the reform steps suggested in a Green and a White Paper in 2005 and 2008 respectively. Section two evaluates the modernisation in the light of the institutional anchoring of neoclassical microeconomic theories, while section three lays bare the driving interest constellation. Section four unravels the reform in merger subunit and the political struggles that preceded it. Section five assesses the growing contestation to the neoliberal course, whilst section six embeds the political responses in the wake of the global economic crisis since 2007 in the broader neoliberal course of regulation.

7.1 The privatisation and (de)centralisation of EC competition regulation

The substance of the EC competition units of regulation remained largely unchanged during the first four decades of the European integration project, with the exception of the introduction of the merger control regulation, as well as a couple of smaller, procedural and enforcement-related reforms in the course of the 1990s. This changed in important ways with the 'modernisation', a package deal of substantive and procedural reform measures that entered into force on 1 May 2004. A comprehensive overhaul of the EC competition unit of regulation already formed a focal point of discussion in the mid 1990s (Hussein and Wright 2009: 750). These discussions resulted in a *White Paper* on the modernisation of the rules implementing Articles 101 and 102 in 1999 (European Commission 1999). The suggested reform, heralded by the Commission as a 'legal and cultural revolution'

(Ehlermann 2000: 537; Monti 2004a), led to Regulation 1/2003, which replaced the longstanding Regulation 17 of 1962.

The new regulation altered the way in which the rules on anticompetitive conduct related to cartels (Article 101) and the abuse of dominance (Article 102) was enforced. Most crucially, it abolished the prenotification system for Article 101 types of commercial intercompany agreements and introduced a decentralised *ex post* private enforcement regime instead. The prenotification and authorisation system had provided an administrative safe-haven procedure for intercompany agreements for more than 40 years: once a transaction was notified, it was automatically legally immune from prosecution by third parties. In the case of a disagreement, private parties had to challenge the decision of the Commission before the court, rather than litigating the companies involved in the agreement. This is why private parties tended to inform the Commission about observed anticompetitive conduct, rather than starting up civil procedures themselves.

The abolition of the prenotification system meant that companies no longer had to ask the Commission for permission prior to concluding contractual commercial intercompany agreements with a Community dimension. Moreover, requests for individual exemptions under Article 101(3) were no longer possible. Rather, companies had to assess themselves whether a particular cooperative agreement fell under the cartel prohibition, or whether it was exempted. Regulation 1/2003 also declared Article 101 in its entirety directly applicable, which meant that national jurisdictions were empowered to enforce EC competition rules for cases categorised as 'affecting cross-border trade' in parallel to their own national rules. In other words, national jurisdictions took over a share of the Commission's work, including major competition cases with a Community dimension. The European Competition Network (ECN) was established in 2002 as one of the key supporting features to ensure the coherent application of the rules, the allocation of the cases, the exchange of information, as well as the coordination of the investigation and prosecution of cases.

In a large part of the literature the 'modernisation' has been portrayed as complex and technical in character, and as the result of 'a debate between technical experts', rather than actual 'power politics' (Hussein and Wright 2009: 740). The Commission similarly justified the reform as a mere technical necessity to deal with the massive backlog of unprocessed notifications of Article 101-type of agreements. Overall, the *ex ante* notification procedure was deemed too time-consuming and bureaucratically cumbersome, laying a heavy burden on the Commission's valuable staff resources, especially alongside welcoming 10 new member states in 2004. As pointed out by a range of scholars and practitioners, the Commission's 'overburdening argument' was however a blunt exaggeration (Riley 2003; Wilks 2005b: 438; Interview with Waelbroek 2008). In the period between 1989 and 1998 the Commission received about 200 notifications annually and as result of a new block exemption system in 1999 this number fell drastically. From 1999 to 2004 the annual average number of notifications was 110, with 473 pending cases only (Monti 2007: 400). The Commission justified the abolition of the pre-notification system with the argument that most of the notified cases concerned relatively harmless agreements anyhow. Commissioner Monti (2004b) argued that 'after forty years of experience, the application of European competition law should be sufficiently clear to business'. He compared the notification procedure to parking a car in a town: 'citizens must know where to park a car and shouldn't have to go to the police station to check first' (ibid.). As a matter of fact, when disregarding conditional exemptions, the prenotification system did not reveal serious infringements. The Commission only prohibited nine notified agreements between 1962 and 1999 (Monti 2007: 397). The interpretation of EC competition rules is however far more complex than the Commission's car parking allegory suggests and the impact of the reform is reaching much further than an ordinary traffic situation.

Regulation 1/2003 only formed the prelude of a much more comprehensive reform project. The subsequent launch of a Green Paper in 2005 and a White Paper in 2008 demonstrated that the profoundly political nature cannot simply be downplayed or denied by referring to discussions between technical experts and their allegedly apolitical or functional remedies of an inefficient system. One of the most central components of the reform trajectory was the introduction and facilitation of a system of private *ex post* enforcement as a complementary device to public enforcement. With the retrenchment of the Commission from its long-standing market supervisory task, companies not only have to watch over themselves, but also over their competitors, distributors and suppliers, bringing observed anticompetitive conduct in civil disputes to the courts. By evoking a situation of mutual private policing, the Commission anticipated the trigger of a certain degree of deterrence that inhibited the owners and managers of companies from engaging in unlawful agreements and hence, to ensure a better compliance with competition rules. Furthermore, by prompting private parties to bring more antitrust infringements to the courts, it hoped to redirect its staff resources to more serious infringements (Monti 2004b). Although private enforcement has always been a possibility, prior to the modernisation, public authorities enforced 95 per cent of the competition cases. Only in 5 per cent of the cases did private actors take the initiative to bring an action to court (Kemper 2004: 9).

The 2005 Green Paper and 2008 White Paper proposed to introduce further legal modifications that would facilitate and boost private enforcement in competition matters in all EU member states. Commissioner Kroes (2005a) was quite overt when saying that 'the comprehensive enforcement of the competition rules is not yet complete – not enough use is made of the courts'. Next to a range of new judicial tools, central in the suggested reform proposals was the introduction of damage actions for the breach of EC competition rules in order to compensate private litigants for the damage suffered (European Commission 2005b; 2008). Thereby, private actions had to become more worthwhile for claimants. The European Court of Justice already levelled the road in this direction by establishing the legal basis for damage actions in two of its rulings. In the *Courage vs Crehan* case (ECJ 2001) and the *Vincenzo Manfredi vs Lloyd Adriatico Assicurazioni Spa* cases (ECJ 2006), the Court stipulated that any individual wronged by an agreement in violation of Article 101(1) must be able to obtain compensation for the economic losses suffered. As rulings by the Court produce a direct effect, individuals could also evoke these rulings before national courts. The 2005 Green and 2008 White paper in essence thus sought to further specify the basis for damage compensation of the previous Court rulings and streamline the prerequisites of the litigation procedures at national and EU level.

The combination of private enforcement, the allocation of enforcement competences at national level, and the establishment of the ECN has far reaching consequences for the content, form and scope of competition units of regulations in all over Europe. As regards *content*, as a consequence of the retrenchment of a public authority and the enhanced reliance on private actors, the Commission could no longer balance the individual decision-making against broader political macroeconomic goals, such as industrial and social policy objectives. By shifting the burden of competition rule enforcement to market actors litigating observed anticompetitive behaviour before EC or national courts, the system became market-based. In combination with the direct applicability of Article 101 and 102 this meant that private litigants could access no less than 27 jurisdictions, with thousands of tribunals. More generally, with the prospect of receiving damage compensation, private claimants might be driven by (pecuniary) self-interest when invoking a claim against anticompetitive behaviour, which by definition entails a political bias towards narrower and more short-term conceptions of the workings of free competition. This is likely to be reinforced by the fact that judges also proceed on a case-by-case basis, without having the authority to evaluate their decision-making against the broader macroeconomic context in which competition takes place.

As regards *form*, the modernisation contributed to make competition regulation in Europe less democratic. The alleged 'decentralisation' of a field that used to be the prerequisite of Commission power in effect centralised more power at EC level. By forming the nodal point of the ECN, the Commission, which is not democratically accountable, reserved far-reaching powers for itself. The enhanced reliance on private 'market intelligence' in spotting and prosecuting anticompetitive practices did not remedy the democratic deficit: competition cases invoked by private litigants before the courts foreclose any preference mediation by social groups other than the litigants and the accused. The EC competition unit thereby continues to be insulated from the influence of the vast majority of European citizens.

With regard to *scope*, what is generally referred to as the 'decentralisation' inherently leads to an enhanced transnationalisation of EC competition rules, to the detriment of national competition units of regulation, which are likely to be marginalised in the long run. Through the ECN, national jurisdictions are structurally integrated into a larger EC level framework and subordinated to the enhanced control of the Commission. Notably, to warrant legal consistency among national competition authorities, Article 11(6) in combination with Article 16 of Regulation 1/2003 entitled the Commission to trespass national jurisdictions. Furthermore, the new regulation required national jurisdictions to report the opening of every new case and send a draft to the Commission before adopting a decision. As there is only one common reference point in the interpretation of EC competition rules, namely that of the Commission and of the case law established by the Courts, the way towards an enhanced scope of EC competition regulation was thereby cleared. This is also revealed in the specific competition law training schemes for national judges financed by the Commission since 2005, meant to streamline the jurisdictional enforcement (Kroes 2005a).

Importantly, the reform brought the EC closer to the US, where private competition enforcement has a tradition of more than a century, and where a range of legal features make it particularly attractive for private litigators to bring competition cases to the courts. In the words of James Rill (2003), former US Deputy Attorney General for Antitrust, the modernisation was 'as close at it could get to the US-style without copying the whole caboodle'. Compared to the EC, the Federal US authorities never played a similarly comforting role as the Commission under the prenotification system. In the US, private litigants came to account for more than 90 per cent of all formal competition cases: for every action pursued by the US authorities before the courts, private actors pursue nine (Wils 2003: 477). A range of features make it attractive to bring cases to the US courts, such as class actions, which allow plaintiffs to group together, sue collectively and share the costs of suing, or pro-plaintiff rules, such as extensive discovery rights, the right to invoke a jury trial, as well as the right of professional litigators to offer contingency fees, or to sell their legal services under a 'no-cure-no-pay' condition. In addition, public enforcement in the US by definition produces a multiplier effect: every public ruling triggers further private lawsuits (Litan and Shapiro 2001: 15). Private actors usually bring complaints to the Federal antitrust institutions first, and once public investigation has proven the necessary evidence, they sue for damage compensation afterwards.

The Green and White Paper of 2005 and 2008 were aimed at institutionalising similar legal features to those of the US. This move towards enhanced convergence was the result of a process that had been initiated by the Commission in the 1990s (see Chapter 8). The full sway of the modernisation still needs to surface, and at the time of writing, no decisions have been taken yet with regard to the suggested legal modifications. Even though there are no official statistics on private antitrust damage actions, so far a range of studies has confirmed that the number of private antitrust litigation cases have steadily increased since the modernisation with many cases still pending and large national differences in the EU–27 (cf. Cook 2008; Renda *et al.* 2007: 41).

7.2 The 'microeconomisation' of EC competition regulation

In many respects the modernisation reinforced the steady trend towards the increased use of ever-more sophisticated neoclassical economic principles and microeconomic (econometric) evidence in the enforcement of EC competition regulation. Judicial interpretations of anticompetitive conduct were increasingly subordinated to economic standards informed by neoclassical economic theory.

This was also reflected in the particular emphasis given to economic efficiency and consumer welfare in the enforcement, which indicated that there was no longer room for a flexible macroeconomic-orientated vision in the interpretation of competition regulations. Efficiency is generally assessed in terms of the lowest possible price for consumers, combined with the highest quality of the goods and services. The use of price theories and price modelling as a central reference point in the assessment of economic efficiency, quintessentially gives precedence to a short-term perspective. The increased importance given to consumer welfare arguments was also revealed in the creation of a new post within the Commission's DG Competition called 'Consumer Liaison Officer' in December 2003, who received the task to ensure a permanent dialogue with European consumers and alerting consumer groups to competition cases. The exclusive focus on citizens as being consumers only deliberately obscures the existence of other social groups organised on the basis of concerns regarding labour or environmental issues.

This development was informed by the strong transatlantic contacts between the Commission and the US competition authorities (see also Chapter 8). In the US, since the 1960s, the maxims and analytical concepts of the Chicago School of Law and Economics influenced generations of US antitrust practitioners, as a result of which microeconomic principles and quantitative econometric data formed the epitome in antitrust enforcement (Wigger 2009; Horn and Mirowski 2009). Throughout the 1990s the Commission increasingly applied microeconomic analytical tools similar to that of the US. Commissioner Monti praised this silent process of convergence as the 'most important success story in the transatlantic relationship', and argued that EC competition regulation was now clearly grounded in 'sound microeconomics' (Monti 2004b). This 'sound' microeconomic vision entailed that the ultimate purpose of public intervention was restricted to safeguarding price competition and efficiency improvements at company level, measured in the form of price reductions.

The increased use of microeconomics was also reflected in the staff composition of the DG Competition. Whereas the DG traditionally hosted more lawyers and judicial experts than economists, exhibiting a ratio of seven to one, over the past decade, a growing number of economists and financial analysts were employed to assist legal competition experts. At present, about half of the Commission's qualified A–grade officials have an academic degree in economics (Monti 2007: 80; Röller and Friederiszick 2005). The sophistication of microeconometric modelling received a major boost under Commissioner Monti, an economist himself. His successor Kroes (2005b; 2005c) also prioritised reforms that facilitated high-quality economic analyses in her agenda. Similarly to the US model, a post called the 'Chief Competition Economist' was established, and entrusted with the mission to scrutinise the Commission's antitrust investigations with a 'fresh pair of eyes' and 'independent economic viewpoints' (Monti 2002a). Accompanied by an entourage of experienced economists called the Economic Advisory Group, the post had the task of guiding the regular staff of lawyers on a case-by-case basis in all dimensions of EC competition regulation, and advising on the future development of the competition unit (Röller 2005: 6).

It was particularly this new cohort of economists that brought EC competition regulation in line with the US enforcement practices (Scheffman and Coleman 2001). The DG Competition maintained strong transatlantic contacts by holding regular bilateral meetings on 'past case work' and 'economic methodology' with economists working at the US Department of Justice and the Federal Trade Commission (Röller 2005: 6). In this vein it seems no coincidence that Professor Lars-Hendrik Röller, who was appointed the first Chief Competition Economist in July 2003, was educated in competition economics in the US.

The impact of Commission staff with a background in neoclassical economics surfaced in the modernisation. The conditions for block exemptions under Article 101 as spelled out in Regulation 1/2003 'shifted from a legalistic approach to an interpretation based on sound economic principles' (Monti 2003). Also the 2008 White Paper brought forth a range of suggestions that sought to standardise microeconomic yardsticks for infringements, and assessments of the soundness of the empirical material used in accusations and court defences. The enhanced use of modern microeconomics and its alleged 'objective scientific foundations' further buttressed the fact that there was no longer room for flexible macroeconomic-orientated visions in the interpretation of competition regulations by discretionary policy-makers and/or bureaucrats. When recalling that 'theory is always for someone and for some purpose' (Cox 1996: 86), we are reminded that neoclassic economic theories are not politically neutral. Economic theories and econometric analyses are by definition predicated upon ideologically held beliefs on how economic reality functions. Reducing real-world complexity to econometric modelling and analyses of empirical data implies that excluded parameters, so-called exogenous variables, simply remain unnoticed in the decision making process. Mathematical economics merely measures what it can measure. Whenever price calculations, as an indicator of consumer welfare, receive priority in the assessment of anticompetitive conduct, other features such as the welfare of employees, and more general employment aspects, the restructuring of certain industries in times of economic downfall, or the protection of the environment are less likely to be considered in the final decision-making. In short, neoclassical economics serves to 'scientifically' legitimate neoliberal policies and practices. In a system of private enforcement, such a 'microeconomisation' is likely to become all-pervasive in Europe, particularly as the growing body of judge-made case law immures certain yardsticks of economic data-gathering methods as the standard for decision-making. Thus, the increased use of microeconomics in combination with the modernisation, and the suggested reform steps, consolidates the neoliberal content, form and scope of European competition regulation.

7.3 The driving forces behind Regulation 1/2003

The support of organised capital for Regulation 1/2003 was not straightforward. Certain elements were fiercely criticised (Interview with Berggren 2005). Even though some business associations long pushed for 'modernising' the application of the EC antitrust rules, they did not favour the chosen direction (UNICE

1995; 1999; 2001). A recurring point of criticism of the existing EC competition unit of regulation was that the enforcement of the rules was vague, inconsistent and complex, exposing companies to the 'arbitrariness' of the Commission. Despite the broad-based interest in lifting regulatory barriers that hampered the free flow of capital accumulation, the administrative character of the prenotification authorisation practice was also widely appreciated, as long as a 'speedy and straightforward processing' was guaranteed (ERT 2002; UNICE 1999; 2001; FRG 1999). Notably the legal immunity granted to intercompany agreements that were notified to the Commission enjoyed general support.

The jeopardy of litigation and the exposure to compensation payments alarmed organised capital at European level (i.e. DIHK 2006; UNICE 2006). The US Chamber of Commerce alerted the European business community on the downsides of an excessive litigation culture (cf. Donohue 2003). The reason was obvious: defence costs, including expensive trial lawyers, potential fines and damage compensation payments, particularly in combination with class actions, as well as the concomitant negative reputation, can be detrimental for companies. Whereas the prenotification system provided companies with a legal check free of charge, specialised services newly needed to be purchased on the market, similar to any other commodity, which added an additional price tag to the compliance with EC competition rules. As a general rule, the more complex a case and the less standardised the problem, the higher the fees will be (Morgan 2005: 167). While larger companies with greater financial resources might deal with litigation rather easily, smaller companies lacking this liquidity can go bankrupt when litigated. The inherently neoliberal character of the retrenchment of a public authority in supervising the market accentuated the situation of legal uncertainty, which made companies more dependent on specialised legal advice and counselling. Already prior to the modernisation, organised capital repeatedly complained that 'the complexity of the rules required extensive expert advice' and 'substantial management time' (UNICE 1999; 2001).

Private professional services companies, often also called law firms, that specialised in the legal and economic questions of the enforcement and interpretation of competition law were the main beneficiaries of private enforcement. As a matter of fact the legal profession was a very active and influential driving force behind the modernisation. Legal experts from the private sector took the initiative for the reform at the Annual Conference of the Fordham Law School in New York in 1996 (Hussein and Wright 2009: 750). They dominated the process leading up to the modernisation, as well as the further legal modifications in the Green and White Paper in 2005 and 2008 – where their responses accounted for almost half of all the formal reactions (European Commission 2006a; 2009a). These responses were overtly mild-mannered, if not wholeheartedly positive, with regard to the introduction of specified damage relief schemes, collective group actions, or special rules on the access to evidence by plaintiffs and the distribution of costs (see for example the contributions of Allen and Overy, Freshfields Bruckhaus Deringer, Linklaters, TILP International, TaylorWessing in Commission 2006; 2009). The stakes were clear: with the introduction of private enforcement, a number of new profitable avenues opened up for selling expertise (Wigger and Nölke 2007; Wigger 2008; 2009).

7.4 The politics of reforming EC merger control

In parallel to the 2004 modernisation in the cartel subunit, the 1989 merger control Regulation 4064/89 was replaced by Regulation 139/2004. Suggestions for reform already reached high on the agenda in the mid-1990s, notably with regard to reducing the turnover thresholds for mergers requiring a Commission ruling (European Commission 1996a: 16). In line with the maxim 'speed is our friend – time is our enemy', organised transnational capital strongly preferred the centralised EC merger regulation above the often more stringent and unclear national procedures, particularly because the one-stop-shop clearance procedures were considered faster and more efficient. In contrast to the Commission, most national competition authorities were under no obligation to stick to clear deadlines, nor did they publish 'reasoned' decisions that provided some guidance for company lawyers. Throughout the 1990s companies increasingly presented so-called borderline mergers in a way that the deal passed the required EC level turnover threshold (The Economist 1993: 124). Member state governments however, steadfastly opposed suggestions to increase the scope of EC merger control, and allowed only minor revisions in the form of a supplementary set of lower turnover thresholds in 1998, which meant that numerous cases continued to be subject to multiple member state rulings.

In 2000 the Commission, backed up by organised capital and the legal profession, initiated the reform process that led to the adoption of the new merger control regulation in 2003 (European Commission 2000). In a Green Paper in December 2001 it outlined possible reform steps. Amongst others, the Commission also asked for suggestions on how to facilitate the inclusion of the views of employees and consumers in ongoing merger control procedures (ibid. 2001b: 55). In a parliamentary debate in October 2003, the socialists, in line with the position of ETUC, called for a 'serious and fully-fledged consultation of employee representatives within the procedures', and for considering 'aspects other than competition in the narrow sense of the word' (European Parliament 2003a; ETUC 2002). The idea to include this element of the centre-left discourse of regulation was however only short lived. In his response, Commissioner Monti considered the input of workers' representatives already sufficient, and argued that the regulation of mergers should not 'be cluttered with measures to stimulate or safeguard employment: there are other instruments for that' (European Parliament 2003a). This was also the view of organised capital, accounting for about half of the 114 written responses to the Green Paper. They feared that the views of employees and consumers in merger cases posed a risk to the competition focus of the Commission's analysis, causing unnecessary uncertainty and delay (UNICE 2002: 8; ERT 2002: 4).

In December 2002 the Commission proposed what it called 'the most far-reaching reform' since the entry into force of the EC merger control regulation in

1990 (European Commission 2002). Commissioner Monti emphasised the business friendly character of the proposal by arguing that merger control was not about blocking mergers, but about ensuring that consumers continued 'to benefit from sufficient innovation, choice and competitive prices' (The Financial Times 2002b). Similar to the overhaul in the cartel subunit, the proposed regulation did not break with the previous neoliberal unit-specific discourse. In the course of 2003 the idea of giving more weight to the views of employees in merger decisions completely disappeared in the discussions. Member state governments did not question the nature of the existing neoliberal type merger control, but disagreed instead over the test basis for controlling mergers (content), and the optimal allocation of cases between the Commission (scope). In terms of *scope*, the Council settled on a solution that allowed companies to request an exclusive Commission review for mergers without 'Community dimension', provided they were otherwise subject to at least three national competition authorities, and that none of the national authorities objected (Article 4(5) of Council Regulation 139/2004). Thereby, more powers were concentrated at Commission level.

In terms of *content*, the test for reviewing mergers was highly disputed. In the 2001 Green Paper, the Commission raised the question of whether or not to retain the 'market dominance' (MD) test of the 1989 merger regulation, or to adopt the so-called alternative 'substantial lessening of competition' (SLC) test. In short, the MD test prohibits a merger if it 'creates or strengthens a dominant position as a result of which effective competition would be significantly impeded in the common market or in a substantial part of it' (Article 2(3) of Regulation 4064/89). The SLC test, which was used in the US, Canada, Australia and had only just been introduced in the UK and Ireland, prohibited mergers that resulted in a 'substantive lessening of competition' (see also Chapter 6). Initially, the question of which test to use was of no central concern. According to the Commission (2001b: 40), the 'experience in applying the dominance test has not revealed major loopholes in the scope of the test. Nor has it frequently led to different results from SLC-test approaches in other jurisdictions'. In its written comments to the Green Paper, the British and Irish governments, in line with economists and the British competition law community, strongly pushed for the SLC test, which was considered 'fundamentally better adapted to merger control, primarily because it is directly grounded in economic analysis' (DTI 2002: para 34; see also Irish Delegation 2002).

The quest for a 'more economic approach' was reinforced by a sequence of rulings by the Court of First Instance between June and October 2002, in which it annulled the Commission's prohibitions in the mergers between Airtours and First Choice, Schneider and Legrand, and Tetra Lavel and Sidel. The Court fiercely criticised the economic analyses underpinning the decision-making by arguing, for instance, in the Airtours judgment that the Commission's decision was 'vitiated by manifest errors of assessment' (CFI 2001: point 21). These rulings, which followed up the consultation period and preceded the Commission's proposal for a revised merger control regulation in December 2002, significantly bolstered the trend towards a 'more economic approach' in the analysis of mergers and most notably, the use of modern microeconomics (see also Christensen *et al.* 2007: 425; Lyons 2004: 249).

While British diplomats strongly pushed in favour of the SLC test (House of Lords 2003), the German diplomats insisted on preserving the MD test and vetoed any other outcome, while negotiators from most other countries were more pragmatic on this issue (Interview Diplomat A and B 2006). Both the *Bundeskartellamt* and organised European capital had already expressed fierce opposition to the SLC test in their responses to the Green Paper. According to the *Bundeskartellamt*, there was no evidence 'for the assertion that the MD test fails to catch merger projects raising competition concerns or that they can be evaluated more comprehensively by means of the SLC test' (Böge and Müller 2002: 498; Bundeskartellamt 2001). The main concern of organised capital was that the new test might create a climate of legal uncertainty for companies intending to merge (BDI 2002: 11; CBI 2002: 2; UNICE 2002: 4; ERT 2002: 2). Overall, they were rather content with the status quo of the existing assessment of mergers. Most notably this was due to the fact that the Commission did not prohibit any mergers between 2002 and May 2004, even though there were arguably sufficient reasons to do so in the cases of the mergers between Carnival and P&O, Sony and BMG, and Oracle and PeopleSoft (Levy 2005: 110; Wall Street Journal 2004).

In a carefully coordinated joint campaign, UNICE and the ERT sought to generate the necessary leverage in the Council. In a letter to its member federations, dated 6 October, UNICE's working group that specialised in competition policy warned that the SLC test widened 'the scope of the present merger control system to an unacceptable extent' (UNICE 2003). It urged its members 'to communicate UNICE's concerns regarding discussions in the Council working party to their national representatives' and 'not to agree to any major changes to the current merger control system' (ibid.). On 21 November 2003, Alain Joly, CEO of Air Liquide, and Wolfgang Kopf, the convenor of the ERT's competition policy working group, wrote a letter to Commissioner Monti, indicating that the MD test was 'entirely compatible with modern economic theory' and expressing their great concern about introducing the SLC test (ERT 2003). Shortly after the ERT's letter on 27 November 2003, the Council reached an agreement on a revised merger regulation. The Spanish and French negotiators worked out a compromise test, the 'significant impediment to effective competition' (SIEC) test, according to which mergers could be blocked only if they posed a 'significant impediment' to competition. The German negotiators only reluctantly accepted the new test. Ulf Böge, the President of the *Bundeskartellamt*, subsequently noted that the SIEC test 'increased legal insecurity for companies' and maintained that there was 'no practical need for this amendment' (Bundeskartellamt 2003). Likewise, Philippe de Buck, Secretary-General of UNICE, expressed that the introduction of a new test was 'unnecessary and disproportionate', leading to severe uncertainty (De Buck 2004).

Notwithstanding the opposition from organised capital, the revised merger control regulation was fully in accordance with the neoliberal unit specific discourse that had informed the content, form and scope of the EC merger control subunit since its inception. Importantly, the hegemony of the neoliberal discourse and the prevalence given to the 'competition only' criterion remained unchallenged, as did the political independence of the DG Competition. The main disagreement between governments concerned specific criteria used in the assessment of mergers, and not the fundamental question of whether or not mergers had to be controlled in line with the neoliberal discourse. The fact that member state governments and the Commission went against the preferences of organised capital does not imply that its role can be neglected more generally. As shown in this and previous chapters, the importance of the capitalist class and notably the transnational capital fraction as a driving force behind the neoliberal-type EC competition regulation, has been vital since the 1980s.

7.5 A renewed moment of contestation to neoliberal EC competition regulation

During the past decade, several elements of the EC competition unit of regulation have been challenged by both friends and foes of the neoliberal discourse of regulation. Generally, organised capital, member state governments and their national competition authorities did not fundamentally contest the neoliberal content, form and scope of the competition unit, but rather advocated different types of neoliberal solutions. Organised capital repeatedly criticised the unit for being a bastion of uncontrollable Commission power, notably because of the Commission's combined role of investigator, prosecutor, judge, jury and executioner, and the lack of checks and balances apart from the European Courts (ERT 2000: 6). Likewise national competition authorities, most notably the *Bundeskartellamt*, feared to become 'semi-autonomous vassals' of the Commission, and moreover pushed for a politically independent 'European cartel office' (Bannerman 2002: 38).

Advocates of positions informed by the centre-left and mercantilist discourses of regulation posed more far reaching challenges to EC competition regulation. From the centre-left perspective, organised labour such as ETUC, but also leftwing parties, contested the Commission's 'competition only' view. They promoted a system that takes into account the effects on employment levels and the views of employees instead. This discourse occasionally surfaced in the reactions of organised labour, such as in the merger between ABB and Alstrom in 2000, where a fifth of the workforce faced redundancy and 2000 French, German, Belgian and Italian workers demonstrated in Brussels, marching 'for a social Europe and against the Commission because they felt that they had no voice in its competition policy' (Erne 2008: 128, 154). Although the protests indicated severe discontent by labour, the Commission did not reverse its decision, nor did it more generally give way to centre-left elements in the EC competition unit. Contestations from the centre-left represented a minority view. It was not taken seriously by decision-making powers. Also in the Parliament, where a vast majority traditionally voted in favour of a centre-left competition regulation, such a view was no longer widely held. For example, in its legislative resolution of 9 October 2003 on EC merger control, the Parliament approved the Commission's proposal for a revised merger control regulation without mentioning social policy considerations in its proposed amendments (European Parliament 2003b).

In addition, contestation was also grounded in the Euro-mercantilist discourse. In the face of ever toughening global competition, critical voices increasingly challenged EC industrial policy. In the past, the DG Industry regularly used to form a political counterweight to the DG Competition's neoliberal course. However, this changed in the late 1980s when its commitment to a strong European industrial policy gave way to 'a new style industrial policy approach', abandoning the 'promotions of Euro-champions', while emphasising competition as a means to generate competitiveness instead (McGowan and Cini 1999: 189). For example in March 2006, The Financial Times (2006a) reported that Italy was 'almost literally cracking up under exposure to competition from Eurozone partners and from China in textiles and shoes', and that 'Paris' was 'reacting with even more fury than Rome at finding that the EU is proving as much a transmission belt bringing the forces of globalisation in as a bulwark keeping them out'.

In reaction, the French and German governments called for a different type of EC competition and industrial policy. Chancellor Schröder noted that EC industrial policy should 'not forget the need for social solidarity and employee participation in decision-making', and differentiate between sectors according to their position in global markets (in the *Financial Times* 2002c). Similarly, the French President Chirac was a strong advocate of European champions and 'a European competition policy that truly takes into account the realities of international competition' (in *EU Observer* 2004). In a joint statement in June 2004, Schröder and Chirac emphasised the need for government intervention to enhance the competitiveness of industrial champions in global markets by setting up a joint industry forum for business leaders to boost industrial cooperation (*International Herald Tribune* 2004). 'Europe's drift to mercantilism' met the staunch opposition of neoliberal hardliners, including the Commission, commentators in the financial press and organised capital. In a letter to the *Financial Times* (2004) titled 'Let the market choose Europe's champions', Internal Market Commissioner Frits Bolkestein responded that he had to pinch himself to himself to make sure he was not back in the 1960s, 1970s or 1980s.

Although the rhetoric of contestation was framed in a Euro-mercantilist idiom, in practice, the countervailing strategies to the enhanced competitive threat and the neoliberal type of competition regulation were more generally of a national mercantilist nature. The genuine fear of losing out from economic globalisation and losing jobs explains why many governments adopted protectionist strategies to boost economic growth. French President Sarkozy evolved as one of the most prominent voices of the national mercantilist counterattack. Already as a Minister of Finance, Sarkozy argued that 'neither France nor Europe can become industrial deserts [...]. It is not a right for the state to help industry. It is a duty' (in Murray 2004: 8).

In a number of cases the French government pursued interventionist policies in order to save large French companies. In the aforementioned case of the company Alstom, a leading French engineering company operating in the sectors of cruise ships and high-speed trains, the French government granted a € 1.2 billion emergency government loan in September 2003 to save it from bankruptcy. When the Commission threatened to block the rescue plan, the French government protested and announced that the Commission was going to be responsible for the loss of 70,000 jobs in that event. This was successful insofar as the Commission eventually approved the subsidy, albeit by imposing conditions (Murray 2004: 14–15). Likewise, as part of a broader national mercantilist strategy, the French government introduced various measures against hostile foreign takeovers, and declared 11 sectors off-limits to foreign investment (The Financial Times 2006b). Illustrative in this regard was the government sponsored merger between the Suez Group and Gaz de France, which was a successful attempt by the French government to avoid the takeover of the Franco-Belgian Suez Group by the Italian company Enel (ibid. 2007c). The Commission ultimately also cleared this merger conditionally, demanding a few divestitures. Nonetheless, the new 'French' company GDF Suez S.A. created 'Europe's second biggest producer of electricity, the continent's biggest gas transport and distribution group and a world leader in the liquefied natural gas market' (The Financial Times 2008).

Also the Italian and Spanish governments put much effort into preventing foreign takeovers, such as in the case of Telecom Italia by Autostrade, or the blocking of Endesa's takeover by German Eon (The Financial Times 2007d). Similarly, the Polish government sought to protect the state-owned PKO Bank Polski by preventing the Italian UniCredit from merging its Polish subsidiary Pekao with a subsidiary of German HVB (ibid. 2006c). The German government similarly struggled hard to preserve a law that protected Volkswagen from being taken over by foreign companies (The Economist 2006). These protectionist moves received every emphasis when the French, Belgian and Spanish governments opposed the hostile takeover bid for the Luxembourg based steel company Arcelor by India's Mittal Steel, which was eventually allowed in June 2006 despite the high-level government involvement (The Financial Times 2006d). Nonetheless, the national mercantilist countermovement to the Commission's neoliberal stance was not sustained by all member states. For example, the British New Labour government, in line with the UK's long neoliberal tradition, openly supported the fight against national protectionism (The Financial Times 2006e).

A renewed challenge to the hegemonic neoliberal course surfaced in the Treaty of Lisbon, following up the European Constitution, which was rejected in popular referenda in France and the Netherlands in 2005. The European Constitution elevated competition to an objective in itself, stating that the EU had to ensure 'an internal market where competition is free and undistorted' (Article 1-3(2)). In the Treaty of Rome, in contrast, the notion of ensuring 'undistorted competition' was spelled out as a means to attain the objectives of Community (Article 3). In the Treaty of Lisbon the prominence of free and undistorted competition as a central objective was reversed again and dropped from the 'objectives' section. It was President Sarkozy who insisted on removing the notion of 'free competition' at the EU Summit in Germany in June 2007. He declared that competition was 'not the meaning of life' and that the word 'protection was no longer taboo' (The Financial Times 2007e). The reactions to this were predictable. The ERT's secretary general considered the move 'food for people arguing in favour of economic nationalism', and BusinessEurope's legal affairs director was worried that this 'had an effect on EU competition policy' (The Financial Times 2007a). Also, commentators from the academia reacted concernedly and warned that 'the evil of protectionism is now, more than ever, alive and kicking' (Bavaso 2007: 3). Despite this upheaval, Sarkozy's move however remained merely symbolic. Nothing changed. The consequence of not including the reference to free and undistorted competition in the 'objectives' section was that the status quo was preserved.

7.6 European competition regulation in the wake of the global financial crisis

The severe economic and financial crisis of the world economy that started in the course of 2007 had important repercussions on the European competition units of regulation. The financial turmoil aggravated after September 2008, most notably after the bankruptcy of Lehman Brothers and the insolvency of several American and European banks, as well as after a range of stock markets found themselves on the edge of collapsing. In response, EU member governments adopted national rescue packages meant to save financial institutions and their depositors. In the vein of the magnitude and acuteness of the crisis and in the absence of concerted action at EU level, national governments acted resolutely and promptly, without awaiting the Commission's approval for state aid granted to the financial sector (Da Silva and Sansom 2009: 28). According to the Commission's State Aid Scoreboard (2009b), the overall aid volume increased from € 66.5 billion or 0.52 per cent of the EU-27 GDP in 2007 to € 279.6 billion or 2.2 per cent of GDP in 2008 (with crises measures excluded, the total aid was 0.54 per cent of GDP).

National rescue packages in the form of capital loans infused in financial behemoths and in industries hit by the credit crunch, as well as other strategies, such as the nationalisation of banks or the sponsoring of defensive mergers, went against the neoliberal type of EC competition regulation of the past decades. The Commission reacted in a proactive manner. In the words of Commissioner Kroes the Commission was 'quick and loud in resisting protectionism' (2009a). In a three-phase approach, the DG Competition first allowed member states to rescue certain financial institutions on the basis of Article 87(2b) in October 2008, a legal waiver for aid remedying 'a serious disturbance in the economy of a Member State' (European Commission 2009c: 3–4). Second, two months later it outlined general standards for recapitalising banks and financial institutions, which had the purpose of ensuring a sufficient volume of lending in the European economies. On this basis, the Commission approved bank state guarantees of more than € 2,900 billion and bank state recapitalisations of more than € 300 billion (Kroes 2009b). As calls for speedy actions were looming large, the Commission gave its approval in an astounding speed. The most remarkable example of this was the approval of the British government's rescue of Bradford and Bingly, which was decided in the record time of 24 hours (Da Silva and Sansom 2009: 28; European Commission 2009d: 9).

In the third so-called 'clean-up phase', the rescued financial sector had to be restructured in order to reverse the damaging effects on competition and to ensure viable business plans for the future. Kroes (2009b) noted in this respect that 'while some banks may have been too big to fail, none are too big to restructure'. Thus, although the Commission acknowledged the need for state aid, it sought to ensure 'a level playing field' and avoid 'subsidy races' among member states (European Commission 2009d). A similar neoliberal tenet was promoted in the cartel subunit. Whereas crisis cartels were allowed in the 1970s, the Commission indicated that this option created a disaster, dragging down economic recovery (Kroes 2009c). In other words, the Commission evolved as a neoliberal-type crisis manager, who effectively coordinated the national supports by simply temporarily enforcing state aid rules in a more flexible manner than hitherto.

Conclusion

This chapter demonstrated that in the course of the early 21st century the neoliberal type competition regulation was consolidated further. The 2004 modernisation, which enacted a partial privatisation and further Europeanisation of competition rule enforcement, institutionally anchored the neoliberal orientation in the cartel and merger subunit of regulation. The enhanced trend towards the use of microeconomic reasoning and ever more sophisticated econometric modelling in the assessment of anticompetitive conduct secured the 'competition only' focus. Neoliberal conceptions of corporate efficiency and consumer welfare increasingly amounted to the sole decisional criteria, which fundamentally broke with the broadly defined macroeconomic and flexible market interventionist orientation that dominated the enforcement practices in the era of embedded liberalism. At the dawn of the century, the resilience of the EC competition unit was put to test when organised European capital and labour, as well as certain governments, expressed their dissatisfaction with different aspects of the competition unit. This did not however result in fundamental changes in its neoliberal content, form and scope. Similarly, the member state governments' responses to the global economic crisis did not cause the Commission to diverge from the neoliberal path, although it temporarily chose to implement the state aid rules with greater flexibility than previously demonstrated.

8 The neoliberal crusade for bilateral and multilateral competition rules

Alongside the constructive and consolidating moments of the neoliberal discourse of regulation, the Commission's DG Competition in alliance with the emerging transnational capitalist class surfaced as a driving force behind a range of bilateral and multilateral competition agreements in the 1990s. Competition regulation was no longer restricted to 'Brussels' and the national level, but formed part of the broader political project of establishing global free markets, free from public and private barriers inhibiting competition. This chapter analyses the political struggles that shaped the globalisation of competition regulation. The first three sections examine the politics underpinning the bilateral competition agreements between the EC and the US competition authorities against the background of enhanced commercial cross-border transactions affecting the transatlantic market place, the emerging transnational capitalist class and its quest for more regulatory convergence. Section four explains the proposal for global competition rules at WTO on the basis of the underlying social power relations, whilst section five analyses the politics of contestation that led to its downfall. Section six explains why the International Competition Network and the bilateral agreements concluded under the 2006 agenda 'Global Europe – Competing in the World' were chosen as alternative routes to proclaim the convergence of competition rules around the world.

8.1 Conflict and cooperation across the Atlantic

The EU–US bilateral cooperation agreements took shape in a macroeconomic context in which transatlantic commercial transactions such as mergers, alliances, joint ventures and other types of intercompany agreements increased in number and magnitude. In 1990, US investment in Europe accounted for half the total earnings of US companies, which held assets of more than US$ 175 billion in Europe, close to half the total of US overseas foreign direct investment at that time (The Economist 1990: 23). In 1994, more than a third of all mergers involved a company from across the Atlantic (Martinez Torre-Enciso and Bilbao Garcia 1996: 7). Once the Commission, equipped with the right to vet mergers, increasingly started to review corporate transactions with a transatlantic dimension, the problem of multijurisdictional overlap came to the fore and therewith, the prospect of divergent rulings and disputes with the US Department of Justice and the Federal Trade Commission. The stalemate in the closing phases of the 1990 GATT Uruguay Round, looming trade wars on bananas, beef, and biotechnological products, and past experiences with protectionism and state aid supporting domestic industries in Europe fuelled US concerns about the prospect of a 'Fortress Europe'. In 1991, Competition Commissioner Brittan considered the transatlantic relationship to be fragile and remarked that 'the US and the Community may well one day soon take different views of a competition case' (in Blumenthal 2005: 1). As a prophylactic measure, the Commission and US authorities formalised three bilateral competition agreements in the course of the 1990s. These agreements formed part of a broader project of concluding a 'significantly strengthened set of institutional and consultative links' as proposed by James Baker, US Secretary of State, in a speech in Berlin in December 1989 shortly after the fall of the Wall (Piening 1997: 108). This led to the Transatlantic Declaration, signed in November in 1990 in Paris, committing the US government and EC to a framework 'for regular and intensive consultation' (ibid.).

The first transatlantic agreement regarding the application of competition rules was concluded in September 1991 between the Commission and the US government (European Commission 1991). As regards *content*, the signatories decided to cooperate in merger control and coordinate and streamline the investigation process on a case-by-case basis. As regards *form*, cooperation had to take place voluntarily and informally, including scheduled meetings to discuss general matters regarding the future course of competition rules on a twice-a-year basis. As regards *scope*, the competition authorities agreed to alert each other on cases that affect 'important interests' of the other party (Article 2). In practice, this meant that they had to keep each other mutually informed on the basis of reciprocal notifications. The principle of 'traditional' or 'negative' comity (Article 5 and 6) constituted the centrepiece of this mutual notification practice. Comity, meaning 'courtesy', 'complaisance' and 'respect', is a non-binding principle in international law, which is generally applied as a mild form of (unilateral) conflict prevention and which in the field of competition rules finds its origin in a series of non-binding OECD recommendations issued from the 1960s onwards (OECD 1967; with revisions in 1973, 1979, 1986, 1995). The primary purpose of the negative comity principle was, according to the Commission (1994a: 72), to avoid 'the possibility or impact of differences between the parties in the application of their competition laws'.

The second transatlantic agreement of June 1998 called the Positive Comity Agreement, went further than the 1991 agreement by allowing the signatories to request the other party to begin investigations in cases outside its jurisdictional reach, if important interests were at stake. It committed them to act 'promptly, responsibly, and diligently in examining allegations at issue', and not to act unilaterally in cases falling under the other party's jurisdiction, unless all means provided by positive comity were exhausted (Pitofsky 1998). In 1999 the Commission and the US competition authorities concluded the Administrative Arrangements on Attendance, an ancillary agreement regulating the attendance of competition officials in each other's staff meetings. The third bilateral agreement of 2002 concerned a set of non-binding best practices on cooperation in reviewing transatlantic mergers. Furthermore, an institutional structure was established to facilitate the transatlantic interagency contacts. Both the US Mission to the European Union in Brussels and the Delegation of the European Commission to the USA in Washington created a special competition division.

The underpinning rationale of the negative and subsequent positive comity principle, as well as the regulated attendance, was similar to the 'one-stop-shop' principle of the EC merger control subunit of regulation (see Chapter 5). It channelled competition cases to only one competition authority, thereby facilitating transatlantic corporate transactions by reducing the jurisdictional overlap. The positive comity was, however, very much Janus-faced and reached further than this. On the one hand, it allowed the signatories to exert influence on each other's jurisdictions by asking the other to start up proceedings in a particular case. On the other hand, it also sought to diminish the problem of extraterritoriality in competition matters, which is fundamentally related to the question of scope. Extraterritorial jurisdiction refers to a situation in which a jurisdiction rules over foreigners, as well as over acts committed outside its own borders. What has generally been the 'privilege' of OECD states, most notably of the US, constitutes one of the 'thorniest' issues in public international law as it violates the 'territoriality' and 'nationality' principles (Gavil *et al.* 2002: 611–20). The intrusion of a foreign jurisdiction into the market organisation of another state is not only an aggressive proceeding, but also lacks the necessary democratic legitimisation. Well-known examples of US extraterritorialism are the embargo politics of the D'Amato and the Helms-Burton Act of March 1996, according to which any (foreign) citizen, company, or even government involved in business transactions with Iran, Libya, and Cuba could be prosecuted under US law. Also in the field of competition regulation, the US record of extraterritoriality cases loomed large. The *United States vs Aluminium Co.* case of 1945 is particularly legendary. It established the Effects Doctrine, which gave the exercise of US extraterritorial jurisdiction a statutory basis by establishing that conduct by foreign business with a significant effect on US import commerce and consumers fell within the application of the Sherman Act (US Supreme Court 1945).

The US practice of extraterritorial application increased considerably from the 1990s onwards (Kolasky 2002b), which generated fierce controversies in Europe. Many governments adopted so-called blocking statutes 'designed to prevent US efforts to assert extraterritorial jurisdiction' prohibiting national companies to comply with the laws of another state and to provide other jurisdictions with information (Calvani 2005). In response to US unilateralism in competition matters, the Commission also started to apply its competition rules more frequently to companies located outside the EU. In 1999 the European Court of First Instance equipped the Commission with its own 'Effects Doctrine' similar to that of the US in its judgment in the *Gencor Ltd vs Commission* case, concerning an appeal against the Commission's decision to block the merger between the two mineral mining companies Gencor from South Africa and

Lonrho from the UK, both companies that operated outside Community-borders and without assets in the EU. The Court ruled that the Commission was authorised to block the deal because it was foreseeable that the proposed concentration 'will have an immediate and substantial effect within the Community' (CFI 1999). Thereby, the Commission was officially entitled to prosecute anticompetitive conduct, irrespective of the companies' national origin as long as it had a major effect on the common market of the EU (Monti 2002b: 71). In other words, due to this ruling the scope of the EC competition unit of regulation was significantly expanded.

Although other competition authorities also started to trespass jurisdictional sovereignty, the extraterritorial application of competition rules evolved foremost as a EC–US play. The new doctrine consolidated the Commission's role as a competition authority with a global reach, creating a certain degree of co-deterrence to the longstanding US practice. Whereas previously the US competition authorities never shied away from applying their competition rules on an extraterritorial basis, they increasingly had to temper their conduct. Thus, the conclusion of bilateral cooperation agreements, most notably the inclusion of positive comity, constituted a political response to the probability of inconsistent rulings and the extraterritorial application of competition rules in the growing number of transatlantic commercial transactions. More than that however, the broader goal of opening up the transatlantic market space and eliminating regulatory constraints, received crucial support from key representatives of the emerging transnational capitalist class.

8.2 United corporate agenda setting for more and faster liberalisation

Previous research identified the US and EC competition authorities as the central driving forces behind the conclusion of the transatlantic bilateral competition agreements, conceptualising them as responses 'to the external challenge of economic internationalisation' (see Damro 2006b: 173). This view however, ignores the critical role played by the emerging transnational capitalist class, which exhibited a strong transatlantic dimension at that time. The presence of US capital in Europe led to an ever-stronger representation of its interests at EC level. US lobby institutions, such as the EU Committee of AmCham, doubled in staff size during the 1990s. As one of the most effective lobbying organisations in Brussels, it issued about 60 policy papers and 10 books in 1998 alone and held countless meetings with Commission officials and members of the Parliament (CEO 1999a). Moreover, it also became a regular source of influence on European organised capital, such as the ERT and UNICE, leading to more consistency in the articulation of corporate interests at EU level (Van Miert 1999).

The process of transnational class formation gained particular momentum with the establishment of the Transatlantic Business Dialogue (TABD) on 11 November 1995 in Seville, Spain. The TABD, which encompassed top executive-level management staff from leading US and European transnational corporations, was the result of an initiative of the US Commerce Department and the European Commission, notably US Secretary of Commerce Ronald Brown, the Commission's Vice President and former Competition Commissioner Sir Leon Brittan and Industry Commissioner Martin Bangemann. The TABD was established with the great support of ERT members and the membership was largely overlapping (Van Apeldoorn 2002: 111). As Reinhard Quick, the TABD's Global Issues Manager noted: 'We work together, we consult with each other. The ERT is part of the TABD network' (in CEO 1999a). In contrast to a traditional lobby group, the TABD was an invited advisor that had the purpose of formulating joint corporate policy positions and facilitating transatlantic capitalist ties. By sending out letters to 1,800 industry officials from the EU and the US, the so-called 'Three B' letters in April 1995 referring to the initials of Brown, Brittan, and Bangemann, the US and EU officials entrusted the member companies with a mandate to identify barriers to transatlantic trade and investment; or, in short, anything that ran against the corporate agenda (Cowles 2000; 2001).

The TABD's subsequent recommendations were informed by the neoliberal discourse of regulation, demanding 'more and faster trade liberalisation' and a 'more business-driven and market-orientated approach' (Brittan 1996; CEO 1999b). Amongst others, the TABD suggested the creation of a free trade zone and a barrier free transatlantic marketplace without 'excessive domestic laws and regulations' and double regulatory requirements (TABD 1996). These suggestions were taken up in the ambitious proposal by Commissioner Brittan to create a Transatlantic Free Trade Agreement (TAFTA) as an analogue to the North American Free Trade Agreement (NAFTA) of January 1994. Once the TAFTA proposal failed to generate the necessary political support, most notably of the French government who refused to give a free rein to Commissioner Brittan in negotiating free trade areas with the US government, a surrogate agreement called the New Transatlantic Agenda (NTA) was adopted in December 1995, following up the Transatlantic Declaration of 1990 (The Economist 1995: 49). The TABD's influence was enormous. Although the NTA's Action Plan did not lead to a free trade zone, it entailed a framework for the progressive reduction and eventual elimination of barriers that hindered the flow of goods, services and capital, thereby incorporating more than 60 per cent of the TABD's recommendations (The Financial Times 1996b: 6). As Timothy Hauser (1997), Deputy Under Secretary for International Trade concluded '[…] virtually every opening move undertaken by the United States and the EU in the last couple of years has been suggested by the TABD'. Importantly, the TABD also succeeded in cancelling, delaying, or watering down business-constraining environmental and consumer-protectionist regulations in the transatlantic realm (Holt 2000).

Competition regulation was one of the TABD's 15 key areas of concern right from the start. In search for quick and business-friendly regulatory procedures, the removal of 'barriers to cross-border mergers and acquisitions both within the EU and across the Atlantic' and the adoption of 'convergent procedures to vet mergers' had priority (TABD 1995: 8; see also 2006: 21). Through substantive and procedural convergence, the TABD hoped to reduce the negative externalities that resulted from complying with different jurisdictions. Parallel investigations were considered to create unnecessary delays and uncertainty, pushing up the costs of transatlantic mergers and rendering them 'a significant transaction risk' (Draghi, Vice Chairman of Goldman Sachs International 2003: 10–11). Similarly, the CEO of Electrolux called the process 'horrendous' as in many cases the businesses of merging companies were frozen for a year or more until both competition authorities reached a decision (The Financial Times 2001: 10).

The EU and US competition authorities took the TABD's request to synchronise and coordinate investigation procedures seriously. In a letter to the TABD Chair, Brittan (1996) confirmed his full personal support and the continuing cooperation of his officials, granting the transatlantic capitalist class privileged day-to-day access to the Commission. The 'tripartite' meetings took place largely behind closed doors and were of an informal nature, thereby evading any form of parliamentary control. TABD interlocutors closely monitored internal working documents of the Commission and issued replies and follow-ups (European Commission 2006b). Although the US Department of Commerce also nurtured the TABD, over time the TABD's alliance with the Commission became much stronger, resulting in the location of the TABD's office near the Commission's headquarters in Brussels (CEO 1999b). As Stephen Johnston, TABD Director, concluded: the 'Commission was cooperative, helping business by giving them the information that they needed', while 'it was business that made recommendations' (in ibid.). One of these recommendations was to make use of the positive comity procedures, while keeping the focus on mergers only (TABD 1995: Section II.10 and II.12; TABD 1997: 6). Only two years later, the Commission presented the draft proposal on positive comity.

The TABD had a stark interest in keeping the prosecution of cartels off the transatlantic cooperation agenda and instead, focus on the merger subunit of regulation only. For this reason, the inclusion of a provision ruling the exchange of confidential information between the competition units became a highly politicised issue. The US authorities were entitled to conclude far-reaching agreements containing provisions on the exchange of confidential agreements with other competition authorities under the International Antitrust Enforcement Assistance Act (IAEAA) that came into force in 1994. When the Commission announced its plans to enter transatlantic IAEAA-type agreement, organised capital fiercely lobbied against it. It feared enhanced exposure to the US jurisdictions, where cartels were seen as a major crime against consumers and prosecuted under criminal law (TABD 1997: 6; ICC 1997, 1999a, 1999b). They stressed that confidential corporate information should only be exchanged in merger cases and only on the basis of prior consent from the companies involved, while institutional safeguards guaranteeing no leakage of sensitive commercial information had to be adopted. These requests were successful and included in Article 3 and Article 4 of the first and the second cooperation agreement, restricting the exchange of information to general matters in the implementation of competition rules, and obliging the competition authorities to protect the confidentiality of this information. Moreover, without the prior permission of companies under investigation to exchange confidential information, officials from the other competition authority were not allowed to participate in hearings. This rendered the mutual notification of merger investigations of the EU and US competition merely an issue of filling in standardised forms with little more than the companies' names (European Commission 1994b). In other words, transatlantic cooperation was entirely dependent on the companies' goodwill to grant waivers for exchanging confidential information concerning their case (Schaub 1998). This explains why transatlantic cooperation has been confined mainly to the field of mergers since the 1990s, where companies have a great incentive to cooperate with the competition units in order to speed up the review procedure and receive consistent rulings.

The TABD's encompassing political influence on economic regulations led to protests by thousands of alterglobalists and civil society movements (The Financial Times 1996b: 6). However, these protests were not successful in limiting the political power of the transnational capitalist class. TABD chair Monod, unimpressed by the protestors, argued in an interview that the 'remarkable success rate justifies the institution's existence all by itself' (in CEO 1999b). Similarly, EU Trade Commissioner Pascal Lamy considered finding 'new ways of getting across the benefits of freer trade' more important than engaging with the demonstrators (The Financial Times 2000: 10). Protests also came from those fractions of capital with a more national or intra-EU, import-competing focus and thus, adherents of positions shaped by the national or Euro-mercantilist discourses of regulation. Representatives of the German industry association, the BDI, and also certain European business leaders organised in UNICE and even in the ERT, did not share the enthusiasm about the TABD's neoliberal agenda (Cowles 2000: 172). Disputes occasionally flared up. As AmCham's chairman Russell reckoned, European transnational companies 'tended to be very much their natural allies', in marked contrast to those 'parts of European industry that are tied very much to the local economies' (in CEO 1999a). Aware of these tensions, the transnational capitalist class sought to accommodate UNICE and small and medium-sized companies with their political agenda by for example, allowing the European Union of Craftsmen and Small and Medium-Sized Enterprises to participate in the TABD's informal framework of political contacts (Carchedi 2001: 125). Also the ERT sought to build closer links with this group as a way to generate broader support (Van Apeldoorn 2002: 112). Furthermore, to avoid the image of extensive US corporate influence, the ERT, rather than the TABD, communicated high-profile policy initiatives to the Commission (in CEO 1999a).

8.3 Towards transatlantic convergence of competition rules

The transatlantic bilateral cooperation resulted in an intensive working-relationship, taking place quietly on an almost daily basis in the form of video-conferences and in-person meetings, generally without raising the awareness of the wider public. This relationship was certainly not conflict-free. Although later downplayed as incidental bumps on the road, the EU–US disputes about the

Boeing–McDonnell Douglas and the GE–Honeywell mergers in 1997 and 2001, as well as about Microsoft's dominant position almost caused trade wars. The situation was similar for all cases: while the US competition authorities gave their approval, the Commission initially intended to block the mergers or in the case of Microsoft, prosecute the company for its abuse of a dominant position. This not only infuriated the companies involved, but also the US government. In the cases of the Boeing–McDonnell Douglas and the GE–Honeywell mergers, the stakes were particularly high as they concerned the US defence sector and related industries such as civil aerospace. As the major purchaser of defence products, the US government had a vital interest in avoiding foreign bidders taking over crucial companies and interfering with US defence interests (Van Miert 2000: 269). With temporarily reduced defence budgets after the end of the Cold War, the US defence sector rapidly restructured by seeking synergies through large-scale mergers. The Commission's plan to ban was inherently linked to the more fragmented European equivalent. For example, in the case of the merger involving the US company Boeing, the world's leading commercial aircraft manufacturer, and McDonnell–Douglas, the second largest US defence supplier, the Commission's blocking was widely seen as a protectionist attempt to safeguard the future economic survival of the state subsidised French, German, British and Spanish Airbus Consortium, the only serious competitor to Boeing in the market for large jet engines. Eventually, a political compromise was reached in which the Commission allowed the deal. The negotiations, however, were reported to have been nerve-wracking. The US threatened with another trade war by filing an official protest with the WTO, limiting flights between the US and France, as well as imposing an import tax on European airplanes. US Vice President Al Gore warned to 'take whatever action is appropriate' to prevent the EU from impeding the merger (The Financial Times 1997: 1). The Commission was also internally divided by a neoliberal and Euro-mercantilist camp, which led to threats of resignation from Competition Commissioner Van Miert (Van Miert 2000).

The political controversies in the Boeing–McDonnell Douglas and the GE–Honeywell mergers were taken as an incident to problematise the 'fundamentally different doctrinal views over the economic purposes and scope of antitrust enforcement' (James 2001). US antitrust officials and scholars alike captured these differences with the adage 'we protect competition, and you protect competitors' (Fox 2003). The EC competition unit of regulation was considered unduly protectionist as it allegedly gave preference to competitor interests above both efficiency and consumer welfare arguments. US authorities observed that sophisticated econometric analyses were absent in the Commission's analysis and proclaimed that sound economics was needed to disentangle trade aspects from competition matters (James 2001). Streamlining the legal standards and the economic thinking that guided the respective merger control subunits and defining 'best practices' was considered essential to ease tensions and take necessary precautions to avoid future conflicts. To translate these endeavours into action, the Transatlantic Merger Working Group was established, composed of several joint subgroups, involving staff members of both agencies who were given the task to identify the possibilities for convergence in the various aspects regarding the content, form and scope of merger control. As US Assistant Attorney General Joel Klein remarked, it was time 'to develop a common language and to adopt a microeconomics-based competition enforcement, even if they could not achieve pure convergence' (Klein 2000).

Thus, what started with 'cooperation' was gradually replaced by a call for more convergence. This call was overtly successful. The Commission soon echoed its US counterparts and declared that 'successful cooperation depends upon rigorous economic analyses based upon strictly legal rules', in order to avoid that trade issues become entwined with competition issues (Schaub 1998). As outlined in Chapter 7, the DG Competition started to employ more economists in this period who adopted microeconometric modelling based on the assumptions of neoclassical economics, most notably the doctrines of the Chicago School (Wigger 2008). Over time, transatlantic cooperation led to a slow but steady process of convergence in which the EU eventually incorporated a broad range of key substantive and procedural features from the US competition model, culminating in the 2004 modernisation (see Chapter 7).

8.4 Multilateralising competition rules: the vanguard role of the European Commission

Initiatives for binding multilateral competition rules have been numerous, yet to date, none were successful. The idea dates back to the Havana Charter of 1947, which aimed at establishing the International Trade Organisation (ITO) as the central pillar of the Bretton Woods regime (see Articles 46–54, United Nations Conference 1948). After the failure of the ITO ratification the idea for multilateral competition rules was re-launched again in the 1960s, again without success however. Except from a few non-binding OECD Recommendations in the 1980s that were limited to the economically successful industrialised world, virtually nothing happened until the mid-1990s.

The efforts to multilateralise competition rules took shape at this juncture were linked to the reinvigorated spirit of fostering worldwide economic integration that emerged after the finalisation of the GATT Uruguay Round at the 1994 Ministerial Conference in Marrakech, after almost eight years of difficult negotiations. Alongside the subsequent reduction of the conventional government imposed tariff and non-tariff barriers and the proliferation of so-called 'trade and …'-issues in the new WTO setting, the inclusion of an agreement on competition rules also seemed tangible. Moreover, the Commission emerged as a strong advocate of a binding multilateral competition agreement already in the very beginning of the decade. Commissioner Brittan's opening speech at the Cartel Conference of 19 June in 1990 in Berlin, shortly after the fall of the Berlin Wall, where he declared the time ripe to address international antitrust convergence (Calvani 2005: 1132), formed the prelude of a series of Commission initiatives. Two years later, at the 1992 Annual Meeting of the World Economic Forum,

Brittan compared 'unfair trade' to cancer and asserted that through establishing multilateral competition rules 'the cancer can be cured before it takes hold' (The Financial Times 1992c: 14). What started with Commissioner Brittan, was given shape under the tenure of Commissioners Van Miert and Monti. The particular configuration of successive competition commissioners at important strategic posts provided the necessary institutional backup in this regard. Brittan's immediate predecessor, Commissioner Sutherland, became Director General of the GATT/WTO and Brittan himself took over the newly established external trade portfolio and became chiefly responsible for the GATT/WTO negotiations. Meanwhile his Director–General Ehlermann was transferred to the WTO's Appellate Body in Geneva in December 1995 where he worked until 2001.

Similar to the bilateral trajectory, the impetus for spreading a global competition culture was advanced by the transnational capitalist class. Ongoing liberalisation made it easier for companies to transnationalise and engage in concentration activities across the globe, which increased the awareness of private and public barriers inhibiting free-market access and thus, further expansion into new product and labour markets. The TABD, the ERT, UNICE and AmCham, as well as the ICC constituted the choir of organised transnational capital favouring more consistency in the regulation of global economic transactions. At the 1994 ERT Summit in Essen, Germany, which was held in parallel to the Council meeting, ERT members urged the political leaders of the EU, including the Commission, to consider a more outward focus on EU competition rules. Together with the TABD, the ERT set the agenda for extending the coverage of the WTO to 'additional relevant areas, such as competition policy in order to address structural impediments to market access which foreign investors might come across' (ERT 1996b; TABD 1996). Multilateral competition rules had to establish 'unimpaired market access on a worldwide scale for foreign goods, services, ideas, investments and business people' (TABD 1995: Section II.13 and II.14). The removal of private market barriers reached high on the agenda. Organised transnational capital regularly complained about the closed Japanese and Korean markets, even though tariff barriers were low (The Economist 1994: 55). The ERT (1993: 10, 14) noted: 'Industry [...] expects more open access to world markets, in return for giving our competitors better access to the Single Market in Europe.' For example, foreign producers were not only restricted from entering Japanese markets by the extensive quota system and special technical and administrative import requirements (Ruigrok and Van Tulder 1995: 42), but also by a lax enforcement of competition of competition rules, which supported closed national production, distribution and retailing networks and other restrictive private practices (The Financial Times 1993b: 2).

Furthermore, the problem of the multijurisdictional overlap became more apparent with the establishment of a growing number of competition units around the world. In 1989, there were only 31, of which 20 were situated in the industrialised OECD and 11 in the developing world (Schoneveld 2003: 434; Gavil *et al.* 2002: 59). At the time of writing, this number had exceeded a hundred. The vast majority of all competition units were established throughout the 1990s, mostly by developing states in South America, marking a wide gap with most of the African continent (except for Zambia, Gabon, and South Africa) and much of Asia (ICPAC 2000: 33). Also, the regional integration projects of Mercosur, the Andean Community and Caricom, the Caribbean Community and Common Market adopted common competition rules (Lee and Morand 2003). As a consequence, organised transnational capital repeatedly complained about the Tower of Babel when having to comply with different national competition units, most notably in the field of merger control. Extreme examples were the case of the planned merger between MCI WorldCom and Sprint, Exxon and Mobil, and GE and Honeywell, which were notified to 37, 20 and 25 different jurisdictions respectively (Bannermann 2002: 55–6). In addition to financial and administrative burdens that accompany multiple filings and varying requirements regarding information, fees and penalties, transnational companies also had a strong interest in eliminating the potential for conflicts arising from extraterritorial competition rule enforcement. As a broad-scale harmonisation was not a viable option, hopes were cherished that national merger control rules and review procedures would at least converge, once free competition and, thus, the right to access new markets was institutionalised at WTO level.

As free competition and free investment were irreversibly coupled, the transnational capitalist class also pushed for a multilateral investment agreement regulating the market access for foreign investors. As the ratio of mergers and acquisitions of the FDI flows amounted to 80 and occasionally even 90 per cent (UNCTAD 2000), a multilateral agreement on investments rules was considered essential for facilitating mergers and acquisitions. Often, domestic investment-blocking statutes such as minority shareholding provisions and other ownership requirements for non-nationals inhibited the freedom of corporate establishment, the acquisition of domestic companies by foreigners and hence, free competition (The Economist 1996: 80). Moreover, the impenetrable regulatory jungle of bilateral investment treaties concluded between the OECD and developing countries was considered a genuine impediment to corporate expansion (The Economist 1994: 55).

The TABD urged the EU and the US authorities to take the lead and make joint efforts within the WTO to harmonise strong and effective competition and investment rules. Yet they also had to cooperate 'closely with the private sector in order to arrive at the most constructive approach in the promotion of a better understanding of the relationship between competition policy and the issue of significant market access in the WTO' (TABD 1996: 7). It found a committed ally in the Commission's DG Competition. The TABD gave direct 'instructions' in an Implementation Table in 1998 on how to proceed in the WTO and was rather satisfied as 'nearly all WTO items identified by the TABD have been taken up' (TABD Implementation Table 1998 in: CEO 1999a).

In June 1994, Competition Commissioner Karel van Miert assigned a group of 'Wise Men' with the mandate to come up with a possible framework for a multilateral competition agreement. This resulted in the 25-page long 'Wise Men Report' of July 1995, or what officially was titled *Competition Policy in the New*

Trade Order: Strengthening International Cooperation and Rules (European Commission 1995). The Commission sought to keep up the appearance of an independent expert report and included the usual disclaimer that the views of the group of experts did not bind the Commission (European Commission 1996b: 1, 22). Except from three 'wise' men, all were Commission staff members however. After some minor modifications and the assistance of his predecessor Brittan, the 'Wise Men' proposal served as a blueprint for the EU to take the lead in adding competition rules to the agenda at the WTO's Ministerial Conference in Singapore in December 1996 (Brittan and Van Miert 1996).

In terms of *content*, the proposal was informed by the neoliberal discourse. It aimed at 'creating and maintaining open and accessible markets' (European Commission 1995: 3), thereby echoing the core interests of the transnational capitalist class. The phenomenon of multijurisdictional overlap was declared 'a major barrier to the expansion of trade and investment', referring to the high transaction costs and increasing uncertainties that companies were suffering from. Similarly, lax implementation or non-enforcement of competition rules was identified as a genuine hindrance in this respect. The report also mentioned the potential conflicts emerging from the practice of extraterritorial enforcement, thereby explicitly referring to the US practice. To generate the necessary political support, the Commission employed rhetoric of social peace, according to which all market players ought to have equal opportunities and, for the sake of free competition, be treated on the same terms as domestic market players. The proposal suggested 'minimum' competition rules in the first place, rather than a full-scale harmonisation. Although a few passages referred to 'consensus' and 'jointly determined principles', the proposal also quite straightforwardly suggested shaping the common competition rules on existing EC rules and enforcement procedures (ibid.: 17).

In terms of *form*, the proposal advocated a 'gradual construction of a plurilateral agreement on a set of jointly determined competition rules' (ibid.: 12–15). Similar to the bilateral cooperation agreements, it suggested establishing a system of mutual notification of cases that affected each other's jurisdictions. At a later stage, it foresaw a new international body that conciliated and arbitrated in the event of disputes and differences' (ibid.: 10), mandated the best-placed competition authority to take action in the case of a multijurisdictional overlap (ibid.: 18), monitored and disciplined the compliance more generally. In terms of *scope*, after the initial inclusion of only the world's major trading partners, the coverage was considered to progressively expand in terms of member states, substance and surveillance competences of the international body (ibid.: 22). Like this, the Commission sought to circumvent the politically cumbersome process of coming to terms with multiple signatories.

When competition became one of the Singapore Issues in 1996, the prospects for a multilateral agreement looked gloomy from the outset. Although a common set of competition principles was not the thorniest issue on the agenda compared to the reduction of tariffs and non-tariff barriers to trade in the agricultural sectors, no consensus could be reached on which components of competition rules had to be discussed. As a result, the newly established Working Group on the Interaction between Trade and Competition Policy was merely entrusted with the mandate to 'study issues raised by Members relating to the interaction between trade and competition policy, including anticompetitive practices, in order to identify any areas that may merit further consideration in the WTO framework' (WTO 1996). As a result of far-reaching disagreements, the Working Group's first report in 1998 lacked the necessary vigour to substantiate serious negotiations (WTO 1998). In November 1999, at the WTO Summit in Seattle, Commissioner Monti put much effort into expanding the Working Group's mandate beyond merely studying the interaction between trade and competition policy, but was ultimately unsuccessful (Monti 2002b: 81). The TABD, especially the US fraction, became more sceptical about the prospect of WTO competition rules (CEO 1999c). To avoid a stalemate, the Commission considerably tempered its proposal. Whereas it initially envisaged a binding competition agreement that was subject to the WTO's dispute settlement mechanism, the emphasis shifted to reaching a voluntary agreement instead. At the subsequent Ministerial Conference in Doha, Qatar in November 2001, a competition agreement was declared a long-term objective and negotiations on the Singapore Issues were postponed until the Ministerial Conference at Cancún, Mexico during 11–14 September 2003.

The Working Group's final report recommended merely some loosely defined 'core principles', outlawing cartels, bid rigging and the nationality-based discrimination between companies. In addition, it entailed stipulations on the transparency of rules and regulations, procedural fairness, due process and recourse to judicial procedures, as well as basic modalities for voluntary cooperation (WTO 2003). At the Cancún Ministerial Conference however, fierce resistance from the US and a number of developing countries led by Brazil and India, albeit for different reasons, brought the negotiations to a halt after only four days. In the subsequent 'July 2004 Package', the Singapore Issues and with them the idea of a binding multilateral competition agreement, were dropped from the WTO agenda without further ado.

8.5 Political contestation and the end of the multilateral competition project

At the 1990 Cartel Conference in Berlin, US competition officials already announced not to go down the road of a binding international competition agreement. Rather than a comprehensive commitment to multilateralism, the US authorities suggested deepening bilateral cooperation agreements in competition matters instead (The Financial Times 1998: 20). US opposition was due to a combination of reasons. To begin with, the US practice of applying its competition rules extraterritorially did not create a pressing need to conclude a multilateral agreement. Furthermore, having long been the only show in town, the US government was not willing to come to terms with the by then 132 WTO member governments, of which the overwhelming majority were developing countries, as well as with the Chinese and Russian government who were still queuing up to enter the WTO. To start negotiations on competition rules was considered premature and counterproductive, leading to a lowest common denominator, which only legitimised weak and ineffective competition rules, all at the expense of trade liberalisation, market access and antitrust enforcement (Klein 2002: 338–9). The disputes in the Boeing–McDonnell Douglas, GE–Honeywell and Microsoft cases reinforced US scepticism in this respect. Furthermore, as WTO rules addressed member state and not company behaviour, the risk of an international body interfering with the longstanding Federal pundits in trust-busting was not considered an option. The US authorities announced that they continued to block a multilateral agreement until there was 'more convergence in enforcement of existing national laws and more experience was gained in cooperative enforcement efforts between national authorities' (Pitofsky 1995). In short, global competition rules had to be defined in Washington and in Washington only, preferably under the leadership of the Department of Justice as 'they were the folks who should take the lead' (Pitofsky 2002: 59; Klein 2002: 338).

Next to US opposition, more than 70 WTO member governments, mostly from the developing world, the US government fiercely opposed to negotiate the Singapore Issues, after which the Cancun Ministerial collapsed after only four days. In the previous Doha Round, competition survived the agenda due to the inclusion of provisions on technical assistance to developing countries (Lee 2005: 23). Officials from developing countries insisted that an 'explicit' consensus was necessary for the launch of future negotiations. Even though the developing world did not form a monolithic block, a range of WTO members joined the position of the 'Kenyan paper' in August 2003, which suggested that the benefits of negotiating a multilateral framework for the Singapore Issues were far from evident, especially as 'many developing countries which were already grappling with the implementation of existing WTO rules, had scarce resources to meaningfully negotiate these issues' (WTO 2003; see also WTO WGTCP 2002a; 2002b; 2003).

Developing states considered a WTO competition agreement a 'Trojan Horse' of further market liberalisation. The inclusion of the proviso of non-discrimination, which constituted the hallmark of the neoliberal discourse of regulation, raised considerable concerns as it formally institutionalised the linkage between free competition and free market access. Inspired by the Most Favoured Nation Treatment, the non-discrimination clause implied that national competition units were not allowed to discriminate between domestic and foreign companies. In other words, any form of preferential treatment or affirmative action targeting domestic companies was outlawed. Thereby industrial or protectionist policies would have been forbidden, giving way to unbridled competition and free-market access. Together with the proposal developed by the Singapore Working Group on Trade and Investment, including the 'right of establishment' through FDI as well as the 'national treatment' principle, transnational capital would have enjoyed unlimited access to valuable natural resources, new product and cheap labour markets, as well as new markets for corporate control through mergers and acquisitions. As a result, structural inequalities in economic power would have been further engrained and the position of transnational corporations consolidated, particularly as companies from the developing world generally lacked similar access to capital, marketing and distribution networks or general expertise. The political bias in favour of creating market access for transnational corporations was also reflected in the issues deliberately excluded from the agenda. Most notably, issues left out were the prosecution of export cartels and antidumping practices, which were mostly applied as a protectionist guise by industrialised governments to restrict cheap imports, especially once import duties or quotas were no real option anymore after the completion of the Uruguay Round.

8.6 The International Competition Network and the Commission's reinvigorated bilateralism

Parallel to the Doha negotiations in 2001 the US competition authorities launched the International Competition Network (ICN), as an alternative route for international cooperation in competition matters. Its purpose was to facilitate substantive and procedural convergence through the voluntary adoption of common standards and 'best practices' through mutual 'policy-learning'. After the downfall of the Cancún Ministerial Conference, the Commission, in tandem with the US, promoted the ICN as the main vehicle to advance a process of convergence in competition matters on a global scale. To date, nearly all national and regional competition authorities from both the developed and developing world take part in the ICN's allegedly 'best practices' and mutual 'policy-learning' machinery.

The idea for the ICN emerged from the International Competition Policy Advisory Committee (ICPAC), established in November 1997 by the US competition authorities in response to European Commission's Wise Men Group. The ICPAC, composed of CEOs, economists, lawyers and public competition officials, was given the task 'to address the global antitrust problems of the 21st Century' (Djelic and Kleiner 2006: 297). In its final report, the ICPAC advised the creation of a 'Global Competition Initiative', meant to promote greater convergence of competition rules without the institutionalisation of a dispute settlement procedure similar to that of the WTO (Klein 2000). The ICPAC was dissolved again in June 2000 after the creation of the ICN was agreed upon.

The ICN was intended as a venue where competition authorities, organised capital, academics, economic and legal experts could discuss matters of competition rules. Organised transnational capital welcomed the proposal with enthusiasm (ERT 2000; see also 2010). This should not come as a surprise, as the ICN's informal organisational structure allowed the companies to play an important role side-by-side with the competition authorities. The Commission agreed to seek advice and welcome contributions from the private sector, the legal professions and individual members of the academic community (Schaub 2002). Similarly, the US authorities believed that the private sector had 'an important role to play in the ICN, not as members but as partners' (US Government 2002). In 2006, the ICN even established a subgroup on 'Business Outreach', which actively sought the contact with organised capital 'in order to benefit from their knowledge, experience, and insights' and to understand business realities (Barnett 2006).

The ICN constituted the perfect means for the diffusion of common norms and procedural standards, allowing the US and EC competition authorities to take over the role of the 'chief socialisers'. Convergence presupposes an identifiable common reference point towards which systemic, legal or regulatory devices are moving. This reference point was set by the established competition authorities of the EC and the US, who were both members of the ICN's steering group responsible for identifying projects and work plans. Moreover, both chaired most of the several other working groups that issued non-binding recommendations. Initially, in line with the interests of organised transnational capital, the ICN primarily targeted the area of merger control in the multijurisdictional context. There were three working groups alone on merger related issues. Meanwhile, working groups have also been formed on cartel investigation and prosecution, as well as on unilateral conduct.

Although the ICN officially declared that it sought to establish consensus through persuasion and deliberation, peer pressure and coercion to adopt the ICN norms and thereby fasten up the process of convergence constituted the order of the day. As remarked by Commissioner Monti (2004c), 'competition authorities and legislators had to move decisively forward with the implementation of the agreed ICN standards'. Anomalies, he continued, had to be eliminated through 'persuasion and other appropriate means' (ibid.). Thus, rather than being a horizontal network of 'equals', the ICN embodied broader structural power inequalities. This is also reflected in the use of a language similar to that used in the field of development aid, including notions such as 'capacity building', 'technical assistance', 'policy advocacy' and the recommendation of 'best practices catalogues' (European Commission 2004: 20) – all notions which imply a mature donor agency giving a young, inexperienced recipient agency a hand in imposing institutional structures to regulate competition. The direction of convergence is inherently neoliberal in nature. As Schaub (2002: 12), Director General for Competition explained: 'The greatest long-term challenge in terms of convergence will be the task of "managing" the worldwide proliferation of antitrust regimes, [...] and we – both the EU and US need to be advocating that competition policy should be used to foster competition, and not as a protectionist instrument, as an instrument of old-fashioned industrial policy, as an instrument of social policy, or whatever'.

In addition to the ICN, the Commission's DG Trade adopted the 'Global Europe: Competing in the World' strategy in 2006, which aimed at compensating for the absence of a multilateral agreement on the Singapore Issues. The 'Global Europe' strategy sought to conclude a new generation of bilateral Free Trade Agreements, Partnership and Cooperation Agreements as well as Association Agreements, which next to trade related aspects also contained provisions on free competition, free investment, rules on intellectual property rights and the access to public procurement markets. Whereas in the past, the

Commission framed its external trade policy vis-à-vis the developing world in the language of development aid, the 'Global Europe' strategy straightforwardly made use of the neoliberal discourse. The overall goal was to open up markets 'in which European companies can compete and providing new opportunities for growth and development' (European Commission 2006c: 2). Bilateralism has become the new road for exporting the neoliberal free market vision to the global realm. This can also be seen in the Commission's Europe 2020 Strategy, in which acting bilaterally 'in order to secure better market access for EU business' became one of the long-term key goals (European Commission 2010a: 21). It should not come as a surprise that the transnational capitalist class welcomes this strategy. In a special report called 'Challenges in EU Competition Policy', the ERT accentuated that 'the EU has to maximise its voice' in the international arena and to fully integrate competition regulation into the EU's external strategy (ERT 2010: 5).

Conclusion

The Commission's bilateral and multilateral trajectories in the conclusion of competition agreements epitomise a further momentum in the construction and consolidation of the neoliberal discourse. The Commission's missionary zeal in exporting a common understanding of free competition and free market access into new regions of the world since the 1990s has been fundamentally driven by the interests of the transnational capitalist class. The EU has become a major protagonist in promoting a 'one size fits all' logic in the global setting of the ICN and the various bilateral trade agreements forming part of the 'Global Europe' strategy. This leaves little scope for organising the national economies in ways that diverge from the neoliberal discourse.

Concluding remarks

When studied from a longitudinal perspective, it appears that the content, form and scope of competition regulation in Europe have undergone a profound transformation since the mid-1980s. The set of discourses that underpinned the competition units of regulation in the post-war years and that subsequently took shape in the 1960s and 1970s, were gradually replaced by a neoliberal discourse in the 1980s. This was related to the more general shift from embedded liberalism towards neoliberalism, which was premised on the transnationalisation of capitalism and the ensuing change in the balance of power between social forces. The capitalist class, most notably its transnational fraction was re-empowered vis-à-vis labour as part of the enduring crisis in the late 1970s. Broader processes of de-industrialisation and technological change, as well as the geographical relocation of production through subcontracting and outsourcing, accompanied declining productivity rates and rising unemployment in Europe. This provided a socioeconomic background that was advantageous for the advocates of neoliberalism to demand units of regulation that were oriented towards creating free markets and free competition, not only in Europe, but also on a global scale.

The transformation of European competition regulation

To fully understand the neoliberal transformation of European competition regulation it is necessary to go back in history. The establishment of competition units of regulation at both national and European level in the era of embedded liberalism formed part of the legacy of the Marshall Plan and political pressures by the US government to open up European markets to US capital. The actual content, form and scope were nonetheless still the contingent outcomes of 'local' political struggles between agents acting on the basis of particular discourses. The competition units of regulation that emerged after the War, all embodied elements of the neoliberal discourse and the national or Euro-mercantilist discourses, and therefore had many features in common.

Competition units of regulation in the era of embedded liberalism

As regards *content*, not only anticompetitive conduct but also social and industrial policy concerns were considered important in the enforcement of competition rules in the era of embedded liberalism. Although competition was deemed desirable in principal, it was not seen as something that had to be preserved at all costs. Particularly, allowing for economic concentration was regarded essential for rebuilding Europe in the immediate post-war years, and later for facing the so-called 'American challenge' of much larger and technologically more advanced companies that tried to gain a foothold in the newly created common market. For this reason, neither EC nor national competition units of regulation initially included merger control subunits. As the overarching purpose of the EC competition unit was to open up and integrate national markets, it entailed a rather tolerant stance towards mergers and various other cross-border intercompany agreements, such as corporate alliances designed to pool R&D investments and various forms of production, distribution, or marketing joint ventures. Thereby, the Commission sought to undermine the mercantilist attempts of governments to promote national champions, and actively stimulated strong European champions instead. At the same time, in most cases, small and medium sized companies were exempted from the necessity to comply with EC competition rules, which *de facto* provided them with a *carte blanche* to engage in various types of corporate alliances. In the course of the economic crisis of the 1970s, companies and industries in despair received permission to engage in crisis cartels and receive state aid, which engendered not only the preservation of companies, but also of jobs. In short, in the era of embedded liberalism, the competition units of regulation formed part of the broader ensembles that sought to facilitate the Fordist accumulation process. Primacy was given to the creation of large and vertically integrated national and European companies, engaged in industrial production of cheap and standardised consumption commodities.

In the late 1960s and 1970s, when there was a scarcity of labour and trade unions were countervailing the power of the capitalist class, a centre-left discourse started to gain some political momentum. At this juncture, the broader commitment to full employment under the Keynesian-type welfare states was to some extent incorporated into the European competition units of regulation. The enforcement of competition rules thereby reflected the wider class compromise between nationally oriented industrial capital and organised labour. This meant that the content of the competition units of regulation was influenced by various, in many respects incompatible, discourses. Competition regulation served multiple purposes, and the enforcement was based on a flexible interpretation, varying from case to case.

As regards *form*, democratically accountable decision-makers played key roles in national regulatory processes, notably in the subunit of merger control. At EC level, there was no room for democratic decision-making. The Commission managed to obtain significant discretionary powers in the enforcement of the competition rules, especially with the adoption of Regulation 17 and the subsequent introduction of the block exemption system. The eventual concentration of power in the EC competition unit of regulation was unprecedented compared to other regulatory fields. As regards *scope,* EC and national competition units largely functioned independently from each other; yet the national units were widely considered the primary locus of regulation. This was particularly the case in the merger control area in the 1960s and 1970s, where national subunits evolved in France, the UK and Germany, whilst no agreement on an EC merger control regulation could be reached.

Competition units of regulation after the neoliberal turn

From the 1980s onwards, neoliberal doctrines gradually came to prevail. The ascendancy of neoliberal ideas was premised on the transnationalisation of production, ownership structures, and a shift in the underlying power balance in favour of capital, most notably the transnational fraction. The resulting neoliberal transformation of the broader ensembles of regulation was however rather uneven and only partial in nature. Neoliberal ideas also took shape in non-linear ways in the field of competition regulation at EC and national level. They evolved through three, to some extent overlapping, discursive moments. In a deconstructive moment, dating back to the late 1970s and early 1980s, neoliberalism emerged as a project that questioned and discredited the social 'embeddedness' of the existing type of European competition regulation. In a constructive moment, which mainly started in the mid-1980s and lasted into the 1990s, the content, form and scope of Europe's competition units of regulation were increasingly underpinned by the neoliberal unit specific discourse. In a third moment, which persisted from the 1990s onwards, the neoliberal-type competition regulation further consolidated, culminating in a far-reaching reform in 2004, which enacted a partial privatisation and a further Europeanisation of the enforcement of competition rules, as well as the promotion of competition rules as a device to open up markets to free competition elsewhere in the world.

As regards *content*, neoliberal competition regulation was based on a 'competition only' vision in all subunits. The Commission and national competition authorities prosecuted cartels much more stringently than before, while also imposing ever higher fines. The Commission no longer tolerated state aid and ordered the privatisation of public monopolies in crucial public utility sectors by endorsing so-called privatisation directives. Furthermore, the EC merger control regulation that was adopted in 1989 entailed a purely neoliberal text. It left no room for industrial and social policy considerations and narrowed the decision-making basis to assessing competition in product markets, rather than taking actual company size as a point of departure. Importantly, the EC merger control subunit was established to facilitate rather than prohibit economic concentration. By eliminating the involvement of several national authorities in the judgment of mergers, the problem of a multijurisdictional overlap was abolished and mergers above a certain annual turnover threshold channelled to the supranational level. As company size was not considered a reason for blocking mergers, the

Commission was subsequently able to clear mergers rather generously. The Commission's enforcement records support this: since the inception of EC merger control, less than 1 per cent of the notified mergers were prohibited. Ever since, transnational corporations seeking to further strengthen their global market position and gain market access through mergers have been the main beneficiaries of the EC merger control subunit. Smaller and often also less competitive companies in contrast, often continued to be subject to multiple national merger control subunits, and were more generally prevented from engaging in cartels and receiving state subsidies as means to face up to the competition by the larger transnational corporations.

As regards *form*, the influence of democratically accountable national decision-makers was significantly reduced. The adoption of the Enterprise Act in 2002 in the UK for instance, narrowed the basis for interventions by the Trade and Industry Secretary in the merger control subunit. More generally, the use of sophisticated microeconomic modelling in the assessment of anticompetitive conduct and the privatisation of the enforcement through private litigation increased considerably. This shift, which consolidated in the 2004 overhaul of the EC competition unit, formed a major step of convergence to the more market-based competition unit of the US. The overhaul was based on the view that 'less regulation is better regulation' and market-based solutions are superior to the interventionist arm of a public authority.

As regards *scope*, competition regulation underwent an increased Europeanisation and globalisation. Whereas national competition authorities enjoyed a certain degree of autonomy in the era of embedded liberalism, the structural integration of national jurisdictions into the European Competition Network, a larger EU-level framework, minimised their independent role in crucial ways. The attempts to conclude a multilateral competition agreement at WTO level and the subsequent establishment of the International Competition Network demonstrate that the hegemony of neoliberalism in Europe has been constituent to the worldwide spread of neoliberal ideas. Through the conclusion of bilateral free trade and free investment agreements around the world, the Commission continues to play an active part in crafting a common understanding about the right to compete freely and hence, ensuring a high degree of corporate freedom and free market access to new (geographical) markets. Table 2 summarises the main characteristics of European competition regulation in the social orders of embedded liberalism and neoliberalism.

Transnational corporations were, and continue to be, not only the main beneficiaries of, but also a key driving force behind, the neoliberal-type of competition regulation. The influence of organised transnational capital was for example crucial for the adoption of the 1989 merger control regulation. At the same time, organised capital has not been in a position to decide on the precise content, form and scope of Europe's competition units. Exemplary is the process leading up to the revision of the merger control regulation in 2003, where organised capital failed to preserve the much cherished 'market dominance' test. Likewise, despite a vigorous political campaign, it could not prevent the introduction of private litigation.

Table 2 Competition regulation in the social orders of embedded liberalism and neoliberalism

	Embedded liberalism	*Neoliberalism*
Content	– Prevalence of 'public interest' criteria, accommodating industrial and social policy objectives – Adopting a tolerant stance towards cartels and state aid measures to industry – Interventionist pro-cooperation and pro- concentration stance	– Prevalence of a narrow 'competition only' focus, allegedly privileging consumer welfare and efficiency objectives – Vigorous rule enforcement and harsh punishment of cartels and state aid measures to industries – Privatisation of public utility sectors – Facilitation of cross-border concentration through the centralisation/coordination of regulatory powers
Form	– Important role reserved for political decision-makers in regulatory processes – Decision-making based on macroeconomics and a multi-goal focus – Public enforcement and administrative supervision	– Key role reserved for independent authorities, marginalising political decision-makers in the regulatory processes – Decision-making based on 'sound' microeconomics and econometric modelling – Facilitation of private enforcement and retrenchment of public authorities
Scope	– Primacy given to national level enforcement – Limited integration of national and supranational competition units – Focus on elimination of intra-EC market barriers	– Significantly reduced importance of national level enforcement – Transnationalisation of competition units of regulation – Focus on elimination of global market barriers

This has important repercussions for how to adequately conceptualise the Commission as a locus of a state-type power. In contrast to the assumption of an overall decline or hollowing out of state autonomy at the expense of transnational corporations that has prevailed in much of the literature since the 1970s, the analysis in this book demonstrated that the Commission enjoys a substantial degree of what Jessop termed operational autonomy (see Chapter 1). This means that instrumentalist or functionalist notions of the Commission as being merely the expression of the preferences of specific class fractions are inadequate. Its powers and regulatory practices are always an imperfect reflection of the broader balance of power between class fractions. For example, since the 1980s, the DG Competition has actively promoted the extension and reproduction of crude notions of free markets and free competition that are central to the neoliberal discourse. In many cases, the Commission actively sought the political support of dominant class fractions, and assumed the role of a coordinator in streamlining the different national (sub)units of regulation with neoliberal ideas. More generally, the Commission enjoys a considerable degree of freedom as long as it acts within the confines of the prevailing general and unit-specific discourse, while being though dependent on the overall political support of the dominant class fractions.

Towards a paradigm shift?

The numerous bailouts and nationalisations of banks and other financial institutions in Europe and the US since 2007 have put the continued survival of the neoliberal growth model into question. In the face of a major global depression, fierce competition and the free play of market forces seem at first sight to have surrendered in favour of a new wave of protectionism. The Commission's sudden tolerance of certain forms of state aid and government sponsoring of defensive mergers also seems to contrast sharply with the neoliberal unit-specific discourse that underpinned European competition regulation during the past three decades. This raises the question of whether we are witnessing the dawn of a major paradigm shift in the field of competition regulation.

This question is certainly not far-fetched. Back in the 1980s and 1990s, the paradigm shift in the content, form and scope of European competition regulation was the result of the deep crisis of the social order of embedded liberalism. At the time of writing (June 2010) however, no conclusive evidence can be given for the advent of yet another paradigm shift. As Chapter 7 demonstrated, so far there are no signs that the Commission's DG Competition diverged from the existing neoliberal path. The initial crisis responses were at most reformist in nature, displaying no radical break with the past. Whereas the enforcement practices in the cartel and merger subunit continued as business as usual, the Commission's 'flexibility' in the regulation of state aid was mainly about allowing member states to rescue finance capital, the dominant fraction in the current social order. Safeguarding financial stability and a 'good' business climate formed the ultimate bedrock for the Commission's decision-making. Even though the crisis continues to deepen, the Commission already proudly heralded its crisis management for having avoided the 'meltdown of the financial system' and for having helped to 'put financial markets back on the path towards normal market functioning' (Lowe 2009: 7). In the meantime, many of the bank nationalisations seem to have been only short-lived, while top managers in the financial sector are once again rewarded with outrageous bonuses and double-digit windfall profit rates from risky investments. In contrast, the Commission has been eager to prevent member state governments from engaging in protectionist 'subsidy races' and staunchly opposed bailouts in the real economy sector. Given the 'Europeanised' nature of the contemporary European competition regulation, national competition units seem to lack the political leeway to sidetrack this path.

There are no indications that the appointment in 2009 of Joaquín Almunia, a former trade union economist and member of the Spanish Socialist Workers' Party, as the new Competition Commissioner will fundamentally change the current nature of EC competition regulation. Important in this regard is that the dominant capital fractions continue to support the DG Competition's crisis strategy. A deconstructive moment similar to that in the crisis of the 1970s is not heaving into sight. The transnational capitalist class and surely its financial fraction, have endorsed the idea of more competition rather than establishing various protectionist shelters as a solution to the crisis. Ideational input for a paradigm shift has not been provided by specialised academics either. In fact, to the contrary, many of them have encouraged European competition authorities not to relax their efforts against protectionism and distortions of competition (for a discussion see Wilks 2009). In short, apart from a few voices considering competition a luxury that is unaffordable in a time of crisis, no clearly articulated counter-project has surfaced so far, leaving the neoliberal discourse and the importance given to competition largely unchallenged.

Arguably, the current moment is one in which 'the old is dying but the new cannot yet be born' (Gramsci 1971: 176). For something new to be born in the field of competition regulation a transformation of the broader ensembles of which the European competition units form part, needs to take place. Such a transformation is most likely if it turns out that the growth model of financialised capitalism no longer 'work'. But even if neoliberalism is intellectually undermined and the growth model it sustains turns out to be irrefutably defeated, for a paradigm shift to take place a reconfiguration of social forces, organised around an alternative project is critical. At this stage however, not even the contours of such a project, around which a new constellation of social forces could form, are visible. As Jessop (2009) observes, 'the speed with which decisions were made effectively marginalized most social forces', notably those of the centre and the left, who seem unable to exploit the crisis and provide a powerful solution to the current neoliberal crisis management.

Outline of an alternative vision for competition regulation

We are habituated to believe that the effects of competition are positive for all of us. Certainly, the opening of markets and enhanced competition has in many ways benefitted consumers in the privileged parts of the world with a huge assortment of innovative and often low-priced products and services. The negative aspects of competition are however significant. The competitive race operates simultaneously at different levels in capitalist societies. Those able to compete set the standards of competition for others, which thwart the existence of comparatively weaker (and usually smaller) competitors. The elimination of competitors inevitably strengthens the winners and reinforces their initial advantages. The centralisation of wealth in the hands of a tiny minority and the oligopolistic nature of competition in certain sectors are a blatant testimony thereof. Examples are the music and film industry and other media outlets, such as newspapers and book publishers, the energy sector, manufacturers of civil passenger aircrafts, the pharmaceutical industry, the industry of wireless communications and grocery markets.

As Marx (1965[1887]: 626) reminds us: 'The battle of competition is fought by cheapening of commodities. The cheapness of commodities depends [...] on the productivity of labour [...]'. The presence of what Marx termed an 'industrial reserve army' creates a chronic insecurity among labour, which is paramount to why resistance to wage repression, unpaid overtime, degradation of working conditions and labour flexiblisation in general is weak. In the event of the growing transnationalisation of production, the bargaining power of labour vis-à-vis that of capital is continuously undermined by geographically segmented, racialised and gendered labour markets (cf. Silver 2003). The right to compete freely in global markets in many ways presupposes the right for corporations, irrespective of ownership and origin, to relocate their production, and thus access (geographically) new and easily controllable labour markets. Transnational corporations enjoy considerable structural bargaining power not only vis-à-vis host governments, corporate affiliates and local competitors, but also labour. Ongoing and ever toughening competition for land, water, energy, other scarce resources and cheap labour is likely to increase the already existing power asymmetries and inequality between the exorbitantly rich and the extremely poor segments within societies and between geographical regions.

Most economists and legal scholars remain nonchalant about the ruinous nature of competition. But it is undeniable that in today's globalised world unbridled competition has serious downsides. Capitalist competition is inducing a ruthless process of capital accumulation that is far from stable, unlimited or unproblematic. In addition to limits of natural resources and energy, sweeping pollution and climate change impose important constraints onto continued economic growth, which in turn further toughens competition. The uncompromising imperative of economic growth sets in motion a vicious spiral causing irreparable damage to the environment. Furthermore, the structural crisis of overaccumulation, induced by underconsumption and overproduction, exposes the underlying stagnation tendency of capitalism as a system. Combined with the exclusion of a significant portion of humanity from capitalist production in the form of un- or underemployment, social tensions and contradictions are likely to increase further. The articulation of credible alternatives to hollow mantras such as 'competition for more competitiveness' is therefore desperately needed. New avenues for shrinking the economies of the privileged North in particular need to be explored, rather than finding solutions for the imperative of infinite economic growth. Downscaling may sound utopian in the current political climate, but continuing down the path hitherto followed is not an option if the planet is to be habitable for humans and other beings in the future.

What is required is a profound transformation of the existing social order and a break with many of the ideas and social practices that have sustained it so far. The search for alternatives needs to take place in various social spheres and spaces simultaneously. Critical intellectuals and academics have a role to play in this process, not only in questioning the sustainability of prevailing institutions and social practices but also in formulating alternatives. A number of outstanding scholars have outlined their visions for a post-neoliberal social order in recent years (e.g. Foster 2009; Hardt and Negri 2009; Harvey 2010). Likewise, since the 1970s the Club of Rome has repeatedly provided an agenda for action, containing a range of ideas, values, strategies and new institutional arrangements that deserves further exploration. Such thoughts about alternatives have, however, not extended into the field of competition regulation yet. This is unfortunate as competition units are essential components of the ensembles of regulation that contribute to reproduce unsustainable social structures of inequality. None of the discourses of regulation identified in this book alongside the neoliberal discourse provides a viable alternative for a sufficiently far-reaching transformation of Europe's competition units. While the national and Euro-mercantilist discourses fail in all respects to meet the challenges ahead of us, the centre-left discourse, despite its socially progressive elements, does not offer a thorough and sufficiently far-reaching solution either. An alternative discourse of regulation informing a qualitative shift in the content, form and scope of future competition units of regulation is urgently needed. The following suggestions might serve as guidance.

As regards *content*, competition units of regulation should seek to ensure fair competition, rather than one-sidedly intensify unlimited and fierce competition at all costs. Fair competition involves equal opportunities and starting points for companies and implies taking into account the societal and environmental consequences of competition. A society, let alone a market, without competition is not something worth striving for, but the negative effects of capitalist competition definitely need to be curbed significantly. An overall restriction of competition therefore forms an unavoidable part of the solution if we want to successfully tackle problems of environmental destruction, climate change and perverse social inequalities. Certainly, the restriction of competition comes at a 'cost' for those who currently benefit from it, namely competitive companies. This will also affect our role as consumers and the possibility to choose from a huge assortment of products and services that may be cheap and entertaining but are environmentally and socially unsustainable. Many products will become more expensive and the pace of innovation may slow down in certain industries, forcing many of us to change our current lifestyles. To stimulate nevertheless a high pace of innovation in sectors providing socially desirable and environmentally viable products and services, public funding structures could be devised.

For competition units to ensure fair competition, new conceptions of what it means to be competitive are needed, namely conceptions that valorise the extra-economic dimensions and comprehensively re-embed economic activities in a way that is more attuned to the needs of society at large. The contemporary subordination of other social spheres to the alleged economic imperative of capitalist competition needs to be fundamentally reversed. This requires a move away from microeconomic price and efficiency modelling, which assesses competition in isolation from other social spheres. The competitive performance of companies should instead be assessed according to various social interest criteria. Such criteria could for example include an assessment of the social usefulness of new products, ecologically sustainable production methods, the safeguarding of employment and employee rights in the corporate governance structure, fair trade practices and investment decisions, as well as solidarity in knowledge transfer and technology sharing. Applied to an alternative merger subunit of regulation, this could consist of viable and sustainable business plans being taken as a point of departure in the decision making, rather than solely efficiency and consumer welfare considerations measured in expected future price reductions. On the basis of such business plans, leveraged buyouts, or mergers and acquisitions conducted for the exclusive purpose of a short-term profit gain through unproductive asset stripping could be ruled out in the future. In addition, as company size matters, not narrowly defined product markets but the actual macroeconomic weight of a company should be decisive in assessing market dominance.

As regards *form*, to remedy the enduring democratic deficit and the growing disenchantment of European citizens with the European integration project, competition units should be profoundly democratised. Currently, European competition authorities are shielded from democratic pressures, even though much is done to make it appear as if this is not the case. For instance, the DG Competition regularly relies on experts as allegedly politically impartial arbiters who seem to look beyond particular short-term interests and who campaign for the public good. The veil of expertise, however, only serves to legitimate a chosen regulatory direction by obscuring and diluting antagonistic positions. Moreover, the Commission's Green and White Papers, inviting responses from interested parties, upholds the illusion that a wide range of agents is able to influence the EC competition unit. The Commission is however not obliged to defend why it disregards some voices in the 'debate', nor does it follow such a practice voluntarily. In contrast, competition authorities applying social interest criteria as judgmental basis should be democratically accountable and genuinely responsive to all inputs by different groups in society. As the 'adequate' degree of competition is dynamic and contingent on the concentration of economic power at a particular junction, the social interest criteria should not be fixed, but be subject to periodic adjustment and democratic re-evaluation. Such constant public attention renders politically independent competition authorities, as they exist today, incompatible with a democratic competition regulation. Precisely because competition regulation is inherently political, it should also be subjected to political mediation.

As regards *scope*, European competition units should continue to operate at different regulatory levels. To ensure the aforementioned democratisation, the current institutional hierarchy, which positions the Commission at the top of the European Competition Network and allowing it to bypass national competition authorities, should be reorganised according to the principle of subsidiarity. Such a new institutional matrix should require competition authorities to take not only each other's views into account, but also that of other social groups. For the purpose of formulating an alternative discourse of regulation, the question of scope is extended here to relate to the nature of competition itself. Competition should not only be fair, but also only exist within well-defined geographical boundaries. This does not imply that inter-territorial competition should be abandoned altogether for all industrial sectors. Rather, imposing geographical limits to fair competition provides, for example, an avenue for local producers of sustainable food products to evade the global war of price competition. This has the more general benefit of significantly reducing long-distance and energy-wasteful transportation. Global competition can make sense for certain products and sectors, but not where it leaves behind mammoth ecological footprints and a legacy of abuses of human rights and labour standards. The logic of competition should be exorcised from certain sectors of common interest. These include utility sectors in the field of energy, water, transport, but also housing, healthcare and education. This does not necessarily imply a full-scale re-nationalisation. Other forms of common ownership are also conceivable. 'Free marketeers' will surely consider this to be a call for protectionism and in one sense it is. The geographical restriction of competition should however not be understood as a return to a mercantilist-type of beggar thy neighbour strategy which seeks to benefit specific industries within a delimited territory at the expense of those on the outside. Rather it is a call for a completely different type of protectionism, namely one that safeguards ecological balances, the common good, democracy and more generally, the vulnerable in society.

An alternative type of competition regulation needs to form part of a much broader transformation of the current social order. Alternative concepts of democratically managed and socialised forms of communal ownership structures have already been proposed. It is time to start deconstructing the one-dimensional neoliberal values of egoism and self-sufficiency and stop seeing them as the alleged natural condition of human beings who compete in a Hobbesian dog-eat-dog world. Such a characterisation is not only mistaken with regard to dogs, but also to human nature. Arguably, a *homo socialis* is indeed as utopian and bathetic as a *homo economicus,* but creating the parameters for a democratically managed socioeconomic order that limits the concentration of economic power and that emphasises solidarity next to fair competition, is as character moulding for a society as the compulsive persistence on competitiveness that dominates the current capitalist system. It is time to put competition into practice in the sense of the Latin word 'competere': to strive and run together and to learn from each other.

Notes

1 Theorising competition regulation: a critical political economy perspective

1 Examples of such theoretical straitjackets are the neorealist theory of Waltz (1979) and the liberal intergovernmentalism of Moravcsik (1998).
2 A vast body of literature identified a number of models or varieties of capitalism (cf. Albert 1993; Coates 2000; Hall and Soskice 2001), and several studies distinguished epochal shifts in the history of capitalism (Harris 2006; Robinson 2004).
3 This process is also known as 'the circuit of capital', which Marx stipulated in the formula M-C-P-C′-M′ in Volume II of *Capital*, referring to a process where money (M) is used to buy commodities (C) that are used in the production process (P) in order to create new commodities (C′), the sale of which results in the generation of more money (M′) than were present at the beginning of the process (Robinson 2004: 15).
4 Classical and neoclassical theorists hold different conceptions of competition. Classical thinkers depart from a behavioural understanding, according to which competition is a guiding force in the process of economic exchanges. According to McNulty (1968: 634), it is understood analogous to the force of gravitation in physical science. Through competition, resources 'gravitate' towards their most productive uses and prices are 'forced' to the lowest sustainable level. Neoclassical theorists, in contrast, adopt a structural point of view, according to which competition refers to a particular imaginary state of affairs, such as perfect competition.
5 See Jessop (2002a: 201) for a general overview of contradictions pervading the basic capital relation.
6 It should be noted that regulation theorists, at least those associated with the Parisian School, use the concept of 'regulation' in a much more inclusive sense to refer to all those extra-economic mechanisms that stabilise the accumulation of capital (see Jessop and Sum 2006: 15, 44; or, Boyer 1990: 117–23 on different Parisian notions of regulation).
7 'Object of regulation' is a concept borrowed from Jessop (see Jessop and Sum 2006: 44, 84).
8 Elsewhere we have referred to unit-specific discourses as 'policy-area specific discourses' (see Buch-Hansen and Wigger 2010; forthcoming).
9 Fractioning also relates to labour. As Bieler (2003: 1–2) notes, 'a white-collar worker in the service industry is clearly in a different fraction of labour than a blue-collar worker at the assembly line of a car manufacturer. Workers they are, however, in that they are forced to sell their labour power, used by capital for the extraction of surplus value and the accumulation of profit.'
10 The term 'owners and managers' of private companies is tricky as the question of who actually owns a company is far from clear-cut, which also blurs the often made separation of ownership and control (cf. Berle and Means 1932). Apart from traditional family-owned and often smaller companies, the situation is particularly complex with

companies that are legal entities and/or stock-market listed. It is often held that shareholders are the rightful owners, while a layer of managers steer and control a company's activities. Shareholders do however not *own* such companies, but merely have a legal claim to a residual profit in the form of dividends and/or interests. The company as a legal entity owns itself. Furthermore, to increase the overall commitment of managers to a company's profit-making goal, managers are often made shareholders themselves, which makes any meaningful separation between owners and managers obsolete: both are capitalists. Having said this, for reasons of simplicity, the term 'owners and managers' is nonetheless applied.

11 These discourses bear some resemblance to the three 'political projects' identified by Van Apeldoorn (2002: 78–82) in his ground-breaking study of the re-launch of European integration in the 1980s and 1990s. Here he distinguishes between (1) a 'neoliberal project' according to which European integration ought to take shape primarily through deregulation and liberalisation of markets; (2) a 'neomercantilist project', emphasising the creation of a strong European 'home market' that needs to be defended against competition from non-European companies; (3) a 'social democratic project' according to which the protection of the European type of welfare state against neoliberalism and economic globalisation stands central. Using the terminology advanced in this book, the three projects were informed, respectively, by the neoliberal, Euro-mercantilist and centre-left discourses of regulation.

2 The origins of European competition regulation I: national level developments

1 Strictly speaking, the term 'trust' refers to the certificates issued by these inter-company networks. Trusts and cartels are often used interchangeably. Compared to cartels and other collusive practices, however, trusts were, at that time, official combinations of companies that jointly managed certain commercial activities. The term trust endured in the notion of 'antitrust policy' to specifically refer to the prohibition of cartels and other restrictive business practices. Until today, US practitioners and academics use the term 'antitrust policy', whereas in Europe and other parts in the world, the more generic analogue 'competition policy' became more widespread.

2 In the 1920s and 1930s, the International Steel Cartel consisting of members from seven European countries controlled a significant proportion of world production and exports.

3 The UK and France were also involved in the decartelisation project of particularly concentrated industries, such as coal and steel production, banking, motion pictures, and chemicals. Yet, in the absence of antitrust rules in these countries, the implementation by these occupation forces was markedly less severe than the approach taken in the US zone. The British did not share the same aversion to cartels as the US Occupation Forces and the French did not prohibit cartels as such. Instead, action could be taken only if an anticompetitive effect could be examined (Harding and Joshua 2003: 87; Wells 2002: 147).

4 Ironically, many sectors of the US industry formed part of the large international industrial cartels in which German corporations, supporting the fascist regime, participated. Examples of US companies engaging in international market sharing 'cooperative agreements' with foreign competitors were General Electric, DuPont, Allied Chemicals, Standard Oil, and Imperial Chemical Industries, which had a strong stake in cartel ties with the German IG Farben (Wells 2002: 46, 75–6).

5 The first plan, the so-called Monnet Plan, identified six key sectors, namely coal, steel, electricity, transportation, agricultural machinery and cement, as the most crucial for the development of the French economy. It outlined a detailed investment programme for each of these sectors (Hall 1986: 142). For a discussion of the content of the various plans and the various ways in which economic steering was carried out, see Hall (1986: 139–91) and Djelic (1998: 135–50).

6 However, the post-war governments were still unable 'to prevent the British economy very quickly resuming the decline which had temporally been suspended by the Depression and the war' (Overbeek 1990: 122). See Coates (2000: 43–52) for an interesting discussion of the reasons for this decline.

3 The origins of European competition regulation II: the supranational level

1 The *Conseil National du Patronat Français* even imposed a 'Commission for German Affairs', whose chief official kept close contact with Robert Schuman, advocating specific competition standards, applicable to German industries only, rather than a wholesale prohibition of horizontal cartel agreements (Karagiannis 2004: 12–13).
2 Jean Monnet attended the negotiation phase as an independent advisor, but did not play a prominent role in the EC Treaty drafting process.
3 Until 1999 this directorate was known as 'DG IV', but was then renamed DG Competition. Throughout this book the DG is referred to as the DG Competition.

4 European competition regulation in the era of embedded liberalism

1 The percentages are based on calculations retrieved from all official decisions on the notified agreements referring to Article 101 and Article 102.

5 The neoliberalisation of European competition regulation

1 A shift towards neoliberalism already took place in the monetary unit of regulation in the mid 1970s. The *Bundesbank* embraced a 'monetarist' unit-specific discourse of regulation, entailing a commitment to ensure low inflation at all costs (Schmidt 2002: 70).
2 One of these two cases became one of the most controversial in the history of German merger control (Wilks and McGowan 1996: 55). The case arose in 1987, when the liberal Minister of Economics, Martin Bangemann, proposed a merger between Daimler Benz and MBB in order to help Airbus, the heavily subsidised airline consortium (Schwartz 1993: 630). The merger would have created a huge conglomerate with 380,000 employees, accounting for 5 per cent of Germany's GDP. The *Bundeskartellamt* blocked the merger, as it led to a dominant position in the airline and defence markets, but the new Minister of Economics, Helmut Haussman overruled the decision in 1989 (Wilks and McGowan 1996: 55).

References

Acheson, D. (1969) *Present at the Creation. My years in the State Department*, 1987 edn, New York: Norton.

Adams, W. and Brock, J.W. (1990) 'Mergers and economic performance: the experience abroad', *Review of Industrial Organization*, 5/2: 175–88.

Akbar, Y. (2003) 'Slip sliding away? The changing politics of European car distribution', *Business and Politics*, 5/2: 175–92.

Albert, M. (1993) *Capitalism Against Capitalism*, London: Whurr Publishers.

Allen, D. (1977) 'Policing or policy-making? Competition policy in the European Communities', in H. Wallace, W. Wallace, and C. Webb (eds) *Policy-Making in the European Communities*, London: John Wiley & Sons.

—— (1983) 'Managing the common market: The Community's competition policy', in H. Wallace, W. Wallace and C. Webb (eds) *Policy-Making in the European Communities*, London: John Wiley & Sons.

Almunia, J. (2010) 'Competition and consumers: the future of EU competition policy', speech 10/247 at the European Competition Day, Madrid, 12 May.

Andriessen, F. (1981) 'Antitrust in the international sphere. Antitrust an endangered species?', speech at the American Bar Association's National Institute on Antitrust, November, Washington. Brussels: Historical Archives of the European Commission.

—— (1982) 'Speech to the *Groupe des Presidents des Grandes Entreprises Europeennes*', Ludwigshafen. Brussels: Archives of the European Commission.

—— (1983a) 'The Role of antitrust in the face of economic recession. State aids in the EEC, 16 September', speech at the Second Oxford International Antitrust Law Conference, Oxford. Brussels: Archives of the European Commission.

—— (1983b) 'Developments in the competition policy of the EEC', speech at the International Political Science Association, London School of Economics, February, Brussels: Archives of the European Commission.

Archer, M.S. (1995) *Realist Social Theory: The Morphogenetic Approach*, Cambridge: Cambridge University Press.

Arestis, P. and Sawyer, M. (2005) 'The neoliberal experience of the United Kingdom', in A. Saad-Filho and D. Johnston (eds) *Neoliberalism. A Critical Reader*, London: Pluto Press.

Armstrong, K. and Bulmer, S. (1998) *The Governance of the Single European Market*, Manchester: Manchester University Press.

Baker, J.B. (2003) 'The case for antitrust enforcement', *Journal of Economic Perspectives*, 17/4: 27–50.

Bannermann, E. (2002) *The Future of EU Competition Policy*, London: Centre for European Reform.

Barnett, T.O. (2006) 'Merger work in the ICN: the challenge of substantive convergence', paper presented at the Fifth Annual Conference of the International Competition Network, Cape Town, South Africa.

Baskoy, T. (2008) *The Political Economy of European Union Competition Policy: A Case Study of the Telecommunications Industry*, London and New York: Routledge.

Baur, J.F. (1980) 'The control of mergers between large financially strong firms in West Germany', *Journal of Institutional and Theoretical Economics*, 136/3: 444–64.

Bavaso, A. (2007) 'An unfortunate turn for Europe', *eCCP Viewpoint*, June.

Bayliss, B.T. and El-Agraa, A.M. (1990) 'Competition and industrial policies with an emphasis on competition policy', in A.M. El-Agraa (ed.) *The Economics of the European Community*, Cambridge: Philip Allan.

BDI (2002) 'Commentary on the Green Paper of the EU Commission of 11 December 2001 on the Review of Council Regulation (EEC) No.4064/89'. Online. Available: <http://ec.europa.eu./competition/consultations/2002_council_regulation/index.html> (accessed 8 June 2010).

Berle, A.A. and Means, G.C. (1932) *The Modern Corporation and Private Property*, 10th edn, New York: Transaction Publishers.

Berghahn, V.R. (1986) *The Americanisation of West German Industry 1945–1973*, New York: Berg.

Bhaskar, R. (1979) *The Possibility of Naturalism. A Philosophical Critique of the Contemporary Human Sciences*, Brighton: The Harvester Press.

Bieler, A. (2003) 'What future union? The struggle for a social Europe', *Queens Papers on Europeanisation*, 1/2003.

Bieler, A. and Morton, A.D. (2001) 'Introduction: neo-Gramscian perspectives in international political economy and the relevance to European integration', in A. Bieler and A.D. Morton (eds) *Social Forces in the Making of the New Europe*, New York: Palgrave.

Bittlingmayer, G. (1985) 'Did antitrust policy cause the great merger wave?', *Journal of Law and Economics*, 28/1: 77–118.

Blumenthal, W. (2005) 'The status of convergence on transatlantic merger policy. Remarks before the ABA section of international law', paper presented at the program on 'Cross-Atlantic Perspectives on Antitrust Enforcement', October, Brussels.

Böge, U. and Müller, E. (2002) 'From the market dominance test to the SLC Test: are there any reasons for a change?', *European Competition Law Review*, 23/10: 495–8.

Bonefeld, W. (2002) 'European integration: the market, the political and class', *Capital & Class*, 26/2: 117–42.

Borth, W., Frank, H., Frei, W., Lindner, A. and Maier, P. (1986) *Zeiten und Menschen. Vom Zeitalter der bürgerlichen Revolutionen bis zum Zweiten Weltkrieg*, Paderborn, Germany: Verlag Ferdinand Schöning.

Bourdieu, P. (1998) 'Utopia of endless exploitation: the essence of neoliberalism', *Le Monde Diplomatique*, 18 December.

Boyer, R. (1990) *The Regulation School: A Critical Introduction*, New York: Columbia University Press.

Branch, A.P. and Øhrgaard, J.C. (1999) 'Trapped in the supranational-intergovernmental dichotomy: a response to Sweet and Sandholtz', *Journal of European Public Policy*, 6/1: 123–43.

Brenner, N., Peck, J. and Theodore, N. (2010a) 'After neoliberalisation', *Globalizations, 7.*
—— (2010b) 'Variegated neoliberalization: geographies, modalities, pathways', *Global Networks* 10/2: 182–222.
Brenner, S. (2009) 'An empirical study of the European corporate leniency program', *International Journal of Industrial Organization*, 27/6: 639–45.
Bright, C. (1996) 'EU competition policy: rules, objectives and deregulation', *Oxford Journal of Legal Studies*, 16/4: 536–59.
Brittan, L. (1996) 'Investment liberalisation: a new issue for WTO. Europe and the challenge of global economy', speech at the Conference of the Confederation of British Industry, Harrogate, November 1996.
Brittan, L. (2000) 'The early days of merger control', in *EC Merger Control: Ten Years On*, London: International Bar Association.
Brittan, L. and Van Miert, K. (1996) 'Towards an international framework of competition rules. Communication to the Council', *International Business Lawyer*, 24: 454–7.
Bryan, D. and Rafferty, M. (2006) *Capitalism with Derivatives*, New York: Palgrave.
Buch-Hansen (2008) *Rethinking the history of European level merger control. A critical political economy perspective*, CBS PhD Series, 26.
Buch-Hansen, H. and Wigger A. (2010) 'Revisiting fifty years of market-making: the neoliberal transformation of European competition policy', *Review of International Political Economy*, 17/1: 20–44.
—— (forthcoming) 'EU competition policy and the ascendency of neoliberalism', in P. Nousios, H. Overbeek and A. Tsolakis (eds) *Globalisation and European Integration: Critical Approaches to Regional Order and International Relations*, London and New York: Routledge.
Budzinski, O. (2002) 'The International Competition Network and its governance of cross-border mergers. An analysis from the perspective of new institutional economics', paper presented at the 2nd CSI-Conference, Innsbruck, November.
Budzinski, O. (2009) 'Monoculture versus diversity in competition economics', *Cambridge Journal of Economics*, 32/2: 295–324.
Bulmer, S. (1994) 'Institutions and policy change in the European Union: the case of merger control', *Public Administration*, 72/Autumn: 423–44.
Bundeskartellamt (2001) 'Prohibition criteria in merger control – dominant position versus substantial lessening of competition?', discussion paper, October, Bonn.
—— (2003) 'Taking stock of 2003'. Online. Available: <http://www.bundeskartellamt.de/wEnglisch/News/Archiv/ArchivNews2003/2003_12_17.php> (accessed 20 April 2010).
Bundeskartellamt (2005) *The Bundeskartellamt in Bonn. Organisation, Activities and History*, Bonn.
—— (2009) 'Übersicht über die bisherigen Anträge auf Ministererlaubnis nach § 24 Abs. 3/§ 42 GWB'. Online. Available: <http://www.bmwi.de> (accessed 29 April 2009).
Burgess, M. (2000) *Federalism and European Union: The Building of Europe, 1950–2000*, London and New York: Routledge.
Büthe, T. (2007) 'The Politics of Competition in the European Union: the First 50 Years', in S. Meunier and K.R. McNamara (eds) *Making History. European Integration and Institutional Change at Fifty*, Oxford: Oxford University Press.
Buxbaum, H.L. (2006) 'German legal culture and the globalization of competition law: a historical perspective on the expansion of private antitrust enforcement', *Issues in Legal Scholarship*, Article 10. Online. Available: <http://www.bepress.com/ils/iss9/art10> (accessed 21 April 2010).

Cable, J. (1979) 'Merger development and policy in West Germany since 1958', *Warwick Economic Research Papers* 150, Coventry: University of Warwick.

Calvani, T. (2005) 'Conflict, cooperation & convergence in international competition', *Antitrust Law Journal*, 72/3: 1127–46.

Canellos, P.C. and Silber, H.S. (1970) 'Concentration in the common market', *Common Market Law Review*, 7: 5–35, 138–66.

Carchedi, G. (2001) *For Another Europe: A Class Analysis of European Economic Integration*, London, New York: Verso.

CBI (1988) 'Memorandum by the Confederation of British Industry: European merger control', August 1988.

—— (2002) 'The European Commission's Green Paper on Review of Council Regulation (EEC) No.4064/89, December 2001 – CBI response', 28 March 2002. Online. Available: <http://ec.europa.eu/competition/consultations/2002_council_regulation/index.html> (accessed 20 April 2010).

CEO (1999a) 'Amcham chimes in with the Brussels corporate choir', *Corporate Europe Observatory*, 1999/3.

—— (1999b) 'Transatlantic Business Dialogue (TABD): Putting the Business Horse Before the Government Cart', Corporate Europe Observatory briefing paper.

—— (1999c) 'Doing business in Berlin. Transatlantic Business Dialogue Annual Conference 1999', Corporate Europe Observatory, November, CEO special report.

CFI (1999) 'Judgment of the Court of First Instance in *Gencor Ltd v Commission*', Case T-102/96, ECR II-753.

—— (2001) 'Judgment of the Court of First Instance in *Airtours v Commission*', Case T-342/99, ECR II-2585.

Christensen, P., Fountoukakos, K. and Sjöblom, D. (2007) 'Mergers', in J. Faull and A. Nikpay (eds) *The EC Law of Competition*, 2nd edn, Oxford: Oxford University Press.

Cini, M. (2000) 'Administrative culture in the European Commission: the cases of competition and environment', in N. Nugent (ed.) *At the Heart of the Union. Studies of the European Commission*, New York: Macmillan.

—— (2006) 'The Europeanization of British competition policy', in I. Bache and A. Jordan (eds) *The Europeanization of British Politics*, Basingstoke: Palgrave.

Cini, M. and McGowan, L. (1998) *Competition Policy in the European Union*, London: Palgrave Macmillan.

—— (2008) *Competition Policy in the European Union*, 2nd edn, London: Palgrave Macmillan.

Clift, B. (2003) 'The changing political economy of France: *dirigisme* under duress', in Cafruny, A.W. and M. Ryner (eds) *A Ruined Fortress? Neoliberal Hegemony and Transformation in Europe*, Lanham: Rowman & Littlefield Publishers.

Coates, D. (2000) *Models of Capitalism. Growth and Stagnation in the Modern Era*, Cambridge: Polity Press.

Cohen, G.A. (1978) *Karl Marx's Theory of History*, 2000 edn, Oxford: Oxford University Press.

Cook, C. (2008) 'Private enforcement of EU competition policy law in member states courts: experience to date and the path ahead', *Global Competition Policy*, 4/2.

Cowles, M.G. (1995) 'Setting the agenda for a new Europe: the ERT and EC 1992', *Journal of Common Market Studies*, 33/4: 501–26.

—— (2000) 'The Transatlantic Business Dialogue and domestic business government relations', in M. Green-Cowles, T. Risse and J.A. Caporaso (eds) *Transforming Europe: Europeanization and Domestic Change*, Cambridge: Cornell University Press.

—— (2001) 'The Transatlantic Business Dialogue. Transforming the New Transatlantic Dialogue', in M.A. Pollack and G.C. Shaffer (eds) *Transatlantic Governance in a Global Economy*, Cambridge: Rowman and Littlefield.

Cox, R.W. (1987) *Production, Power and World Order*, New York: Columbia University Press.

—— (1994) 'Forum: Hegemony and Social Change', *Mershon International Studies Review*, 38/2: 361–76.

—— (1996) *Approaches to World Order*, Cambridge: Cambridge University Press.

Damro, C. (2006a) *Cooperation on Competition in Transatlantic Economic Relations. The Politics of Dispute Prevention*, New York: Palgrave.

—— (2006b) 'Transatlantic competition policy: domestic and international sources of EU-US Cooperation', *European Journal of International Relations* 12/2: 171–96.

Da Silva, A.G. and Sansom, M. (2009) 'Antitrust implications of the financial crisis: a UK and EU view', *Antitrust*, 23/2: 24–31.

Davies, N. (1996) *Europe. A History*, Cambridge: Oxford University Press.

Dean, K., Joseph, J., Roberts, J.M. and Wight, C. (2006) 'Realism, Marxism and method', in K. Dean, J. Joseph, J.M. Roberts and C. Wight (eds) *Realism, Philosophy and Social Science*, New York: Palgrave.

De Buck, P. (2004) 'Modernising European merger policy: a business view', *Les Petites Affiches*, No. 139.

Deringer, A. (2003) 'Verordnung Nr.17/62 und Verordnung Nr.1/2003 – die historische Perspektive', paper presented at the Seminar 'Ein halbes Jahrhundert Europäisches Wettbewerbsrecht', Brussels, July. Online. Available: <http://www.freshfields.com/practice/comptrade/publications/deringer/de.asp> (accessed 20 April 2010).

DIHK (2006) 'Stellungnahme zum Grünbuch der Europäischen Kommission: Schadenersatzklagen wegen Verletzung des EU-Wettbewerbsrechts'. Online. Available: <http://ec.europa.eu/competition/antitrust/actionsdamages/green_paper_comments.html> (accessed 20 April 2010).

Dinan, D. (1999) *Ever Closer Union. An introduction to European integration*, New York: Palgrave.

Djelic, M.L. (1998) *Exporting the American Model: The Postwar Transformation of European Business*, Cambridge: Oxford University Press.

Djelic, M.L. (2002) 'Does Europe mean Americanization? The case of competition', *Competition and Change*, 6/3: 233–50.

Djelic, M.L. and Kleiner, T. (2003) 'The International Competition Network – illustrating the evolution of transnational governance', in M.L. Djelic and K. Sahlin-Andersson (eds) *Transnational Governance. Institutional Dynamics of Regulation*, Cambridge: Cambridge University Press.

—— (2006) 'The International Competition Network: moving towards transnational governance', in M.L. Djelic, and K. Sahlin-Andersson (eds) *Transnational Governance. Institutional Dynamics of Regulation*, Cambridge: Cambridge University Press.

Dolan, M.B. (1983) 'European restructuring and import policies for a textile industry in crisis', *International Organization*, 37/4: 583–615.

Donohue, T.J. (2003) 'Legal reform press conference of the U.S. Chamber of Commerce'. Online. Available: <http://www.uschamber.com/press/speeches/2003/030918tjd_legalreform.htm> (accessed 20 April 2010).

Dormois, J.P. (2004) *The French Economy in the Twentieth Century*, Cambridge: Cambridge University Press.

Dörn, G.B. and Wilks, S. (1996) *Comparative Competition Policy. National Institutions in a Global Market*, Cambridge: Oxford University Press.

Draghi, M. (2003) 'US-EU regulatory convergence capital markets issues', speech at the Second Meeting of the Transatlantic Strategy Groups, Bertelsmann Foundation, February, Gütersloh.

DTI (1988) 'Memorandum by the Department of Trade and Industry', October 1988, Parliamentary Archives of Westminster.

—— (2002) 'Commission Green Paper on the Review of Council Regulation (EEC) No 4064/89. United Kingdom response', London, March 2002. Online. Available: <http://ec.europa.eu/competition/consultations/2002_council_regulation/index.html> (accessed 8 June 2010).

Dumez, H. and Jeunemaître, A. (1996) 'The convergence of competition policies in Europe: internal dynamics and external imposition', in S. Berger and R. Dore (eds) *National Diversity and Global Capitalism*, Cambridge: Cornell University Press.

ECJ (2001) *Courage v Crehan*, Case C-453/99, ECR I-6297.

—— (2006) *Vincenzo Manfredi and others v Lloyd Adriatico Assicurazioni SpA et al*, Joined cases C-295/04 to C-298/04, ECR I-6619.

Economist (1973), 'Gunning for mergers', August 4.

—— (1988) 'Wanted: a new referee for European fair play', 5 November 1988.

—— (1990) 'A faraway continent of which we need to know more', 8 December.

—— (1993), 'Getting Away With Merger', 12 June.

—— (1994) 'A disquieting new agenda for trade', 16 July.

—— (1995) 'Who ya gonna call?', 5 August.

—— (1996) 'Economics focus: free trade, fettered investment. Should global trade rules treat foreign direct investment in the same way as conventional trade?', 14 September.

—— (2006) 'Freedom fried', 11 February.

EC Summit (1972) 'Final declaration of the conference of the heads of States or of Governments of the member States of the Enlarged Community', *Bulletin of the European Communities*, 10–1972, Paris.

Edwards, J. and Ogilvie, S. (1996) 'The universal banks and German industrialization: a reappraisal', *Economic History Review New Series*, 49/3: 427–46.

EESC (1982) 'Opinion on the amendment to the proposal for a Council Regulation on the control of concentrations', *Official Journal of the European Communities*, C252/15, 27 September 1982.

Eekhoff, J. and Moch, C. (2004) 'Competition – the Core of a Market Economy', in J. Eekhoff (ed.) *Competition Policy in Europe*, Cambridge: Springer.

Ehlermann, C.D. (2000) 'The modernization of EC antitrust policy: a legal and cultural revolution', *Common Market Law Review*, 37: 537–90.

Ehrmann, H.W. (1954) 'The French trade associations and the ratification of the Schuman Plan', *World Politics*, 6/4: 453–81.

Eickhof, N. and Isele, K. (2005) 'Eine Politökonomische Analyse des Einflusses wettbewerbspolitischer Leitbilder auf die Europäische Fusionskontrolle', Volkswirtschaftliche Diskussionsbeiträge, Potsdam: Universität Potsdam.

Erne, R. (2008) *European Unions. Labor's Quest for a Transnational Democracy*, Cambridge: Cornell University Press.

ERT (1988a) 'Merger control: ERT standpoint on the proposed EC regulation', Brussels, 1 June.

—— (1988b) 'Press statement. Merger regulation', Brussels, 15 June.

—— (1993) 'Beating the crisis. A charter for Europe's industrial future', Brussels: European Roundtable of Industrialists.
—— (1994) 'Freedom to compete. Competition policy issues for European business', Brussels: European Roundtable of Industrialists.
—— (1996a) 'Benchmarking for policy-makers. The way to competitiveness, growth and job creation', Brussels: European Roundtable of Industrialists.
—— (1996b) 'Investment in the developing world: new openings and challenges for European industry', Brussels: European Round Table of Industrialists, Brussels: European Roundtable of Industrialists.
—— (2000) 'ERT proposals for reform of EU competition policy', Brussels: European Round Table of Industrialists. Online. Available: <http://www.ert.be/doc/0001.pdf> (accessed 20 April 2010).
—— (2002) 'ERT competition policy task force, response to the "Green Paper on the review of Council Regulation (EEC) No 4064/89" (12 December 2001)'. Online. Available: <http://ec.europa.eu/competition/consultations/2002_council_regulation/index.html> (accessed 8 June 2010).
—— (2003) 'Letter from Alain Joly and Wolfgang Kopf to Mr Mario Monti', 21 November.
—— (2004) 'Building a Political Europe. 50 Proposals For Tomorrow's Europe', Brussels: European Round Table of Industrialists.
—— (2010) 'Challenges in EU competition policy', Brussels, European Round Table of Industrialists. Online. Available: www.ert.be/doc/01721.pdf (accessed 26 May 2010).
ETUC (2002) 'Position of the ETUC on the: Green Paper on the Review of Council Regulation (EEC) No. 4064/89 (presented by the Commission)', Brussels.
Eucken, W. (1938) *Wozu Nationalökonomie?*, Cambridge: Felix Meiner Verlag.
Eucken, W. and Hensel, K.P. (1952) *Grundsätze der Wirtschaftspolitik*, Tübingen: Mohr und Siebeck.
Europe Daily Bulletin (1988), 22 December 1988.
European Commission (1970a) *Industrial Policy in the Community*, Memorandum to the Council, Brussels: European Commission.
—— (1970b) 'Commission Notice of 27 May 1970 concerning agreements, decisions and concerted practices of minor importance which do not fall under Article 85(1) of the Treaty establishing the European Economic Community (De Minimis Notice)', Official Journal C64/1.
—— (1972) *First Report on Competition Policy*, Brussels and Luxembourg: Commission of the European Communities.
—— (1973) 'Proposal for a regulation (EEC) of the Council on the control of concentrations between undertakings', *Official Journal of the European Communities*, C92/1, 31 October 1973.
—— (1974) *Third Report on Competition Policy*, Brussels and Luxembourg: Commission of the European Communities.
—— (1977) *Sixth Report on Competition Policy*, Brussels and Luxembourg: Commission of the European Communities.
—— (1980) *Ninth Report on Competition Policy*, Brussels and Luxembourg: Commission of the European Communities.
—— (1981a) *Tenth Report on Competition Policy*, Brussels and Luxembourg: Commission of the European Communities.

—— (1981b) 'Amended proposal for a Council Regulation on the control of concentrations between undertakings (merger control regulation)', COM(81) 773 final, Brussels, 9 December.

—— (1984) 'Amended Proposal for a Council Regulation on the control of concentrations between undertakings', COM(84) 59 final, Brussels, 3 February 1984.

—— (1985a) *Completing the Internal Market: White Paper of the Commission*, COM(85) 310, Luxembourg: Office of Official Publications of the European Community.

—— (1985b) *Fourteenth Report on Competition Policy*, Brussels and Luxembourg: Commission of the European Communities.

—— (1986) 'Commission Decision of 23 April 1986 relating to a proceeding under Article 85 of the EEC Treaty (IV/31.149 – Polypropylene)', *Official Journal* L230/1.

—— (1988) *Seventeenth Report on Competition Policy*, Brussels and Luxembourg: Commission of the European Communities.

—— (1989) *Eighteenth Report on Competition Policy*, Brussels and Luxembourg: Commission of the European Communities.

—— (1991) 'Agreement between the European Communities and the government of the United States of America regarding the application of their competition laws', *Official Journal* (L 95 of 27.04.1995).

—— (1992) *Twenty-first Report on Competition Policy*, Brussels and Luxembourg: Commission of the European Communities.

—— (1994a) 'Court judgments: case 327/91 Judgment of the Court 9 August 1994 agreement between the Commission and the United States Regarding the application of their competition laws', *EC Competition Policy Newsletter* 1/3.

—— (1994b) *EC Competition Policy Newsletter*, 1/Spring.

—— (1995) *Competition Policy in the New Trade Order: Strengthening International Cooperation and Rules*, Brussels.

—— (1996a) *Green Paper on the Review of the Merger Regulation*, COM(96) 19 final, Brussels.

—— (1996b) 'XXVIth Report on Competition Policy. Part Three', Brussels: DG Competition.

—— (1999) *White Paper on the Modernisation of the Rules Implementing Articles 81 and 82 of the EC Treaty*, COM(99), 027, Brussels.

—— (2000) *Report from the Commission to the Council on the Application of the Merger Regulation Thresholds*, COM(2000) 399 Final, Brussels.

—— (2001a) 'Commission unveiled EU scoreboard on state aid', Press Release IP/01/1032, Brussels, 19July.

—— (2001b) *Green Paper on the Review of Council Regulation (EEC), No 4064/89*, COM(216701) 745/6, Brussels.

—— (2002) 'Commission adopts comprehensive reform of EU merger control', Press Release IP/02/1856, Brussels.

—— (2004) 'Communication from the Commission to the Council and the European Parliament. The EU approach to the Millennium Round: Summary'. Online. Available: <http://trade.ec.europa.eu/doclib/docs/2006/december/tradoc_111111.pdf> (accessed 20 April 2010).

—— (2005a) 'State aid: Commission outlines comprehensive five year reform of state aid policy to promote growth, jobs and cohesion', Press Release IP/05/680, Brussels, 7 June.

—— (2005b) *Green Paper on Damages Actions for Breach of the EC Antitrust Rules*, COM (2005) 672, Brussels.

—— (2006a) 'Comments on Green Paper'. Online. Available: <http://ec.europa.eu/competition/antitrust/actionsdamages/green_paper_comments.html> (accessed 20 April 2010).

—— (2006b) 'The Trans-Atlantic Business Dialogue (TABD). Entrepreneurial diplomacy between EU and US business and governments'. Online. Available: <http://ec.europa.eu/enterprise/enterprise_policy/business_dialogues/tabd/thetabd.htlm> (accessed 2 January 2008).

—— (2006c) *Global Europe: Competing in the World. A Contribution to the EU's Growth and Jobs Strategy*, DG External Trade, Brussels.

—— (2007a) 'State aid: latest scoreboard analyses harm done by illegal aid', press release IP/07/955, Brussels, 28 June.

—— (2007b) *Report: State Aid Scoreboard*, COM(2007) 347 final, Brussels, 28 June.

—— (2008) *White Paper on Damages Actions for Breach of the EC Antitrust Rules*, COM(2008) 165, Brussels.

—— (2009a) 'Comments on White Paper'. Online. Available: <http://ec.europa.eu/competition/antitrust/actionsdamages/white_paper_comments.htm> (accessed 20 April 2010).

—— (2009b) '*State Aid Scoreboard, Spring 2009 Update. Special Edition on State Aid Interventions in the Current Financial and Economic Crisis*', COM(2009) 164, Brussels.

—— (2009c) 'Temporary community framework for state aid measures to support access to finance in the current financial and economic crisis', 2009/C83/01. Online. Available: <http://ec.europa.eu/competition/state_aid/reform/reform.html> (accessed 20 April 2010).

—— (2009d) 'Competition and Financial Markets. Roundtable 3 on Real Economy: The Challenges for Competition Policy in Periods of Retrenchment', OECD, DAF/COMP/WD(2009)12/ADD2, 10 February.

—— (2010a) *Europe 2020. A European Strategy for Smart, Sustainable and Inclusive Growth*. Online. Available: <http://ec.europa.eu/eu2020/index_en.htm> (accessed 26 May 2010).

—— (2010b) 'Cartel Statistics. Situation as of 19 May 2010'. Online. Available: <http://ec.europa.eu/competition/cartels/statistics/statistics.pdf> (accessed 16 June 2010).

—— (2010c) 'Merger Statistics. 21 September 1990 to 31 May 2010'. Online. Available: <http://ec.europa.eu/competition/mergers/statistics.pdf> (accessed 16 June 2010).

European Council (1962) 'EEC Council Regulation No 17: First Regulation implementing Articles 85 and 86 of the Treaty', *Official Journal*, P 013, 21/02/1962.

—— (1963) *European Yearbook / Annuaire Européen, Volume 11, 1963 Council of Europe*, Cambridge: Martinus Nijhoff Publishers.

—— (2000) 'Presidency conclusions', Lisbon European Council, 23 and 24 March.

European Parliament (1974) 'Debates of the European Parliament. Regulation on the control of concentrations between undertakings (vote)', *Official Journal of the European Communities*, 171/February: 70–83.

—— (2003a) 'Debate in the Parliament over the Report by Mr Della Vedova'. Online. Available: <http://www.futurdeleurope.parlament.gv.at/sides/getDoc.do?pubRef=-//EP//TEXT+CRE+20031008+ITEM-011+DOC+XML+V0//EN&language=HU> (accessed 20 April 2010).

—— (2003b) 'European Parliament legislative resolution on the proposal for a Council regulation on the control of concentrations between undertakings: "the EC merger regulation" (COM(2002) 711 – C5-0005/2003 – 2002/0296(CNS))', Brussels, October.

EU Observer (2004) 'France calls on EU to support "industrial champions" ', 30 August.

Evenett, S.J. (2003) 'The cross border mergers and acquisitions wave of the late 1990s', *NBER Working Paper, W9655*.

Eyre, S. and Lodge, M. (2000) 'National tunes and a European melody? Competition law reform in the UK and Germany', *Journal of European Public Policy*, 7/1: 63–79.

Fear, J. (2006) 'Cartels and competition: neither markets nor hierarchies', *Working Paper Harvard Business School*, 07/11.

Feldenkirchen, W. (1992) 'Competition policy in Germany', *Business and Economic History*, 21/2: 257–69.

Fennema, M. (1982) *International Networks of Banks and Industry*, The Hague: Martinus Nijhoff Publishers.

Financial Times (1982) 'Brussels at odds with Bonn over steel aid', 23 December.

—— (1985) 'Brussels Takes Aim at Restrictive Practices. The Competition Commissioner Talks to Paul Cheesright', 27 March.

—— (1987) 'A Skilful Run for the Line. William Dawkins Meets Peter Sutherland. European Commissioner for Competition Policy', 28 September.

—— (1989) 'Brussels Flexes Its Muscles to Take a Swing At State Subsidies', 20 November.

—— (1991) 'International Mergers & Acquisitions: Directive Attacked', 18 November.

—— (1992a) 'Bangemann hits out at competition "ayatollahs" ', 11 February.

—— (1992b) 'EC Merger regime defies expectations of critics', 3 September.

—— (1992c) 'Competition and GATT', Editorial, 4 February.

—— (1993a) 'Commissioner Aims to Broaden Scope of EC Competition Policy', 15 January.

—— (1993b) 'Van Miert Calls for GATT Rules on Business Barriers', 9 October.

—— (1996a) 'The Threat from Without: The FT Interview Helmut Maucher', 29 October.

—— (1996b) 'US, EU Closer on Telecoms and IT Accord', 11 November.

—— (1997) 'Boeing Warns of Trade War if Merger is Blocked', 14 May.

—— (1998) 'No Monopoly on Antitrust: Personal View', 13 February.

—— (2000) 'Protests Make a Mark on World Trade Leaders', 20 November.

—— (2001) 'Corporate Chiefs Call For Cheaper Antitrust Process', 17 May.

—— (2002a) 'Monti's trials: Europe's competition commissioner faces a barrage of criticism from governments, companies and judges', 13 June.

—— (2002b) 'Monti unveils "business-friendly" merger reform', 12 December.

—— (2002c) 'Shaping industry on the anvil of Europe', 29 April.

—— (2004) 'Let the market choose Europe's champions', 14 June.

—— (2006a) 'Welcome to the world of block-thy-neighbour', 4 March.

—— (2006b) 'France in new moves to defend companies', 2 March.

—— (2006c) 'Bank merger battle grows as Brussels warns Poland', 9 March.

—— (2006d) 'India asks Chirac to be fair to Mittal', 21 February.

—— (2006e) 'UK Minister slams French protectionism', 1 February.

—— (2007a) 'Dismay over competition shift', 22 June.

—— (2007b) 'Deal volumes suffer sharp fall', 21 December.

—— (2007c) 'The deals they don't like', 20 April.

—— (2007d) 'A losing battle to defend champions', 20 April.

—— (2007e) 'Kroes vows to maintain "firm and fair" line on competition', 25 June.

—— (2008) 'GDF Suez merger overcomes two years of political roadblocks and diversions', 17 July.

Flinders, M. (2006) 'Public/private: the boundaries of the state', in C. Hay, M. Lister and D. Marsh (eds) *The State. Theories and Issues*, New York: Palgrave.

Foster, J.B. (2009) *The Ecological Revolution. Making Peace with the Planet*, New York: Monthly Review Press.

Foster, J.B. and Magdoff, F. (2009) *The Great Financial Crisis. Causes and Consequences*. New York: Monthly Review Press.

Fox, E.M. (2003) 'We protect competition, you protect competitors', *World Competition*, 26/2: 149–65.

Freyer, T.A. (2006) *Antitrust and Global Capitalism, 1930–2004*, Cambridge: Cambridge University Press.

FRG (1999) 'Statement by the government of the Federal Republic of Germany on the White Paper of the European Commission on the modernisation of the rules implementing articles 81 and 82 of the EC Treaty'. Online. Available: <http://www.bundeskartellamt.de/wEnglisch/download/pdf/StellungBReg.pdf> (accessed 20 April 2010).

Gallo, J.C., Dau-Schmidt, K., Craycraft, J.L. and Parker, C.J. (2000) 'Department of Justice antitrust enforcement, 1955–1997: an empirical study', *Review of Industrial Organization*, 17/1: 75–133.

Garnier, A. and Asselineau, C. (1991) 'Merger control in France', in S. Cromie (ed.) *Merger Control in Europe*, Cambridge: IFR Publishing Ltd.

Gavil, A.I., Gavil, A.I. and Baker, J.B. (2002) *Antitrust Law in Perspective: Cases, Concepts and Problems in Competition Policy*, American Casebook Series, New York: Thomson West.

Gaughan, P.A. (2002) *Mergers, Acquisitions, and Corporate Restructurings*, New York: John Wiley & Sons, Inc.

Gehler, M. and Von der Gröben, H. (2002) 'Europäische Integration aus historischer Erfahrung. Ein Zeitzeugengespräch mit Michael Gehler/Hans von der Gröben', *Zentrum für Europäische Integrationsforschung Discussion Paper*, Cambridge: Rheinische Friedrich-Wilhelms-Universität.

George, K. (1990) 'UK competition policy: issues and institutions', in W.S. Comanor, K. George, A. Jacquemin, F. Jenny, E. Kanzenbach, J.A. Ofrover and L. Waverman (eds) *Competition Policy in Europe and North America. Economic Issues and Institutions*, Cambridge: Harwood Academic Publishers.

Gerber, D.J. (1998) *Law and Competition in Twentieth Century Europe. Protecting Prometheus*, New York/Oxford: Clarendon Press.

Geroski, P.A. (1989) 'European industrial policy and industrial policy in Europe', *Oxford Review of Economic Policy*, 5/2: 20–36.

Giersch, H. (1985) 'Eurosclerosis', *Kiel Discussion Papers* 112.

Gill, S. and Law, D. (1989) 'Global hegemony and the structural power of capital', *International Studies Quarterly*, 33/4: 475–99.

Gillingham, J. (2003) *European Integration, 1950–2003*, Cambridge: Cambridge University Press.

Giocoli, N. (2009) 'Competition versus property rights: American antitrust law, the Freiburg school, and the early years of European competition policy', *Journal of Competition Law & Economics*, 00/0: 1–40.

Glyn, A., Hughes, A., Lipietz, A. and Singh, A. (1990) 'The rise and fall of the golden age', in S.A. Marglin and J.B. Schor (eds) *The Golden Age of Capitalism. Reinterpreting the Postwar Experience*, Cambridge: Clarendon Press.

Goddard, C.R. (2003) 'Defining the transnational cooperation in the era of globalization', in C.R. Goddard, P. Cronin and K.C. Dash (eds) *International Political*

Economy. State Market Relations in a Changing Global Order, 2nd edn, London: Palgrave Macmillan.

Gourevitch, P. (1986) *Politics in Hard Times. Comparative Responses to International Economic Crises*, Cambridge: Cornell University Press.

Goyder, D.G. (1993) *EEC Competition Law*, 2nd edn, Oxford: Clarendon Press.

—— (2003) *EEC Competition Law*, 4th edn, Oxford: Clarendon Press.

Gramsci, A. (1971) *Selections from Prison Notebooks*, Cambridge: Lawrence and Wishart.

Grant, C. (1994) *Delors: Inside the House that Jacques Built*, Cambridge: Nicholas Brealey Publishing Ltd.

Gray, S.J. and McDermott, M.C. (1989) *Mega-Merger Mayhem. Takeover Strategies, Battles and Controls*, Cambridge: Paul Chapman Publishing.

Gutteridge, T. (2000) 'European Round Table (ERT): Agenda setting for the EU', *Corporate Watch*, 12/Autumn: 16–18.

Haas, E.B. (1958) *The Uniting of Europe. Political, social, and economic forces 1950–1957*, Cambridge: Stanford University Press.

Hager, W. (1987) 'Political Implications of US-EC Economic Conflicts (II): Atlantic Trade: Problems and Prospects', *Government and Opposition*, 22/1: 49–63.

Hall, P. (1986) *Governing the Economy. The Politics of State Intervention in Britain and France*, Cambridge: Polity Press.

Hall, P. and Soskice, D. (eds) (2001) *Varieties of Capitalism: The Institutional Foundations of Comparative Advantage*, Cambridge: Oxford University Press.

Harding, C. and Joshua, J. (2003) *Regulating Cartels in Europe: A Study of Legal Control of Corporate Delinquency*, Cambridge: Oxford University Press.

Hardt, M. and Negri, A. (2009) *Commonwealth*, Cambridge, MA: Harvard University Press.

Harris, J. (2006) *The Dialectics of Globalization. Economic and Political Conflict in a Transnational World*, Newcastle Upon Tyne: Cambridge Scholars Publishing.

Harrison, R.J. (1974) *Europe in Question: Theories of Regional International Integration*, Cambridge: George Allen & Unwin.

Harvey, D. (2005) *A Brief History of Neoliberalism*, Cambridge: Oxford University Press.

—— (2010) *The Enigma of Capital. And the crises of capitalism*, Cambridge: Profile Books.

Hassel, A. and Beyer, J. (2001) 'The Effects of Convergence: Internationalisation and the Changing Distribution of Net Value Added in Large German Firms', *MPIfG Discussion Paper*, 7/1.

Hattersley, R. (1978) *A Review of Monopolies and Mergers Policy. A Consultative Document*, presented to the Parliament by the Secretary of State for Prices and Consumer Protection by Command of Her Majesty, London.

Hauser, T. (1997) 'Testimony before the House Committee on ways and means, hearing on the New Transatlantic Agenda', Washington, D.C., July. Online. Available: <http://comm-docs.house.gov/committees/ways/hwmw105-20.000/hwmw105-20_0f.htm> (accessed 20 April 2010).

Hay, C. (1996) *Re-Stating Social and Political Change*, Buckingham and Philadelphia: Open University Press.

—— (2002) *Political Analysis. A Critical Introduction*, New York: Palgrave.

Hay, C., Lister, M. and Marsh, D. (eds) (2006) *The State. Theories and Issues*, New York: Palgrave.

Hay, C. and Rosamond, B. (2002) 'Globalization, European integration, and the discursive construction of economic imperatives', *Journal of European Public Policy*, 9/2: 147–67.

Hayward, J.E.S. (1995) *Industrial Enterprise and European Integration. From National to International Champions in Western Europe*, Oxford: Oxford University Press.

Heall (2005) 'Abuse of codex alimentarius cartel and the Berlin tribunal ... Can we stop it?'. Online. Available: <http://www.heall.com/medicalfreedom/codexabuse.html> (accessed 7 August 2007).

Hildebrand, D. (2002) 'The European school in EC competition law', *World Competition*, 25/1: 3–23.

Hix, S. (1999) *The Political System of The European Union*, Cambridge: Macmillan.

Hobsbawm, E. (1994) *Age of Extremes: The Short Twentieth Century 1914–91*, Cambridge: Michael Joseph.

Hoeren, T. (1999) 'Europäisches Kartellrecht zwischen Verbots- und Mißbrauchsprinzip. Überlegungen zur Entstehungsgeschichte des Art. 85 EGV', in U. Hübner (ed.), *Festschrift für Bernhard Großfeld*, Heidelberg.

Hoffmann, S. (1982) 'Reflections on the Nation–State in Western Europe Today', *Journal of Common Market Studies*, 21/Nos 1,2: 21–37.

Holman, O. (2004) 'Asymmetrical regulation and multidimensional governance in the European Union', *Review of International Political Economy*, 11/4: 714–35.

Holt, N. (2000) '2,000 march in Chicago against summit of CEOs', *Asheville Global Report*, Online. Available: <http://www.agrnews.org/issues/200/nationalnews.html#nation1> (accessed 20 April 2010).

Horn, L. (2009) *Corporate Governance Regulation in the European Union – Towards a Marketisation of Corporate Control*, Dissertation, Vrije Universiteit Amsterdam.

Horn, R. von and Mirowski, P. (2009) 'Reinventing monopoly and the role of corporations: Chicago School of Law and Economics', in P. Mirowski and D. Plewhe (eds) *The Road from Mont Pèlerin: The Making of the Neoliberal Thought Collective*, Harvard: Harvard University Press.

House of Lords (1974) 'Report of Sub-Committee "B" (Trade and Treaties)', Report E/B/74-5/1, Parliamentary Archives of Westminster.

House of Lords (1989) 'Examination of witnesses', Select Committee on the European Communities, 17 January, Parliamentary Archives of Westminster.

—— (2003) 'Debate in the European Standing Committee C'. Online. Available: <http://www.publications.parliament.uk/pa/cm200203/cmstand/euroc/st031110/31110s02.htm> (accessed 20 April 2010).

Hudson, R. (2003) 'European integration and new forms of uneven development', *European Urban and Regional Studies*, 10/1, 49–67.

—— (2005) *Economic Geographies*, Cambridge: Sage.

Hussein, K. and Wright, K. (2009) 'Bringing regulatory processes back in: the reform of EU Antitrust and merger control', *West European Politics*, 32/4: 738–55.

ICC (1997) 'Policy statement ICC comments on EU-US positive comity agreement law and practices relating to competition', 12 March. Online. Available: <http://www.iccwbo.org/id370/index.html> (accessed 19 June 2010).

—— (1999a) 'Letter to the International Competition Policy Advisory Committee from ICC'. 21 May 1999. Online. Available: <http://www.iccwbo.org/home/competition/letter_icpac.asp> (accessed 2 January 2008).

—— (1999b) 'Recommendations to the International Competition Policy Advisory Committee (ICPAC). Online. Available: <http://www.iccwbo.org/home/statements_rules/statements/1999/icpac_confidential_info.aspht> (accessed 2 January 2008).

ICPAC (2000) *Final Report*, United States Department of Justice. Online. Available: <http://www.justice.gov/atr/icpac/finalreport.htm> (accessed 19 June 2010).

International Business Times (2006) 'Acquisitions made in 2006 set new records', 22 November.

International Herald Tribune (2004) 'France-China deals awaken Europeans', 11 October.

IoD (1988) 'Memorandum by the Institute of Directors', December. Parliamentary Archives of Westminster.

Irish Delegation (2002) 'Response of the Irish delegation to the merger Green Paper'. Online. Available: <http://ec.europa.eu/competition/consultations/2002_council_regulation/index.html> (accessed 8 June 2010).

James, C.A. (2001) 'Reconciling divergent enforcement policies: where do we go from here?', speech at the 28th Annual Conference on International Law and Policy, Fordham Corporate Law Institute, New York. October. Online. Available: <http://www.usdoj.gov/atr/public/speeches/9395.pdf> (accessed 20 April 2010).

Janssen, B.D. (2000) 'The Pacc of economic change in Europe', speech at the Annual Meeting of the Trilateral Commission, Tokyo. Online. Available: <http://www.trilateral.org> (accessed 20 April 2010).

Jenny, F. (1990) 'French competition policy in perspective', in W.S. Comanor, K. George, A. Jacquemin, F. Jenny, E. Kanzenbach, J.A. Ofrover and L. Waverman (eds) *Competition Policy in Europe and North America: Economic Issues and Institutions*, London: Harwood Academic Publishers.

Jenny, F. and Weber, A.P. (1975) 'French antitrust legislation: an exercise in futility?', *The Antitrust Bulletin*, 20.

Jessop, B. (1990) *State Theory. Putting the Capitalist State in its Place*, Cambridge: Polity Press.

—— (1997) 'Capitalism and its future: remarks on regulation, government and governance', *Review of International Political Economy*, 4/3: 561–81.

—— (2000) 'The crisis of the national spatio-temporal fix and the tendential ecological dominance of globalizing capitalism', *International Journal of Urban and Regional Research*, 24/2: 323–60.

—— (2002a) *The Future of the Capitalist State*, Cambridge: Polity.

—— (2002b) 'Capitalism, the regulation approach, and critical realism', in A. Brown, S. Fleetwood and J.M. Roberts (eds) *Critical Realism and Marxism*, London and New York: Routledge.

—— (2005) 'Critical realism and the Strategic-Relational Approach', *New Formations*, 56/Autumn: 40–53.

—— (2006) 'The third way: neo-liberalism with a human face?', Lancaster E-prints, also published in *New Labour und die Modernisierung Großbritanniens*, Augsburg: Wissener Verlag.

—— (2009) 'A Return to "Business as Usual"? Asa Globalog'. Online. Available: <http://blog.theasa.org/?p=226> (accessed 21 May 2010).

Jessop, B. and Sum, N.-L. (2006) *Beyond the Regulation Approach*, Cornwalls: Edward Elgar Publishing.

Johnson, D. and Turner, C. (2006) *European Business*, London and New York: Routledge.

Karagiannis, J.A. (2004) 'Ein Keim, der wachsen muß. German antitrust as the first Europeanised policy (1950–1957)'. Online. Available: <http://www.epsnet.org/2004/pps/Karagiannis.pdf> (accessed 8 April 2010).

Kemper, B. (2004) 'Private enforcement of EU and national competition law', paper presented at the European Competition Day, October, Amsterdam.

Kenworthy, L. (2008) 'Are industrial policy and corporatism compatible?', *Journal of Public Policy*, 10/3: 233–65.

Klein, J. (2000) 'Time for a global competitive initiative?', presented at the EC Merger Control 10th Anniversary Conference, September, Brussels.

Klein, J. (2002) 'Expanding Our Web of Bilateral Agreements', in C.A. Jones and M. Matsushita (eds) *Competition in the Global Trading System*, Dordrecht, The Netherlands: Kluwer Law International.

Klein, N. (2007) *The Shock Doctrine. The Rise of Disaster Capitalism*, London: Penguin Books.

Kniazhinsky, V. (1984) *West European Integration: its policies and international relations*, Moscow: Progress Publishers.

Knudsen, D.C. (1996) *The Transition to Flexibility*, Dordrecht: Kluwer Academic Publishers.

Kolasky, W.J. (2002a) 'Comparative merger control analysis: six guiding principles for antitrust agencies – new and old.' Online. Available: <http://149.101.1.32/atr/public/speeches/10845.htm>(accessed 20 April 2010).

Kolasky, W.J. (2002b) 'US and EU competition policy. Cartels, mergers and beyond.' Online. Available: <www.usdoj.gov/atr/public/speeches/9848.pdf> (accessed 20 April 2010).

Kon, S.D. (1980) 'The delicate balance between municipal law and community law in the application of articles 85 and 86 of the Treaty of Rome', in L. Hurwitz (ed.) *Contemporary Perspectives on European Integration. Attitudes, Nongovernmental Behaviour, and Collective Decision Making,* London: Aldwych Press.

Kroes, N. (2005a) 'Taking competition seriously – anti-trust reform in Europe', speech 05/157, at the International Bar Association/European Commission Conference, Brussels, March.

—— (2005b) 'Effective competition policy – a key tool for delivering the Lisbon strategy', speech 05/73 at the EMAC Open Meeting of Coordinators, Brussels, February.

—— (2005c) 'Building a competitive Europe – competition policy and the relaunch of the Lisbon strategy', speech 5/78, at the conference at Bocconi University, Milan, February.

—— (2007) 'European competition policy in a changing world and globalised economy: fundamentals, new objectives and challenges ahead', speech at the GCLC/College of Europe Conference on '50 years of EC Competition Law', Brussels, June.

—— (2009a) 'Lessons learned from the economic crisis. Address to Committee on Economic and Monetary Affairs, European Parliament', Brussels, September.

—— (2009b) 'Competition law in an economic crisis', speech 09/385 at the 13th Annual Competition Conference of the International Bar Association, Fiesole, September.

—— (2009c) 'Tackling cartels – a never-ending task', speech 09/454 at the Anti-Cartel Enforcement: Criminal and Administrative Policy, Brasilia, October.

Kryda, G.M. (2002) 'The competition criterion in British merger control policy', *Policy Studies Journal*, 30/2: 252–69.

Laurent, P.-H. (1970) 'Paul-Henri Spaak and the diplomatic origins of the common market 1955–1956', *Political Science Quarterly*, 85/3: 373–96.

Lee, J.S. (2005) 'Towards a development-oriented multilateral framework on competition policy', *Bepress Legal Series*, 785: 1–22.

Lee, M. and Morand, C. (2003) *Competition Policy in the WTO and FTAA: A Trojan Horse for International Trade Negotiations?*, Ottawa: Canadian Centre for Policy Alternatives.

Letwin, W. (1981) *Law and Economic Policy in America: The Evolution of the Sherman Antitrust Act*, Chicago: University of Chicago Press.

Leucht, B. (2009) 'Transatlantic policy networks in the creation of the first European anti-trust law: mediating between American anti-trust and German ordo-liberalism', in W. Kaiser, B. Leucht, and M. Rasmussen (eds) *The History of The European Union. Origins of A Trans- And Supranational Polity, 1950–72*, London and New York: Routledge.

Leucht, B. and Seidel, K. (2007) 'Ruptures and continuities in European competition policy, 1950–1962', paper presented at the Conference on European Competition Policy 1930–2007 at the University Paris IV-Sorbonne, Paris, September.

Levy, N. (2005) 'Mario Monti's legacy in EC merger control', *Competition Policy International*, 1/1: 99–132.

Lindblom, C.E. (1977) *Politics and Markets*, New York: Harper Colophon.

Link, W. (1978) *Deutsche und amerikanische Gewerkschaften und Geschäftsleute, 1945–1975. Eine Studie über transnationale Beziehungen*, Düsseldorf: Droste.

Lipietz, A. (1983) *The Enchanted World. Inflation, Credit and the World Crisis*, London: Verso.

—— (1992) *Towards a New Economic Order. Postfordism, Ecology and Democracy*, Cambridge: Polity Press.

Litan, R.E. and Shapiro, C. (2001) 'Antitrust policy and the Clinton administration', *Center for Competition Policy Working Paper*, CPC01-22.

Lovett, A.W. (1996) 'The United States and the Schuman Plan. A study in French diplomacy 1950–1952', *The Historical Journal*, 39/2: 425–55.

Lowe, P. (2009) 'Competition Policy and the Global Economic Crisis', *Competition Policy International*, 5/2: 1–24.

Lynch, F.M.B. (1984) 'Resolving the paradox of the Monnet Plan. National and international planning in French reconstruction', *The Economic History Review*, 37/2: 229–43.

Lyons, B.R. (2004) 'Reform of European merger policy', *Review of International Economics*, 12/2: 246–61.

McGowan, L. (1996) 'Unmasking a federal agency: the European Commission's control of competition policy', *European Business Review*, 96/5: 13–26.

—— (2005) 'Europeanization unleashed and rebounding: assessing the modernisation of EU cartel policy', *Journal of European Public Policy*, 12/6: 986–1004.

—— (2007a) 'Theorising European integration: revisiting neo-functionalism and testing its suitability for explaining the development of EC competition policy?', *European Integration Online Papers*, 11/3.

—— (2007b) 'In Search of theoretical explanations: Reflections on the European Commission's Fifty Year War against Cartels', paper presented at the International Conference on European Competition Policy 1930–2005, Paris, 14–15 September 2007.

McGowan, L. and Cini, M. (1999) 'Discretion and politization in EU competition policy: the case of merger control', *Governance: An International Journal of Policy and Administration*, 12/2: 175–200.

McGowan, L. and Wilks, S. (1995) 'The first supranational policy in the European Union: competition policy', *European Journal of Political Research*, 28/2: 141–69.

McLachlan, D.L. and Swann, D. (1967a) *Competition Policy in the European Community. The rules in Theory and Practice*, Oxford: Oxford University Press.

—— (1967b) *Concentration or Competition. A European Dilemma?*, London: Chatham House.

McNulty, P. (1968) 'Economic theory and the meaning of competition', *Quarterly Journal of Economics*, 72/November: 639–56.

Maher, I. (2000) 'Re-imagining the story of European competition law', *Oxford Journal of Legal Studies*, 20/1: 155–66.

Martinez Torre-Enciso, I. and Bilbao Garcia, J. (1996) 'Mergers and acquisition trends in Europe', *International Advances in Economic Research*, 2/3: 279–86.

Marx, K. (1965[1887]) *Capital, Vol. 1*, Moscow: Progress Publishers.

—— (1966[1894]) *Capital, Vol. III*, Moscow: Progress Publishers.

—— (2006[1891]) *Wage Labour and Capital, Value, Price and Profit*, United States of America: International Publishers Co.

Mazey, S. (1996) 'The development of the European idea: from sectoral integration to political union', in J. Richardson (ed.) *European Union. Power and Policy-Making*, London and New York: Routledge.

Menon, A. and Hayward, J. (1996) 'States, industrial policies and the European Union', in H. Kassim and A. Menon (eds) *The European Union and National Industrial Policy*, London and New York: Routledge, 267–90.

Messina Declaration (1955) *The Messina Declaration*. Online. Available: <http://www.eccfp.edu.mk/files/rezultati/The_Messina_Declaration_1955_EN_pdf.pdf> (accessed 8 April 2010).

Michalet, C.-A. (1974) 'France', in R. Vernon (ed.) *Big Business and the State*, Cambridge, MA: Harvard University Press.

Milward, A. (2000) *The European Rescue of the Nation-State*, 2nd edn, London and New York: Routledge.

Mirowski P. and D. Plewhe (eds) (2009) *The Road from Mont Pèlerin. The Making of the Neoliberal Thought Collective.* Harvard: Harvard University Press.

Monnet, J. (1950) 'Memorandum to Robert Schuman', Paris, 30 November 1950. Online. Available: <http://www.ena.lu/mce.cfm> (accessed 8 April 2010).

—— (1978) *Memoirs*, New York: Doubleday & Company, Inc.

Monti, G. (2007) *EC Competition Law*, Cambridge: Cambridge University Press.

Monti, M. (2002a) 'Merger control in the European Union. A radical reform', speech 02/545 at the European Commission/IBA Conference on EU Merger Control, Brussels.

—— (2002b) 'Cooperation between competition authorities. A vision for the future', in C. Jones and M. Matsushita (eds) *Competition Policy in the Global Trading System*, The Hague: Kluwer Law International.

—— (2003) 'EU competition policy after May 2004', speech 03/489 at the Fordham Annual Conference on International Antitrust Law and Policy, New York.

—— (2004a) 'The EU gets new competition powers for the 21st century', *Competition Policy Newsletter* Special Edition.

—— (2004b) 'Private litigation as a key complement to public enforcement of competition rules and the first conclusions on the implementation of the new merger regulation', speech 04/403 at the 8th IBA Annual Competition Conference, Fiesole.

—— (2004c) 'International antitrust – a personal perspective', speech 04/449 at the Fordham Corporate Law Institute.

Moravcsik, A. (1998) *The Choice for Europe: Social Purpose and State Power from Messina to Maastricht*, New York: Cornell University Press.

Morgan, E.J. (2001) 'A decade of EC merger control', *International Journal of the Economics of Business*, 8/3: 451–73.

Morgan, G. (2005) 'Transnational actors, transnational institutions, transnational spaces: the role of law firms in the internationalization of competition regulations', *CSGR Working Paper* 167/05: 1–28.

Möschel, W. (2001) 'The proper scope of government viewed from an ordoliberal perspective: the example of competition policy', *Journal of Institutional and Theoretical Economics*, 157: 3–13.

Moschonas, A. (1996) 'The logic of European integration', in G.A. Kourvetaris and A. Moschonas (eds) *The Impact of European Integration. Political, Sociological and Economic Changes*, London: Praeger.

Motta, M. (2004) *Competition Policy. Theory and Practice*, Cambridge: Cambridge University Press.

Mueller, D.C. (1997) 'Merger Policy in the United States: A Reconsideration', *Review of Industrial Organization*, 12: 655–685.

Murray, A. (2004) *A Fair Referee? The European Commission and EU Competition Policy*, London: Centre for European Reform.

Neumann, F. (1942) *Behemoth. The Structure and Function of National Socialism 1933–1944*, New York: Oxford University Press.

Neumann, M. (2001) *Competition Policy. History, Theory and Practice*, Cheltenham: Edward Elgar.

Neven, D., Seabright, P. and Papandropoulos, P. (1998) *Trawling for Minnows: European Competition Policy and Agreements Between Firms*, London: Centre for Economic Policy Research.

Nogués, P. (2009) 'France: the new French competition authority'. Online. Available: <www.mondaq.com> (accessed 20 April 2010).

OECD (1967) *Recommendation on Cooperation between Member Countries on Restrictive Business Practices Affecting International Trade*, Paris.

—— (2005) 'Competition Law and Policy in the European Union', Country Studies, Report prepared by M. Wise for the OECD. Paris.

Ollman, B. (2003) *Dance of the Dialectic. Steps in Marx's Method*, Chicago: University of Illinois Press.

Ougaard, M. (2004) *Political Globalization. State, Power and Social Forces*, New York: Palgrave.

Overbeek, H. (1990) *Global Capitalism and National Decline*, London: Unwin Hyman.

—— (2000) 'Globalisation and Britain's Decline', in R. English and M. Kenny (eds) *Rethinking British Decline*, London: Macmillan.

—— (2002) 'Globalisation and governance. Contradictions of neo-liberal migration management', *HWWA Discussion Paper*, 174, Hamburg Institute of International Economics.

—— (2004) 'Transnational class formation and concepts of control: towards a genealogy of the Amsterdam project in international political economy', *Journal of International Relations and Development*, 7/2: 113–41.

Overbeek, H. and Van der Pijl, K. (1993) 'Restructuring capital and restructuring hegemony: neoliberalism and the unmaking of the post-war order', in H. Overbeek (ed.) *Restructuring Hegemony in the Global Political Economy*, London and New York: Routledge.

Paines, A. and Reynolds, M. (1988) 'United Kingdom', in *Merger Control in the EEC*, Deventer: Kluwer Law.

Patomäki, H. (2002) *After International Relations. Critical Realism and the (Re)Construction of World Politics*, London and New York: Routledge.

Pedersen, K.R. (1996) 'Re-educating European management: the Marshall Plan's campaign against restrictive business practices in France, 1949–53', *Business and Economic History*, 25/1: 267–74.

Piening, C. (1997) *Global Europe: The European Union in World Affairs,* London: Lynne Rienner.

Pitofsky, R. (1995) 'International antitrust: an FTC perspective', speech at the 22nd Annual Conference on International Antitrust Law & Policy, Fordham University Law School, New York.

—— (1998) 'Competition policy in a global economy – today and tomorrow', speech at the European Institute's 8th Annual Transatlantic Seminar on Trade and Investment, Washington, D.C.

—— (2002) 'Antitrust cooperation, global trade, and US competition policy', in C.A. Jones and M. Matsushita (eds) *Competition Policy in the Global Trading System*. The Netherlands: Kluwer Law International.

Polanyi, K. (1992[1944]) *The Great Transformation*, 2nd edn, Boston: Beacon Press.

Pollack, M.A. (1998) 'The engines of integration? Supranational autonomy and influence in the European Union', in W. Sandholtz and A.S. Sweet (eds) *European Integration and Supranational Governance*, Oxford: Oxford University Press.

Poulantzas, N. (1975) *Classes in Contemporary Capitalism*, London: NLB.

Prasad, M. (2005) 'Why is France so French? Culture, Institutions, and Neoliberalism, 1974–1981', *American Journal of Sociology*, 111/2: 357–407.

Prodi, R. (2001) 'Looking towards Laeken', speech 01/590 at the plenary session of the European Parliament, 28 November, Brussels.

Renda, A., Peysner, J., Riley, A. and Rodger, B. (2007) 'Making antitrust damages more effective in the EU: welfare impact and potential scenarios', report for the European Commission, Contract DG COMP/2006/A3/012.

Resch, A. (2005) 'Phases of competition policy in Europe', *Institute of European Studies*, Paper 050401.

Reuters (2008) 'Global M&A Falls in 2008. Ends 5 Years of Growth', 22 December.

Riesenfeld, S.A. (1960) 'The legal protection of competition in France', *California Law Review*, 48/4: 574–95.

Riley, A. (2003) 'EC antitrust modernization: the commission does very nicely – thank you!', *European Competition Law Review*, 24/11: 604–15.

Rill, J. (2003) 'Overhaul merger regime may not come up smelling roses', *European Voice,* 9/39.

Robinson, W.I. (2004) *A Theory of Global Capitalism. Production, Class, and State in a Transnational World*, London: Johns Hopkins University Press.

Röller, L.H. (2005) 'Using economic analysis to strengthen competition policy enforcement in Europe'. Online. Available: <http://www.concorrencia.pt/Download/Paper_Lars.Roller_13052005.pdf> (accessed 20 April 2010).

Röller, L.H. and Friederiszick, H.W. (2005) 'Ökonomische Analyse in der EU Wettbewerbspolitik', Brussels: European Commission.

Ross, G. (1995) *Jacques Delors and European Integration*, New York: Oxford University Press.

Ruggie, J.G. (1982) 'International regimes, transactions, and change: embedded liberalism in the postwar economic order', *International Organization*, 36/2: 379–415.

Ruigrok, W. and Van Tulder, R. (1995) *The Logic of International Restructuring*, London and New York: Routledge.

Rupert, M. (2007) 'Marxism and critical theory', in T. Dunne, M. Kurki and C. Wight (eds) *International Relations Theories. Discipline and Diversity*, Oxford: Oxford University Press.

Ryner, M. (2003) 'Disciplinary neoliberalism, regionalization, and the social market in German restructuring', in A.W. Cafruny and M. Ryner (eds) *A Ruined Fortress? Neoliberal Hegemony and Transformation in Europe*, Lanham: Rowman & Littlefield Publishers.

Sauter, W. (1997) *Competition Law and Industrial Policy in the EU*, Oxford: Oxford University Press.

Scharpf, F.W. (2002) 'The European social model: coping with the challenges of diversity', *Journal of Common Market Studies*, 40/4: 645–70.

Schaub, A. (1998) 'International cooperation in antitrust matters: making the point in the wake of the BOEING/MDD proceedings', *EC Competition Policy Newsletter* 1998/1. European Commission, Brussels.

—— (2002) 'Cooperation in competition policy enforcement between the EU and the US and new concepts evolving at the World Trade Organization and the International Competition Network', European Commission, Brussels.

Scheffman, D. and Coleman, M. (2001) 'Dialogue and consultation facilitates convergence in the analyses of mergers in the US and EU'. Online. Available: <http://www.ftc.gov/be/convergence.pdf> (accessed 20 April 2010).

Schinkel, M.P., Carree, M. and Günster, A. (2004) 'European antitrust policy: an empirical analysis of commission decisions and their appeals histories, 1964–2001', paper presented at the 2004 EARIE Conference, Berlin.

Schmidt, S.K. (1998) 'Commission activism: subsuming telecommunications and electricity under European competition law', *Journal of European Public Policy*, 5/1: 169–84.

Schmidt, V. (2002) *The Futures of European Capitalism*, Oxford: Oxford University Press.

Schmitt, H.A. (1964) 'The European Coal and Steel Community: operations of the first European antitrust law, 1952–1958', *Business History Review*, 38/1: 102–22.

Schmitter, P. (1991) 'The European Community as an emergent and novel form of political domination', working paper no. 26, Juan March Institute, Madrid.

Schmitz, S. (2002) 'The European Commission's decision in GE/Honeywell and the question of the goals of antitrust law', *Journal of International Economic Law* 23/3: 539–96.

Schoneveld, F.R. (2003) 'Cartel sanctions and international competition policy: cross-border cooperation and appropriate forums for cooperation', *World Competition*, 26/3: 433–71.

Schröter, H. (1996) 'Cartelization and decartelization in Europe, 1870–1995: rise and decline of an economic institution', *The Journal of European Economic History*, 25/1: 129–53.

Schuman, R. (1950) 'The Schuman Declaration of 9 May 1950'. Online. Available: <http://www.ena.lu/schuman_declaration_paris_1950-020000152.html> (accessed 8 April 2010).

Schumpeter, J. (1947) *Capitalism, Socialism and Democracy*, 2nd edn, New York: Harper & Brothers Publishers

Schwartz, E. (1993) 'Politics as usual: the history of European Community merger control', *Yale Journal of International Law*, 18/2: 607–62.

Scott, A., Hviid, M., Lyons, I. and Bright, C. (2006) *Merger Control in the United Kingdom*, Oxford: Oxford University Press.

Seabrooke, L. (2006) *The Social Sources of Financial Power. Domestic Legitimacy and International Financial Orders*, Ithaca and London: Cornell University Press.

Seidenfuss, K.U. and Kathawala, Y. (2005) 'Voluntary export restraint (VER) without market restraints?', *European Business Review*, 17/3: 217–23.

Servan-Schreiber, J.J. (1968) *The American Challenge*, London: Hamish Hamilton.

Silver, B.J. (2003) *Forces of Labour: Workers' Movements and Globalisation Since 1870*, Cambridge: Cambridge University Press.

Sklar, M.J. (1988) *The Corporate Reconstruction of American Capitalism, 1890–1916. The Market, the Law, and Politics*, Cambridge: Cambridge University Press.

Slot, P.J. (2004) 'A view from the mountain: 40 years of developments in EC Competition Law', *Common Market Law Review*, 41/2: 443–73.

Smith, A. (2003[1776]) *The Wealth of Nations*, New York: Bantam Classics.

Smith, E.O. (1994) *The German Economy*, London and New York: Routledge.

Souam, S. (1998) 'French competition policy', in S. Martin (ed.) *Competition Policies in Europe*, Amsterdam: Elsevier Science.

Stanford, J. (2008) *Economics for Everyone. A Short Guide to the Economics of Capitalism*, London: Pluto Press.

Suleiman, E.N (1975) 'Industrial policy formation in France', in S.J. Warnecke and E.N. Suleiman (eds) *Industrial Policies in Western Europe*, New York: Praeger Publishers.

TABD (1995) 'Transatlantic Business Dialogue: overall conclusions'. Online. Available: <http://static.tabd.com/manilaGems/1995SevilleCEOReport.pdf> (accessed 20 April 2010).

—— (1996) 'The Chicago declaration'. Online. Available: <http://static.tabd.com/manilaGems/1996ChicagoCEOReport.pdf> (accessed 20 April 2010).

—— (1997) 'TABD priorities for the mid-year summit'. Online. Available: <http://www.tabd.com/ceo_reports> (accessed 20 April 2010).

—— (2006) 'Towards a barrier-free transatlantic market. Report and recommendations to the 2006 EU-US summit leaders'. Online. Available: <http://static.tabd.com/manilaGems/TABDreport14March07FINAL.pdf> (accessed 20 April 2010).

Thyssen, F. (1941) *I Paid Hitler*, New York: Farrar & Rinehart.

The Times (1987) 'Britain eases mergers stand', 30 November.

UNCTAD (1996) *World Investment Report. Investment, Trade and International Policy Arrangements*, New York: United Nations.

—— (2000) *World Investment Report. Cross-border Mergers and Acquisition and Development*, New York: United Nations.

UNICE (1974) 'Proposition d'un reglement (C.E.E.) du Conseil sur le controle des concentrations', January 1974.

—— (1982) 'Amended proposal for a Council Regulation on the control of concentrations between undertakings', position paper, June 1982.

—— (1987) 'Merger control at Community level', UNICE Declaration, November 1987.

—— (1989) 'Draft regulation regarding the control of concentrations', Note, November 1989.

—— (1995) 'Modernising EU competition policy, re-focussing the scope and administration of article 85 and reform of state aid control', discussion paper, September.

—— (1999) 'UNICE comments, executive summary on the modernization of EC competition law', position paper, Brussels.

—— (2001) 'UNICE comments on the modernization of EC competition law. Proposal for a Council regulation implementing Articles 81 and 82 of the Treaty. Com (2000) 582 Final', position paper, Brussels.

—— (2002) 'UNICE supplementary comments on the modernization of EC competition law. Proposal for a Council regulation implementing Articles 81 and 82 of the Treaty. Status: 26 July 2002', position paper, Brussels.

—— (2003) 'Urgent – review of community merger policy: recent developments'. Letter from UNICE Working Group on Competition, 6 October, Brussels.

—— (2006) 'Comments on Green Paper "Damages actions for breach of the EC antitrust" ', Executive Summary, Brussels.

United Nations Conference (1948) 'Final Act of the United Nations Conference on Trade and Employment: Havana Charter for an International Trade Organization'. Online. Available HTTP: http://www.worldtradelaw.net/misc/havana.pdf (accessed 20 April 2010).

US Government (2002) 'Competition policy and deregulation group. Submission of the United States United States', Merida, May. Online. Available: <http://www.apeccp.org.tw/doc/Workshop/w2002/008.htm> (accessed 20 April 2010).

US Supreme Court (1945) *United States v. Aluminum Co. of Am.*, 148 F. 2d 416 (2d Cir. 1945).

Utton, M. (2000) 'Fifty years of U.K. competition policy', *Review of Industrial Organization,* 16/3: 267–85.

Van Apeldoorn, B. (2000) 'Transnational class agency and European governance: the case of the European Round Table of Industrialists', *New Political Economy*, 5/2: 157–81.

—— (2002) *Transnational Capitalism and the Struggle Over European Integration*, London and New York: Routledge.

—— (2004) 'Theorizing the transnational: a historical materialist approach', *Journal of International Relations and Development*, 7/2: 142–76.

Van Apeldoorn, B. and Horn, L. (2007) 'The marketisation of European corporate control: a critical political economy perspective', *New Political Economy*, 12/2: 211–35.

Van der Pijl, K. (1984) *The Making of an Atlantic Ruling Class*, London: Verso.

—— (1989) 'Ruling classes, hegemony, and the state system', *International Journal of Political Economy*, 19/3: 7–35.

—— (2006) *Global Rivalries from the Cold War to Iraq*, New York: Verso.

Van der Wurff, R. (1993) 'Neo-liberalism in Germany? The "Wende" in perspective', in H. Overbeek (ed.) *Restructuring Hegemony in the Global Political Economy. The Rise Of Transnational Neo-Liberalism in the 1980s*, London and New York: Routledge.

Van Miert, K. (1998) 'European competition policy', paper for the Management Policy Council, Brussels – De Warande. Online. Available: <http://ec.europa.eu/comm/competition/speeches/text/sp1998_053_en.html> (accessed 19 June 2010).

—— 'European Competition Policy', speech at the 29th Annual Fordham Corporate Law Institute, New York, 1999.

—— (2000) *Mijn jaren in Europa*, The Netherlands: Lanoo.

Venturini, G. (1971) *Monopolies and Restrictive Trade Practices in France*, Leyden: Sijthoff.

Verdun, A. (1999) 'The institutional design of EMU: a democratic deficit?' *Journal of Public Policy*, 18/2: 107–32.

Vickers, J. (2004) 'Merger policy in Europe: retrospect and prospect', *European Competition Law Review*, 25/7: 455–63.

Voillemot, D. and Michel, A. (1988) 'France', in *Merger Control in the EEC*, Deventer: Kluwer Law.

Von der Gröben, H. (1962) 'Vier Jahre Gemeinsamer Markt', *IX. Table Ronde des Problemes de L'Europe*, 12 May, Strassbourg: Historical Archive of the European Commission.

—— (1963) 'Wettbewerb und Programmierung als Instrument der Wirtschaftspolitik im Gemeinsamen Markt', Vortrag vor der List-Gesellschaft in Frankfurt am Main, 8 June, Brussels: Historical Archives of the European Commission.
—— (1964) 'Die Entwicklung der EWG und ihre Auswirkungen auf die Wirtschaftsverfassung in den Mitgliedstaaten', Vortrag vor der Berlin Conférence Européenne des Entreprises Publiques, 14 September, Brussels: Historical Archives of the European Commission.
—— (1965a) 'Möglichkeiten und Grenzen politischer Einigung durch wirtschaftliche Integration', Vortrag vor dem Übersee-Club in Hamburg, 22 January, Brussels: Historical Archives of the European Commission.
—— (1965b) 'Competition Policy as a Part of Economic Policy in the Common Market', address to the European Parliament, Strasbourg, 16 June, Brussels: Historical Archives of the European Commission.
—— (1987) *The European Community. The Formative Years*, Brussels: The European Perspectives Series.
Wallerstein, I. (2000) 'A left politics for the 21st century? or, theory and praxis once again', *New Political Science*, 22/2: 143–59.
Wall Street Journal (2004) 'No Curtain Call for the Full Monti', 4 October.
Waltz, K.N. (1979) *Theory of International Politics*, New York: McGraw-Hill.
Wanniski, J. (1992) 'The future of Russian capitalism', *Foreign Affairs*, 71/2: 17–25.
Warlouzet, L. (2005) 'At the core of European power. The origins of competition policy (1957–1964)'. Online. Available: <http://www.heirs-eu.org/documents/heirscolloquium2005.pdf> (accessed 8 April 2010).
—— (forthcoming) 'Historical institutionalism and competition policy. The Regulation 17/62 (1962–2002)'.
Washington Post (2006) 'Acquisitions Made in 2006 Set New Record', 20 November.
Weitbrecht, A. (2005) 'EU merger control in 2004 – an overview', *European Competition Law Review*, 26/2: 67–74.
Wells, W. (2002) *Antitrust and the Formation of the Postwar World*, New York: Columbia University Press.
Went, R. (2002) *Enigma of Globalization: A Journey to a New State of Capitalism*, London and New York: Routledge.
Wigger, A. (2008) *Competition for Competitiveness. The Politics of Transformation of the EU Competition Regime,* Dissertation, Vrije Universiteit Amsterdam.
—— (2009) 'The political role of transnational experts in shaping EU competition policy. Towards a pan-European system of private enforcement', *Legisprudence*, 3/3: 251–75.
Wigger, A. and Nölke, A. (2007) 'Enhanced roles of private actors in EU business regulation and the erosion of Rhenish capitalism: the case of antitrust enforcement', *Journal of Common Market Studies*, 45/2: 487–513.
Wight, C. (2006) *Agents, Structures and International Relations. Politics as Ontology*, Cambridge: Cambridge University Press.
Wilks, S. (1999), *In the Public Interest. Competition Policy and the Monopolies and Mergers Commission*, Manchester: Manchester University Press.
—— (2005a) 'Agency escape: decentralization or dominance of the European Commission in the modernization of competition policy?', *Governance*, 18/3: 431–52.
—— (2005b) 'Competition policy. Challenge and reform', in H. Wallace, W. Wallace and M. Pollack (eds) *Policy-Making in the European Union*, 5th edn, Oxford: Oxford University Press.

—— (2007) 'Agencies, networks, discourses and the trajectory of European Competition enforcement', *European Competition Journal*, 3/2: 437–64.

—— (2009) 'The impact of the recession on competition policy: amending the economic constitution', *International Journal of the Economics of Business*, 16/3: 269–88.

Wilks, S. and Bartle, I. (2002) 'The unanticipated consequences of creating independent competition agencies', *West European Politics*, 25/1: 148–72.

Wilks, S. and McGowan, L. (1996) 'Competition policy in the European Union. Creating a federal agency?', in G.B. Doern and S. Wilks (eds) *Comparative Competition Policy: National Institutions in a Global Market*, Oxford: Clarendon Press.

Wils, W. (2003) 'Should private antitrust enforcement be encouraged in Europe?', *World Competition*, 26/3: 473–88.

Wise, M. (2005a) 'Competition Law and Policy in Germany', *OECD Journal of Competition Law and Policy*, 7/2: 7–66.

Wise, M. (2005b) 'Competition law and policy in France', *OECD Journal of Competition Law and Policy*, 7/1: 7–81.

Witschke, T. (2001) 'The first antitrust law in Europe – success or failure? Origins and application of the merger control policy of the High Authority of the European Coal and Steel Community 1950–1963', working paper, European University Institute, Florence.

—— (2003) *Gefahr für den Wettbewerb? Die Fusionskontrolle der Europäischen Gemeinschaft für Kohle und Stahl (EGKS) und die 'Rekonzentration' der Ruhrstallindustrie 1950–1963.* Dissertation, European University Institute, Florence.

Wood, E.M. (2003) *Empire of Capital*, New York: Verso.

Woods, N. (2001) 'International political economy in an age of globalization', in J. Baylis and S. Smith (eds), *The Globalization of World Politics. An Introduction to International Relations*, Oxford: Oxford University Press.

Woolcock, S. (1989) 'European mergers: national or community controls?', *RIIA Discussion Papers* 15, The Royal Institute of International Affairs.

Woolcock, S., Hodges, M. and Schreiber, K. (1991) *Britain, Germany and 1992: The Limits of Deregulation*, London: Pinter Publishers/The Royal Institute of International Affairs.

WTO (1996) 'The Singapore Ministerial Declaration.' Online. Available: <http://www.wto.org/english/news_e/pres96_e/wtodec.htm> (accessed 20 April 2010).

—— (1998) 'Annual report of the Working Group on the Interaction between Trade and Competition Policy to the General Council.' Online. Available: <http://www.wto.org/english/tratop_e/comp_e/comp_e.htm> (accessed 20 April 2010).

—— (2003) 'Report (2003) of the Working Group on the Interaction Between Trade and Competition Policy to the General Council.' Online. Available: <http://www.wto.org/english/tratop_e/comp_e/comp_e.htm> (accessed 20 April 2010).

WTO WGTCP (2002a) 'Communication from Korea to the Working Group on the Interaction of Trade and Competition Policy.' Online. Available: <http://www.wto.org/english/tratop_e/comp_e/wgtcp_docs_e.htm> (accessed 20 April 2010).

—— (2002b) 'Communication from India to the Working Group on the Interaction of Trade and Competition Policy.' Online. Available: <http://www.commerce.nic.in/trade/international_trade_papers_nextDetail.asp?id=32> (accessed 20 April 2010).

—— (2003) 'Communication from Thailand to the Working Group on the Interaction of Trade and Competition Policy.' Online. Available: <http://www.wto.org/english/tratop_e/comp_e/wgtcp_docs_e.htm> (accessed 20 April 2010).

Wyatt, D. and Dashwood, A. (1980) *The Substantive Law of the EEC*, London: Sweet & Maxwell.

Interviews

Andriessen, F. (former EC Competition Commissioner), 22 April 2006, The Hague.

Berggren, E. (Senior Adviser UNICE), 20 October 2005, Brussels.

Brittan, L. (former EC Competition Commissioner), telephone interview, 6 February 2006.

Davignon, E. (former Commissioner responsible for industrial affairs and former member of the ERT), 1 June 2006, Brussels.

Diplomat A (involved in the negotiations over the revision of the merger control regulation), February 2006.

Diplomat B (involved in the negotiations over the revision of the merger control regulation), February 2006.

Faull, J. (former member of Leon Brittan's cabinet), 24 March 2006, Brussels.

Sutherland, P. (former EC Competition Commissioner and member of the ERT), telephone interview, 26 April 2006.

Waelbroeck, D. (competition lawyer at Ashurst Office in Brussels involved in major EC cases), 24 November 2005, Brussels.

Index